Principles of Population and Development

Key Text

REFERENCE

Principles of Population and Development

with Illustrations from Asia and Africa

NIGEL CROOK

EDITED BY
IAN M. TIMÆUS

Oxford University Press
1997

Oxford University Press, Walton Street, Oxford OX2 6DP

Oxford New York
Athens Auckland Bangkok Bogota Bombay
Buenos Aires Calcutta Cape Town Dar es Salaam
Delhi Florence Hong Kong Istanbul Karachi
Kuala Lumpur Madras Madrid Melbourne
Mexico City Nairobi Paris Singapore
Taipei Tokyo Toronto

and associated companies in
Berlin Ibadan

Oxford is a trade mark of Oxford University Press

Published in the United States
by Oxford University Press Inc., New York

British Library Cataloguing in Publication Data
Data available

Library of Congress Cataloging in Publication Data
Crook, Nigel.
    Principles of population and development: with illustrations from
Asia and Africa/Nigel Crook; edited by Ian M. Timaeus.
    Includes bibliographical references and index.
    1. Population—Asia—Case studies.   2. Population—Africa—Case
studies.   3. Population—Economic aspects—Case studies.   I. Title.
HB3633.A3C76   1997   304.6'095—dc20   96-28079
ISBN 0-19-877488-5 (pbk)
ISBN 0-19-877489-3.

1 3 5 7 9 10 8 6 4 2

Typeset by Best-set Typesetter Ltd., Hong Kong
Printed in Great Britain
on acid-free paper by Biddles Ltd, Guildford & King's Lynn

Preface

This book provides an introduction to population and development issues that focuses on the developing world. It should be of interest to students of economics, population studies, development studies, geography, economic history, and related disciplines. While it is intended primarily for under-graduates and for Masters students encountering this field for the first time, others wanting an introduction to the subject should find it useful too.

Nigel Crook was keen to produce a text for Asian and African scholars, as well as one for those in the UK and USA. This is the first book of its type to draw heavily on the economic and demographic history of Asia for its em-pirical material. It is also unusual in the degree of attention it devotes to the ideas of economists, demographers, and others writing about countries now in the course of economic development rather than about Europe's demographic history. For example, the book discusses Chayanov on Russia, Malthus on Asia, Hung on China, Henry George on India, and Marx, Malthus, and Ricardo on economic and demographic development generally.

Each chapter in the book follows a similar pattern. Theories and ideas about population and development are introduced first. Empirical and quantitative material and case studies follow. Demographic measures and principles mentioned in the text are explained fully in boxes. This approach makes the need to learn some formal (quantitative) demography more apparent (and the process more appealing) than when it is discussed in isolation or before substantive issues.

Nigel Crook submitted the manuscript of this book to Oxford University Press in 1994. The Press accepted it for publication shortly after his death in May 1995. During his illness, Nigel asked me whether I would see the book into print if he was unable to do so himself. I agreed and this volume is the outcome.

This is Nigel Crook's book and not mine. In editing it, I have been con-servative about matters of substance and authorial style, although I have allowed myself more freedom regarding presentation. As a result, I have not acted on many suggestions made by the publisher's readers that Nigel prob-ably would have adopted if he had been able. I have implemented most of the readers' minor suggestions and corrections but ignored more radical requests to widen the scope of the book. I hope that those who read the draft manuscript so carefully will forgive me but my concern was not to distort the author's intent by trying to improve on his work.

The book developed out of courses for students of economics, geography, and development studies at the School of Oriental and African Studies,

Preface

University of London, where Nigel Crook was Senior Lecturer in Economics. Its roots in the lecture hall are reflected in the book's informal, conversational style. I have attempted to preserve this while editing the text, as it yields a uniform and accessible approach. However, I have modified some of the more oratorical phrasing that to my eye looked wrong once it had been transferred from speech to print. The boxes on formal demography seemed to me to need a final polish with particular attention to their layout. This component of the book was subjected to heavier-handed editing than the rest of the manuscript.

It is customary for the preface of a book to acknowledge those who have contributed to its genesis and production. I cannot identify all the friends, colleagues, and students that Nigel Crook would have wanted to thank. Therefore I prefer not to mention any names at all. I also am grateful to everyone whose ideas or practical help benefited the text. You know who you are.

Nigel Crook's work was characterized by the fusion of his careful scholarship with his commitment to supporting the struggle of the poor for a better life. He was a stimulating and supportive teacher who inspired a series of able undergraduates to pursue postgraduate studies and careers in demography. This book reflects these themes in Nigel's academic career. It discusses issues of both intellectual and practical importance. I hope that it will engender some of Nigel's profound concern about them in its readers.

IAN TIMÆUS

Contents

List of Boxes

List of Figures

List of Figures

List of Tables

Part I

Population and Subsistence: Theories and Evidence

1 | Theories of Population and Subsistence

We start with Thomas Malthus. He was not the first theoretician to write about population. As we shall see, a Chinese scholar had tackled the same question just before him. Nevertheless, Malthus is surely the best-known figure in this field. He was born in 1766, and *An Essay on The Principle of Population* (cited hereafter as *First Essay*) was published in 1798. This is what he has to say about the relationship between population and subsistence—first on natural increase[1] in a population without a subsistence constraint:

In the United States of America, where the means of subsistence have been more ample, . . . and the checks to early marriages fewer, than in any of the modern states of Europe, the population has been found to double itself in twenty-five years.

This ratio of increase, though short of the utmost power of population, . . . we will take as our rule, and say, that population, when unchecked, goes on doubling itself every twenty-five years or increases in a geometrical ratio.

Now consider what Malthus claims in the *First Essay* about increase in the means of subsistence or, basically, food. The language is a little bit quaint, but the point is clear:

Let us now take any spot on earth, this Island for instance [i.e. Britain], and see in what ratio the subsistence it affords can be supposed to increase. We will begin with it under its present state of cultivation.

If we allow that by the best possible policy, by breaking up more land and by great encouragements to agriculture, the produce of this island may be doubled in the first twenty-five years, I think it will be allowing as much as any person can well demand.

In the next twenty-five years, it is impossible to suppose that the produce could be quadrupled. It would be contrary to all our knowledge of the qualities of land. The very utmost that we can conceive, is, that the increase in the second twenty-five years might equal the present produce. Let us then take this for our rule . . . and allow that, by great exertion, the whole produce of the Island might be increased every twenty-five years, by a quantity of subsistence equal to what it at present produces. The most enthusiastic spectator cannot suppose a greater increase than this. In a few centuries it would make every acre of land in the Island look like a garden.

Yet this ratio of increase is evidently arithmetical.

These are remarkable words. Malthus claims, from his experience of studying the American people, that populations increase geometrically and that, by casually observing the British countryside, we can say that food supply increases arithmetically. In fact his comment that in a few centuries every acre of Britain would look like a garden seems to suggest that he thought even this process was unlikely to be sustained. Actually, if he had been around today he would have seen that (from the air at least) much of southern England does look like a garden.

We can visualize the difference between arithmetic and geometric rates of increase from the drawings in Figure 1.1. The upper line of rectangles can be thought to represent fields of food grains. Every twenty-five years a new field equal in size to the one that we started with is added. This is the arithmetic progression. The lower line of rectangles can be thought to represent the population of a village. Every twenty-five years that population doubles, which means that on the second and subsequent increases it adds to itself a new mass of people that is larger than the population with which we started. If we graph these progressions over time, the arithmetic forms a straight line sloping upwards, whereas the geometric forms a sloping line that gets steeper and steeper (see Figure 1.2).[2] The mathematics of this process are explained in Box 1.1.

Whether these relationships are valid remains important today. Food is absolutely necessary for life and still constitutes 70 to 80 per cent of expenditure and consumption of most of the people of Asia and Africa. Nevertheless, would we be right to conclude, as did Malthus, that poverty and starvation can be explained by this tendency of population increase to outstrip food increase?

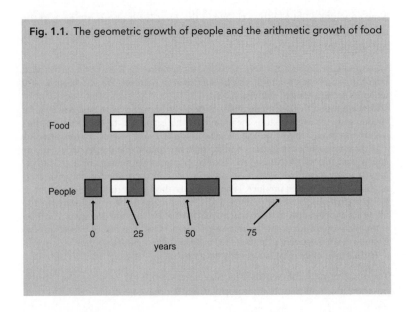

Fig. 1.1. The geometric growth of people and the arithmetic growth of food

Fig. 1.2. Relationship between the geometric growth of people and the arithmetic growth of food

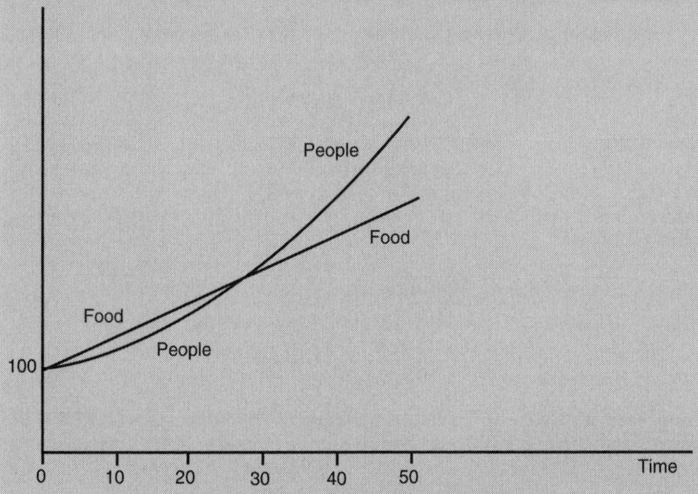

Note: We start both series indexed at 100. For food this could be 100 million tonnes, for population 500 million people. In this example, the percentage growth in food is initially greater than the percentage growth in people but it diminishes over time.

Even when Malthus was writing in the eighteenth century, some economists argued that this relationship was not the cause of poverty and starvation. W. Godwin, for example, believed that poverty could be averted if food was distributed correctly. It was the lack of appropriate institutions for doing this that was the problem. Malthus's own father apparently agreed with Godwin and the father and son engaged in furious argument. This argument has continued down the centuries and is still with us today. Sometimes it is conducted as an exercise in rhetoric and sometimes as an exercise in logic; we will try to keep to the latter.

Malthus's technical-economic argument

We should look at Malthus's argument in a little more detail, as there are two or three strands to it that should not be confused. The following quotation is from his *A Summary View on the Principle of Population* (cited hereafter as *Summary View*), written in 1830, and shows how his ideas developed. First, he is prepared to agree that increasing the food supply is not just a question of taking in more land:

BOX 1.1. MEASURES OF GROWTH

Consider the following data for China:

Food grain production:	1964	184 million tonnes;
	1982	356 million tonnes.
Population:	1964	694 million persons;
	1982	1,002 million persons.

Note that population census years may not be typical agricultural years. One can exaggerate (or underestimate) growth rates by selecting unrepresentative years at the beginning and end of a period. The simplest measure of change and growth is the percentage change over the period. This is calculated as follows:

For food:
$$\frac{356-184}{184} \times 100 = 93\%.$$

For population:
$$\frac{1,002-694}{694} \times 100 = 44\%.$$

From here it is easy to calculate the rate of arithmetic growth. Take the percentage change and divide by the number of years in the interval:

For food: $93\% \div 18 = 5.2\%$ a year.

For population: $44\% \div 18 = 2.4\%$ a year.

Here, the average annual increase in food production in absolute rather than percentage terms is $5.2\% \times 184 = 9.6$ million tonnes and, for population, 16.6 million.

Putting this algebraically, if:

P_t = Population at year t,

P_0 = Population at year 0 (the beginning of the period), and

a = the absolute annual increase,

then the arithmetic progression looks like this:

$P_t = P_0 + at.$

The geometric progression assumes that the increase is always a fixed proportion of the population (or food) level reached the year before. If:

r = the proportional increase,

the geometric progression looks like this:

$P_t = P_0(1+r)^t.$

A little algebra shows that the rate of geometric increase (r) is obtained from population numbers at 0 and t as follows:

$$r = \left(\frac{P_t}{P_0}\right)^{\frac{1}{t}} - 1.$$

BOX 1.1. continued

We do not elaborate this in any further detail because populations do not increase by a proportional amount at the end of each year. This would imply that all births and deaths occurred in one split second at midnight on New Year's Eve. In fact births and deaths take place throughout the year: the population grows continuously. If the additions are proportional to the population reached a split second earlier, a continuous geometric progression results, which is known as exponential growth. We first give the formula for this and then illustrate its use.

The formula for exponential growth is:

$$P_t = P_0 e^{rt},$$

where e is a mathematical constant approximately equal to 2.718.

With a little algebra one can show how to calculate r, the annual average proportional rate of growth (assuming growth is exponential) or, in short hand, *the growth rate*.

$$r = \left[\log_e (P_t / P_0)\right] \div t,$$

where $\log_e$ is the natural logarithm, sometimes written ln instead. For population growth in the Chinese example:

$$r = \left[\log_e (1,002/694)\right] \div 18 = 0.02,$$

or 2 per cent a year. Similarly, assuming that the growth in food production is exponential (and one has to assume this if we want to make a comparison with population growth), the rate of food growth in the example is:

$$r = \left[\log_e (356/184)\right] \div 18 = 0.037,$$

or 3.7 per cent a year.

Since 356/184 = 1.93, which is close to two, food production nearly doubles in eighteen years through sustained growth at this rate. Clearly, if food production continued to grow at 3.7 per cent a year, food would keep on doubling every eighteen years. The same would be true of population or indeed anything that grew at 3.7 per cent a year: it would nearly double in quantity every eighteen years.

This suggests that this equation has another useful demographic purpose. If food production had doubled exactly in the equation above, we would have had simply $\log_e 2$ (instead of $\log_e 1.93$). $\log_e 2$ is 0.693, which is the natural logarithm of anything that doubles. So, if the population is growing at 2 per cent a year, we can calculate its doubling time as follows:

$$0.02 = 0.693 \div t.$$

Hence:

$$t = 0.693 \div 0.02 = 35.$$

Thus, the doubling time for a population growing at 2 per cent a year is thirty-five years. If China's population had continued to grow at 2 per cent a year after 1982, it would have reached two billion by the year 2017. The equation for finding doubling times is therefore:

BOX 1.1. continued

$$t = 0.693 \div r,$$

where r is the annual rate of growth.

Finally, note that taking logs of the equation $P_t = P_0 e^{rt}$ converts the function into a straight line:

$$\log_e P_t = \log_e P_0 + rt.$$

The slope of the line, r, measures the annual average exponential rate of change. Therefore, the growth of two measures that grow exponentially (e.g., food and population) may be compared simply by examining the steepness of the slopes on a graph, provided that the units of measurement are the same. This can best be achieved by indexing them (see Box 2.1).

The main peculiarity that distinguishes man from other animals, in the means of his support, is the power which he possesses of very greatly increasing those means. But this power is obviously limited by the scarcity of the land—by the great natural barrenness of a very large part of the surface of the earth—and by the decreasing proportion of produce which must necessarily be obtained from the continual additions of capital applied to land already in cultivation.

Secondly, as this quotation makes clear, he points out that one will eventually run out of usable land. Economists are familiar with the first argument: technically it is known as the diminishing returns to a factor of production. Look at Figure 1.3. The vertical axis measures quantities of food grown on the land. The horizontal axis measures hours of labour applied to work on the land. Successive increases in labour inputs yield more food, but the increase diminishes and may cease if workers start to get in each other's way. Now, suppose that more land is taken in to cultivation: how could we represent the new relationship between labour and food produced on the same diagram? Simply shift the curve upwards. This gives us some breathing space—more food for the same amount of work. As we start increasing labour hours again, the same problem of diminishing returns to labour occurs again. Eventually, if one keeps on taking in land, one hits the end of the world, so to speak. This process continues today, for instance in villages in parts of West Africa bordering on the desert. The quotation from Malthus is about the effects of increasing the capital applied to the land, meaning tools or animal-drawn equipment. Yet the same story holds: if one uses too many oxen and ploughs in a single field the yield will cease to increase. We might classify these strands in the argument as the static Malthusian theory.

The other strand in Malthus's argument is the one with which we started. The food product curves shift upwards over time and labour gets added as the population increases over time. If the latter occur too rapidly in comparison with the former, we arrive on the flat portion of a given curve, where additional labour cannot increase the food supply. Suppose that at that point the population is living at subsistence level—that is consuming the

Fig. 1.3. Relationship between input of labour and output of food, illustrating the Malthusian position

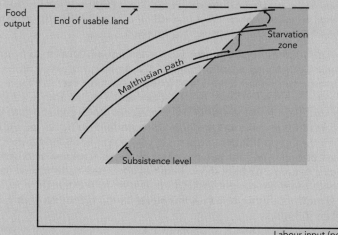

Note: Land is held fixed on each curve, but is increased as the curve shifts upward; technology and capital are held fixed all the time.

minimum of food needed for survival. Increase the population and some-body (or everybody) starves. Starvation continues until agriculture can be organized to take in more land. The belief that agriculture can only increase arithmetically is sufficient to support this general line of reasoning. Figure 1.2 makes it clear why. However steep the arithmetic slope, the geometric curve always becomes steeper eventually.[3]

Nineteenth-century criticisms of Malthus's argument

Consider for a moment what are the main weaknesses in Malthus's argu-ment. It did not take very long for economists and others to point some of them out. His contemporary Godwin was optimistic about the prospects of increasing agricultural yields and so providing more food. 'The parts al-ready cultivated are capable of immeasurable improvement', he said, an assertion that Malthus thought was stupid: 'How little has Mr Godwin turned his penetrating mind to the real state of man on earth', Malthus replied. But it was a geographer by the name of Alison who, in 1840, soon after Malthus had written his *Summary View*, really posed the critique suc-cinctly. After all, why did Malthus assume, after only casual observation, that agricultural output increased in an arithmetic progression? Instead Alison asserted:

> Let us assume that the increase in yield due to increase in labour does not always rise in proportion to the labour: there still remains a third element . . . science. Science increases in proportion to the knowledge bequeathed it by the previous generation . . . and thus also in geometric progression.

There is indeed a challenge here. Economists nowadays call this increase in applied knowledge, technical progress. If technical progress advances in a geometric progression, there is hope for the population. Yet this hope rests on another assumption—that the rate of increase of technical knowledge is faster than the rate of increase of the population. Look again at Figure 1.2 and compare it with Figure 1.4. Figure 1.4 shows food output increasing in a geometric progression because of the application of scientific knowledge: this might consist of new varieties of seeds, better fertilizers, and better cropping patterns. We have shown here two alternative paths of food output, both geometric progressions. One is always steeper than the population growth. The other is always less steep. In the latter case Malthus's problem still arises.[4]

It was Engels (the famous collaborator of Karl Marx) who brought Alison's point to the fore. The mid-nineteenth century saw a violent outbreak of criticism of Malthus's ideas, mainly from the early Marxists, to which we will

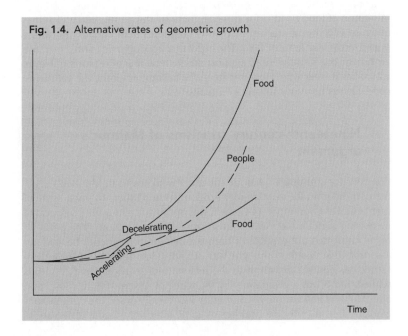

Fig. 1.4. Alternative rates of geometric growth

return. Nevertheless, other economists also held views on the rate of technical progress in agriculture and in the economy as a whole. In fact, it is still
one of the hottest debates among economists. John Stuart Mill believed this
was a vital force, but felt that its rate of increase might slow. (Consider the
effect on the upper curve in Figure 1.4 if it did.) Instead of all this guesswork,
to try to find out what these rates of increase were in practice might have
been useful. We return to this suggestion.

A twentieth-century critique

An even more intriguing idea on how technical progress took effect was put
forward much later by the economist Ester Boserup. Alison had discussed
how fast scientific knowledge could grow. Boserup was concerned with how
fast that scientific knowledge would be applied to the practical problem of
producing food. The application of scientific knowledge, or of an invention,
is known technically as an innovation.

Boserup suggested that the very problem of population being faced with
the prospect of running out of food would spur people to apply technical
knowledge faster. What she proposed in her writings of the 1960s was that
increasing population density (increasing numbers of people per acre of
land) was a stimulus to technical progress in agriculture.

For an indication of what this would mean to Malthus, look at Figure 1.5.
In Malthus's scheme of things more population, implying more labour to
work the land, pushes the agricultural economy in the direction of the lower
arrow. It passes the point of starvation before sufficient new land or improvements in cultivation can take place to push food output upwards
again. With Boserup, as the increasing population approaches starvation
point, it simultaneously devises ways of avoiding the crisis by introducing
new agricultural practices, pushing the economy upwards in advance.
Technical progress is a *response* to increasing densities of population (and
consequent fears of food shortage). In technical language, in her theory
technical progress becomes endogenous.

The point that Boserup was making is even stronger than this. She argued
that technical progress in agriculture can only take place if certain critical
densities of population on the land are reached. So population growth is
necessary for agricultural progress. This is truly turning Malthus on his
head. For instance, she argued that no one is going to clear land for settled
agriculture using manure to maintain yields if the population density is less
than fifteen people per square kilometre or so. At somewhere around fifty
people per square kilometre such innovations begin to take place. Much of
Africa had densities of less than fifteen per square kilometre when she was
writing. At the other extreme, Java in Indonesia and Japan had densities of
500 people per square kilometre or more. In the outer islands of Indonesia

Fig. 1.5. Relationship between input of labour and output of food, illustrating Boserup's position

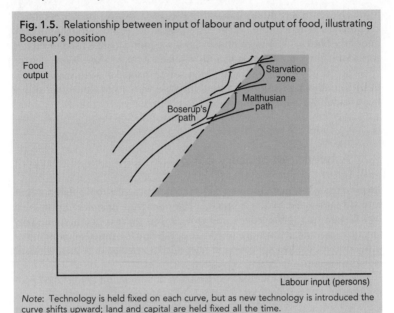

Note: Technology is held fixed on each curve, but as new technology is introduced the curve shifts upward; land and capital are held fixed all the time.

where population densities were low, quite primitive forms of food production were still practised—the forest was cut and burnt. Similarly, Boserup points out that the first major technical innovations in European food production, such as short fallowing and planting of root crops with a high calorific content per acre, came in the Low Countries, which were the most densely populated part of the continent.

Before the machine age, all technical progress had to be labour intensive: this made sense, as labour was relatively cheap. Thus, the connection between population pressure and technical progress was a close one. Still, the technical innovations were often sufficient to push the economy or the production of food well ahead of the population. Boserup seems less clear on this point: did population pressure cause technical innovations that raised the long-term trend in output per head before the use of manufactured inputs in agriculture? Did these early innovations lead to food surpluses or did they merely prevent a deterioration in output per head to the point where starvation would have occurred?[5] These are very important theoretical questions, and we cannot take them much further here. Boserup does note that while the Low Countries could feed themselves, other parts of north-western Europe went through periodic bouts of starvation. There was greater potential to avoid the Malthusian problem in the new agricultural system of the Low Countries, because of its high population density not despite it, as Malthus would have argued.

Some modern economists argue that population growth, at least in moderation, may be a good thing. Their arguments generally relate to industrializing economies, and some of their observations were first made by Marx in the middle of the nineteenth century. One of their points concerns infrastructure like roads or railways. An economist will not recommend the construction of a highway unless one can guarantee enough users (whose goods can be transported more cheaply by truck down a highway than on the backs of thousands of donkeys). It often follows that a large population must live close to the highway to make it profitable to build.

More extravagant claims have been made by other political economists such as Hoselitz. It has been argued that, even today, the pressure of population on resources may stimulate the adoption of modern farming techniques. These innovations may be sponsored by the State rather than adopted spontaneously by individual farmers. The introduction of new high-yielding varieties of seed into parts of Asia, for instance in the Indian Punjab in the 1960s, was promoted strongly by the Government and international agencies. Their action may have been precipitated by a panic when the State realized how fast the population was growing and how inadequate were existing methods of food production.

Although Boserup may be right, there are other responses to population growth besides technical innovation.[6] Where it is available, one is simply that the population takes in more land. This point is made by one of Boserup's major critics, Grigg. We will look at Chinese and Russian examples of this later. Secondly, improved techniques of working the land that raise yields (output per acre) may be induced by factors other than population growth or density.[7] For example, the compulsion to pay taxes or rents demanded or increased by a new landlord or a new colonizer will force peasants to find ways of increasing their yield. George, writing critically of Malthus in the late nineteenth century, and for once focusing attention on the condition in the colonies, especially India, made this point. It still holds today. Indeed, some modern agricultural political economists believe that it is the compulsion to pay rents and to repay debt that primarily accounts for the high yields that are often produced on small peasant farms.

What is the evidence?

It seems that we ought to be able to assess the various contentions about rates of agricultural progress and population growth by looking at some data. After all, we can now look back over a long period of much change in the world's economies. Malthus was not so lucky, though he did not look very hard at what was happening under his nose either. How could we test the theory of arithmetic versus geometric growth? We could plot some figures, say for India or China, and see whether they represented the curve and the straight line (illustrated in Figure 1.2). But suppose, as J. S. Mill suggested, that the rate of agricultural growth was slowing, could we really decide whether we had a geometric progression, an arithmetic progression, or something in between?

Look at the statistics plotted for India or China in Figure 1.6 and see what

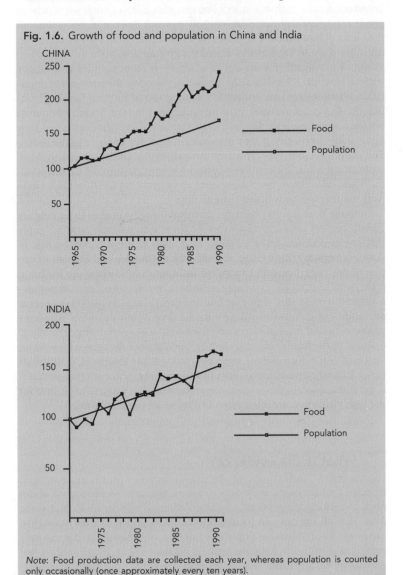

Fig. 1.6. Growth of food and population in China and India

Note: Food production data are collected each year, whereas population is counted only occasionally (once approximately every ten years).

they suggest about the rates of growth of population and food supplies during the last forty years. As Box 1.1 shows (and Figures 1.2 and 1.4 also illustrate), it is the slope of the curve that enables us to distinguish rates of growth (from a common indexed starting-point).[8] Since 1950 the growth rate of food seems to have exceeded the growth rate (the natural increase) of population, by a small margin. The calculation in Box 1.1 confirms this for China.

Malthus on the adjustment of population to food supplies

We have already suggested one way in Malthus's way of thinking in which population might adjust, so to speak, to limited food supplies: when the average product of labour falls below the subsistence level of consumption per head people begin to starve. The increase in mortality reduces the population and the cycle begins again. This mortality is called a 'positive check' in Malthus's scheme of things.

Rather unhelpfully, he went on to define his positive check as anything that 'tends[s] in any way prematurely to shorten the duration of human life'. Apart from starvation and famine, this includes such things as insufficient clothing (to keep out the cold), bad nursing of children, excesses of all kinds, great towns and manufactured goods, the whole train of common diseases and epidemics, wars, infanticide, and plague. Presumably he did not believe that all these factors were caused by excessive population growth: or did he? We shall return to this question shortly. Nevertheless, bear in mind that some historians have argued that population growth and subsequent migrations have been responsible for the spread of disease and for nations going to war. These positive checks all amount to 'misery' for the human race, to use Malthus's expression.

On the other hand, there are the 'preventive checks' to population growth. These include birth control within marriage, delayed marriage, and abstaining from marriage altogether. Very curiously, in his *First Essay* Malthus ignored the possibility of delayed marriage. Of birth control within marriage he disapproved heartily. This is difficult for us to understand nowadays, as we are conditioned by our own way of thinking. To us birth control seems a sensible way of reducing population growth and most religious or ethnic groups are prepared to practise at least some methods of birth control. In Malthus's day though, or at least in Malthus's mind, birth limitation was associated closely with 'sinful' activities. (We should remember that Malthus was a parson.) 'Improper arts' (presumably abortion, which is clearly a preventive check) were the recourse of people who needed to prevent the outcome of 'irregular connections' such as adultery. Barrier methods of contraception like condoms were resorted to for 'the sort of intercourse that renders some of the women of large towns unprolific', that is to say by men visiting prostitutes. Though that was the end of the story for Malthus, there was more to birth control than this even in Malthus's day.

It was theoretically possible, Malthus acknowledged, for couples to abstain from sex. That was moral but hardly a happy solution to the population problem. All the other preventive checks were described as 'vice'. So in Malthus's *First Essay* the population problem could be resolved only by solutions that were either miserable or vicious. It seems that economics was already a dismal science in the 1780s.

Fortunately, by the time he wrote the *Summary View* in 1830, Malthus had come to realize the potential of 'abstinence from marriage, either for a time or permanently'. This he called a 'moral restraint'. This we shall see was and is still a very important way in which populations control their growth.

As individuals felt themselves being constrained by poverty (as they moved towards the crisis of subsistence in Figure 1.3), they responded by waiting until times improved before marrying. As a result, their first births were delayed a year or so. Thus, fewer births occurred in years when some individuals were waiting for better times. Therefore, population growth slowed a little. This gave time for more land to be taken into cultivation to meet the growing population. Thus, the crisis was averted.

An important policy issue arose from this system of adjustment. England had a system of poverty relief in the form of the Poor Laws, which guaranteed that the local authority would provide accommodation and work for the destitute in the local workhouse. Malthus thought that this was a bad scheme. It interfered with the 'natural' mechanism of the positive and preventive checks, by which the destitute would be unable to bring up children and so the population (in the poorest part of society) would diminish. Instead it spread the poverty around, so to speak, by making the middle and richest classes contribute through their local parish to the upkeep of the poorest. The outcome, Malthus observed, might be that we all end up starving. It was not a very charitable point of view from a churchman who had enjoyed the luxury of a private education. Such schemes as the Poor Laws have continued to operate in essence in several countries until the present. For example, in parts of India employment guarantee schemes ensure that work will be provided for food or cash. We discuss these when we look at measures to avoid mass starvation. Like Malthus, some economists and politicians today criticize such efforts to prevent destitution.

The economist David Ricardo, a contemporary of Malthus, described the adjustment process as it would affect a whole society. In his *The Principles of Political Economy and Taxation*, written in 1817, Ricardo distinguishes short-term fluctuations in the real wage rate from its long-term equilibrium value, which he calls the 'natural price' of labour, writing:

It is when the market price of labour exceeds its natural price that the condition of the labourer is flourishing and happy, that he has it in his power to command a greater proportion of the necessaries and enjoyments of life, and therefore to rear a healthy and numerous family. When, however, by the encouragement which high wages give to the increase of population, the number of labourers is increased, wages again fall to their natural price, and indeed from a reaction sometimes fall below it.

This, the reader will notice, is a theory of long swings or cycles in the relationship between real incomes and population growth. It implies that marriages may be contracted earlier, children may be born earlier, and more of them survive when real incomes are rising (presumably because labour productivity is rising: the product curves are shifting upwards in Figure 1.3 faster than the progress along them). After a time, however, the result is more rapid increase in the number of boys and girls entering the labour market (the movement along the product curve becomes faster than the upward shifts). The result is a fall in the marginal product of labour and so a fall in real wages. This, we may observe (even if Ricardo did not), not only discourages early marriages and early childbearing but also leads to malnutrition and deaths of children. Both preventive and positive checks may be made endogenous to the economic system, as economists would say. Malthus came to believe that preventive checks had become more important than positive checks as a mechanism for maintaining the equilibrium in Western Europe. This was probably correct, and was a less dismal prognosis for the future than that implied by the *First Essay*. Yet late twentieth-century Malthusians have returned to the dismal frame of mind.

Reformulation of the institutional arguments

We have noted that from the early days of the debate about Malthus's ideas, Godwin had put the blame for poverty and malnutrition on the management of society by the State. Ricardo advanced a similar idea when looking at the developing countries of the world (as we call them today). When population presses upon resources in those parts of the world, 'the evil proceeds from bad government, from the insecurity of property, and from a want of education in all ranks of the people. To be made happier they require only to be better governed and instructed, as the augmentation of capital, beyond the augmentation of people, would be the inevitable result.' Note that Ricardo is arguing that, while population increase may be a problem in the developed countries (which are well governed), it is less likely to be the source of economic backwardness in the developing countries (which are badly governed). This seems to stand modern Malthusianism on its head.

The role of the State was also pointed out by a contemporary of Malthus, whom he never knew and who never knew him. In 1793, just a few years before Malthus published his first essay, Hung Liang-Chi wrote two essays: *Reign of Peace* and *Livelihood*. He too believed, presumably from observations in China, that population tended to multiply faster than the means of subsistence, in so far as the latter were limited by land area. The only solution, he writes, is for the government 'to exhort the people to develop new land, to practise more intensive farming, to transfer people from congested areas, . . . to prohibit extravagant living and the consumption of luxuries'. This is a more optimistic conclusion than that of Malthus, but it coincides with Godwin's view that the distribution of resources had something to do with poverty: clearly only the rich consumed luxuries. Godwin, Ricardo, and Hung share the view that the State has an independent role to play. This was not a view shared by Malthus's Marxist critics (at least not with reference to capitalist society): to these we turn shortly.

Finally, as already mentioned, George argued towards the end of the nineteenth century that the poverty one heard about in India was due to the tyrannous extraction of agricultural surplus by the landowning princes and the severe taxation imposed by the British colonial authorities. He was a distinctly sarcastic critic of Malthus, as can be judged from an amusing passage in his famous book *Progress and Poverty* of 1879:

It begins with the assumption that population tends to increase in a geometrical ratio while subsistence can at best be made to increase in only an arithmetic ratio—an assumption just as valid, and no more so, than it would be, from the fact that a puppy doubled the length of his tail while he added so many pounds to his weight, to assert a geometric progression of the tail and an arithmetic progression of the weight . . . the savants [wise men] of a previously dogless island might deduce the 'very striking consequence' that by the time the dog grew to a weight of fifty pounds his tail would be over a mile long and extremely difficult to wag, and hence recommend the prudential check of a bandage as the only alternative to the positive check of constant amputations.

Marx's critique of Malthus

It was Marx who advanced the most elaborate alternative model of the relationship between poverty, starvation, and population growth. He was outspoken in his denial that there was a general law of population and poverty in the manner proposed by Malthus.

Marx published his famous treatise, *Capital*, in 1867 when many improvements in agriculture in England had taken place and when the economy was coming through the first phase of the Industrial Revolution. Marx believed that poverty was tied up closely with these two processes, rather than with population growth itself.

The changes in rural and urban England that Marx observed were social as well as economic. This is what distinguishes his analysis (and that of his collaborator, Engels). Not only were innovations in agriculture taking place and more intensive use being made of the land, but changes in the relationships between different social groups were also occurring. Spurred on by the prospects of agricultural growth and prosperity, the wealthier landowning farmers began to look for ways of accumulating surplus cash from the sale of produce, so that they could invest in agricultural machinery or buy more land. These investments would enable them to grow even more food for sale and make even more profit. In their desire to maximize their profit from farming, such farmers looked for ways of using labour as efficiently and cheaply as possible. Often this could be achieved by doing away with tenant farmers and hiring agricultural labourers as and when they were needed. The tenant farmers were simply pushed off the land. This practice of hiring and firing amounted to an entirely new relationship between farm workers and farm owners. The process just outlined is a simplified description of what Marx called the development of capitalism.

The landless labourers were at times unemployed, leading to a rapid descent to poverty. Someone like Malthus, viewing this poverty, might think that overpopulation due to excessive population growth existed. The Marxists argued that such poverty resulted from the development of capitalism. Under a different economic system, like the one that came before (feudalism) or the one they thought would come afterwards (socialism), this overpopulation would not necessarily have occurred. That is why they called it 'relative overpopulation', or 'relative surplus population'.

As the manufacturing enterprises grew, the same profit-making strategies were implemented in the industrializing regions. Instead of using small workshops employing family labour, entrepreneurs realized they could make more money by building larger factories, mechanizing some jobs, and hiring labourers as and when they needed them. Of course they would always need some labourers to operate the machines, but if consumer demand for their products fell off at any time, they could fire some workers temporarily and reduce their output. When business picked up, they could hire some workers to enable them to produce to full capacity again. The workers who were fired had to wait around for another job. Why did business cycles of this kind occur? This is a much-debated question and is of equal relevance today. The more rapid oscillations might have been related to the agricultural cycles described already. If people went without enough food during a harvest failure, presumably they could not afford to buy manufactured clothes either. But, whatever the cause of cycles, whether long or short, if most businesses went into a depression at the same time, many labourers would be thrown out of work together. Marx's understanding of the process is summarized as follows, in Volume I of *Capital*:

The dynamic characteristic of modern industry, viz. a decennial cycle (interrupted by smaller oscillations) of periods of average activity, production at high pressure, crisis, and stagnation, depends on constant formation, the greater or less absorption, and the re-formation of the industrial reserve army of the surplus population.

Here again was a relative surplus population, likely to suffer poverty and even starvation. Its occurrence was linked fundamentally to the capitalist system of industry. Indeed, Marx went further than this. Business could not operate successfully without this relative surplus population: for how else could it easily hire labourers as and when the business cycle picked up? The 'reserve army', as he called it, was necessary to capitalism. Modern economists have used the term frictional unemployment to describe this requirement. Furthermore, economists would recognize that a pool of unemployed (which is another modern expression for the reserve army) tends to keep wages down. Why did these people not migrate back to the countryside? The reply lies in another question: what would they do there if there was already a relative surplus labour force in agriculture?

Marx also perceived a long-run tendency for industrial capitalists to substitute capital for labour by adopting the latest technology.[9] This meant that labourers were continually being thrown out of work and into the pool of unemployed. Some would be re-employed eventually as other businesses expanded or started up. It is debated whether the reserve army got larger over time. That debate need not concern us here.

Marx used three distinct terms to describe different segments of the relative surplus population. The unemployed agricultural labourers were called the latent overpopulation; the urban unemployed, thrown out of work, were called the floating overpopulation; and the family workers in small workshops, who would soon be absorbed in the capitalist system, he called the stagnant overpopulation.

As can be seen, Malthus has been turned on his head again. Poverty and starvation result from a failure in labour demand, rather than an excessive increase in labour supply. The relative merits of these interpretations continue to be debated today in the context of the economic development of Asia and Africa.

Malthus on the evidence

Malthus stated his theory as if it were a universal law, and not an idea with only limited applicability. In his *Second Essay*, published in 1803, he put together all the evidence he could find from the writings of others (including explorers and anthropologists) on the experience of populations throughout the world. This unfortunately is the weakest part of his work. He was so determined to support his theory—and if it really was a law it had to be supported by every instance he could come across—that his judgement was severely compromised in the effort. To give an example, he commented on the population of Tierra del Fuego at the tip of South America from the evidence of the diaries of his contemporary, Captain James Cook. This was hardly an area containing many people—then, as now, it was probably among the least populous wildernesses in the world. The people were extremely poor by all accounts and Malthus drew the hasty conclusion that this was evidence of too great a population pressing on meagre resources. Only in a very literal and static sense could one say that this was true. Moreover, if the solution was to impose preventive checks to slow the rate of population increase (which was probably already close to zero), the population would rapidly dwindle into non-existence. This is not, one feels, a very helpful analysis or conclusion. Another example illustrates Malthus's single-mindedness. Montesquieu, the French philosopher, had recorded how among the Malabar Nayas, a caste residing in south-western India (present-day Kerala), only the eldest brother married. Montesquieu thought this was to enable the younger brothers to serve in the military. Malthus rejoined (without any evidence) that it was due to 'the fear of poverty arising from a large family'.

Everywhere that Malthus looked, he saw misery, vice, and occasionally prudential checks, such as in the example just quoted, but he refused to entertain alternative explanations. We shall try to avoid such prejudice as we follow through selected cases in the demographic history of Asia (see Chapter 3).

Notes

1. Demographers use the term 'natural' to distinguish population increase resulting from an excess of births over deaths from growth in population due to migration as well. In practice, the words 'population growth' are often used to mean natural increase, the assumption being that migration is negligible.
2. This means that the proportional (or percentage) increase in population (which is constant in a geometric progression) must at some point become greater than the proportional increase in food (which is diminishing in an arithmetic progression), even if the proportional increase in food started off greater (see Figure 1.2).
3. Actually Malthus need not have assumed an arithmetic growth of food supply to support his argument that population growth outstrips the growth of food. It was only necessary to show that the geometric growth of food was slower than the geometric growth of the population.
4. In technical jargon this means that Alison's solution, the geometric increase in scientific knowledge, is a necessary but not a sufficient condition to prevent the ultimate occurrence of the Malthusian problem. Taking logs of the two geometric functions, we can see from the slope of the lines that the proportional increase in food is less than the proportional increase in population. Box 1.1 shows the mathematics of this for exponential growth rates.
5. Boserup does argue that, at roughly the same levels of technological development, high-density countries have lower output per head than low-density countries. She also argues that, in order to achieve these high yields per acre, men, women, and children have to work longer hours. Even so, output per head seems to fall, but starvation is averted. It is easier to imagine output per person-hour falling and, as a result, longer hours are necessary in order to maintain output per head.
6. To put it another way, population growth may be necessary, but not sufficient, for agricultural innovation.

7. Technically speaking, population growth may not even be necessary for agricultural innovation to take place.
8. The illustration is fairly impressionistic. Annual data for food output will reflect annual fluctuations and not lie on a curve or a straight line. Econometric techniques are required to fit a geometric (or exponential) curve to the data. Then, by taking logs, the slopes can be compared, as indicated in Box 1.1.
9. Neo-classical economists tell us that profit maximizers only do this if wages rise. Reality is probably more complicated. Not all productivity-raising technological changes are 'labour-using' like Boserup's agricultural innovations. In industrial production such options sometimes simply do not exist. Many major productivity improvements inevitably employ more capital per unit of labour than before.

2 | Adjustment of Households to Food Supplies and Other Resources

Introduction

Aggregate food supply seems to have grown at a faster rate than population in most areas of the world over the last half century. This was illustrated for China and India in the last chapter (Figure 1.6). The projections of agronomists are optimistic about the continuation of this trend. Furthermore, demographers have become increasingly confident that there is going to be a deceleration in the rate of population growth: data from the larger countries of Asia give reason to believe this is so and similar evidence is emerging from Africa. Does this mean that poverty and starvation are on their way out? It seems unlikely.

We have already discussed the ideas of those economists who emphasize that the distribution of resources is the critical factor in understanding poverty. We now discuss how households and their members gain access to food and how they manage their households and make decisions regarding family formation and investments in physical resources like land.

The key concept is that of effective demand. Every individual needs food for survival. That need is only realized in practice if the individual can lay claim to the food. His or her claim may be a moral one, a contractual one, or one involving purchasing power in the market-place.

Let us give one stark example. Several Asian countries have embarked on programmes of offshore fishing. Some development plans have pointed out how important fish is as a source of protein for a poor population. However, the fishermen are often wage labourers, paid cash wages by the fishing company concerned. The fish caught is sold for canning and consumption overseas where it fetches a high price. The fishermen's wages are insufficient to buy that fish, though they may be sufficient to buy a great deal more rice than they were able to buy before the fishing programme was started. This shows that the programme has been of some benefit to them. It also illustrates that the effective demand of the fishermen is crucial in deciding whether they can consume the fish that they catch.

Food allocation within the family

We can discuss what we mean by effective demand by starting with the family. Everyone of whatever age or sex needs food. Table 2.1(a) indicates approximately how much food they each need in comparison with an adult male (aged between 15 and 54 years). It is not always appreciated that very young children need as much as a third or a half of the adult food intake. How would we calculate effective demand? An economist might be tempted to relate this to the work that a person can contribute to the household economy. For instance, the work potential of children aged less than ten years is rather small, though in some societies children perform important tasks like looking after farm animals. Similarly, the work potential of elderly family members is small. Table 2.1(b) illustrates this, again taking the adult male's work potential as the norm or index. Figure 2.1 shows the cost of

Table 2.1. Indices of estimated calorie needs and potential work

(a) Estimated calorie needs (adult male = 1.0)

Age	Male	Female
0–4	0.3	0.3
5–9	0.5	0.5
10–14	0.8	0.7
15–54	1.0	0.8/1.0[a]
55–59	0.9	0.7
60–64	0.8	0.6
65+	0.7	0.6

[a] Lactating or pregnant women.

Source: Adapted from the United Nations 'medium-consumption' profile.

(b) Potential work (adult = 1.0)

Age	Index
0–4	0.0
5–9	0.1
10–14	0.3
15–19	0.9
20–54	1.0
55–64	0.6
65+	0.4

Source: Author's estimates derived from several sources.

Fig. 2.1. Consumption and production profiles by age

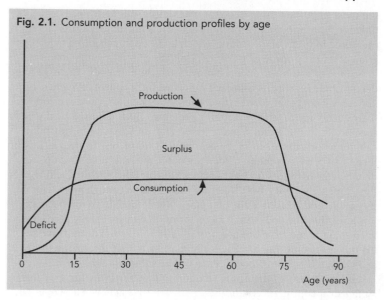

feeding family members by age along with their earning power, on the assumption that an adult male can earn twice as much as it costs to feed him. This explanation of effective demand treats a household like a firm. Presumably elderly people, who make little contribution to the household economy, would be half-starved if they were not allowed to consume more than they contribute. Usually, however, entitlement to food is partly of a moral nature. Social norms require one to look after one's old people. Social norms on feeding differ from society to society. In societies where women have an inferior status to men, they may get less to eat although pregnant and lactating women need as much food as (or more than) active adult males. Similarly, young girls are not always allocated as much food as young boys. This may be rationalized on the grounds that they do less work. Yet what work they are allowed to do is socially determined. Social norms (encapsulating age and gender power relations) change over time. Sex differentials in child mortality, which may result from insufficient food, are becoming smaller as development proceeds, even in those South Asian countries where they were once quite substantial.

Protein-energy malnutrition

There used to be considerable concern about whether different societies consumed enough protein. Nowadays nutritionists believe that calories are the most important thing to count. Put simply, the body needs energy to function hour by hour and the more active it is the more it needs. Energy is measured in terms of the calorie, which is the energy required to heat one gram of water by one degree Celsius. Thus the calorific content of food is an indication of how much energy it provides the human body. There is a huge debate about how many calories are needed by people of different stature, and we will not get involved in this. The same food that provides calories for daily energy needs usually contains proteins, which are used by the body specifically to build and replace tissue and muscle. One might think of calories as consumption (in the economist's sense) and protein as investment. Out of its daily intake of food (income), the body uses most up immediately (consumption) and sets aside a little for body-building and repairs (investment, net and gross). Nearly all diets contain enough protein for this, if enough food is taken in the first place. But, if food intake drops to a very low level, then the body uses it all up for its immediate energy needs just to keep going, in the same way as a poverty-stricken person cannot save any of his or her income. So, all that really matters is that the calorie intake is sufficient. If it is, then protein intake will be sufficient also.[1]

It is true, however, that some vitamins and minerals are not available in sufficient quantity in certain diets, perhaps especially when people have migrated to new environments and are not immediately aware of what is available. It is also important to note that people who are forced to live on fewer calories than is ideal are often seriously deficient in the intake of particular vitamins or minerals. This may result in death or disability although they have enough energy to keep going. The most outstanding example is vitamin A deficiency, which leads to blindness. This affliction is especially common among children: in the 1970s 10 per cent of children in rural India were reckoned to be afflicted in this way. Vitamin A is particularly concentrated in some green vegetables.

Iron is also often deficient in a low-calorie diet. This leads to anaemia, a common disability (especially among women, who lose iron when menstruating). The majority of preschool children were believed to be anaemic in India in the 1960s, as were most expectant mothers, who pass on this important mineral to their babies. The result was that at least 10 per cent of maternal deaths could be attributed to this cause.

In the past, vitamin D deficiency was a problem. The vitamin is contained in milk, for example, and is produced in the body by exposure to sunlight. In nineteenth-century Europe, children who were sheltered from the light by being kept in workshops for child labour, in cities enshrouded in smog, grew up crippled by rickets, that is, insufficient bone growth.

A deficiency in nutrients like thiamine, which is part of the vitamin B chain and is needed to release energy from carbohydrates, can occur if food is subjected to particular processes of manufacture. For example, polishing rice so that the outer layers of the grain are lost may result in the disease known as beri-beri, which was common in colonial Burma, for example.

It can be seen, therefore, that insufficient food may lead to specific diseases long before people die of starvation. Probably the most important case in point relates to the immunity people acquire against disease. It is increasingly being understood that recovery from many diseases is enhanced by adequate nutrition. In particular, a synergistic relationship exists between diarrhoeal disease and malnutrition. A child who is malnourished and becomes infected with bacteria that thrive in the gut will conquer those bacteria less quickly than a well-nourished child. This means that his or her diarrhoea lasts longer and may become life threatening if the child becomes dehydrated. In addition, a child with diarrhoea usually suffers from lack of appetite and is unable to digest food efficiently. Thus, it gets even weaker and less able to resist the progress of the bacteria. Diarrhoeal disease is one of the greatest killers in the world of children aged under five.

Effective demand and the 'green revolution'

We have looked at how effective demand for food may operate through family distribution mechanisms to affect the survival chances of different family members. Now consider how households may find their collective effective demand changing as they are subjected to commercialization and other features of economic change. We have mentioned that improving the production of a food like fish might not mean that the fishermen had any opportunity to eat the fish. Here we give a more elaborate example of why growth in food production may fail to benefit certain economic groups or classes unless their effective demand in the market is also raised.

In the 1960s a 'green revolution' (to which we alluded in Chapter 1) began to take hold in parts of north-west India and the Pakistan Punjab. These agricultural areas had a history of high productivity (partly due to a well-developed canal irrigation system) and for some time farmers had been organizing their farms on capitalistic lines. These farmers were politically powerful also. When the governments concerned began to encourage the adoption of new high-yielding seeds in these areas, they also agreed to subsidize production on these farms and to ensure a high price for their product, which was mainly wheat.

Wheat is expensive in India and wheat bread is consumed mainly by the middle class, particularly the urban middle class who favour white sliced bread in the western style. The poor eat either bread made from coarse grains (not wheat) or rice. The rich can easily obtain enough protein through eating bread (as wheat has about 12 per cent of protein in it)[2] and also tend to consume milk and meat, which are both rich in proteins. The poor would need to eat a great deal of rice, preferably brown rice, to obtain enough protein (white rice, that is milled rice, has about 8 per cent). This represents a bulky diet that is not very suitable for young children. Traditionally, however, the poor have eaten pulses (known as dal in India) along with their rice. These are rich in protein (containing about 25 per cent) and iron, and provide a balanced diet when taken with rice. Children can easily take in enough protein if they eat dal. Moreover, it is a cooked food and hygienic (if it is not watered down) since cooking kills off many of the harmful bacteria that are found in unclean environments.

The new policies meant that farmers could make increased profits by growing more wheat. As land dedicated to growing pulses was less profitable, they tended to turn it over to wheat. The result can be seen in Table 2.2, which gives indices for total cereals, pulses, and population (Box 2.1 shows how an index is calculated). Readers can calculate the annual average (compound) growth of each and see how their availability changed. Between 1961 and 1971, production of wheat per head rose by one-quarter, whereas that of pulses fell by one-third. Economists will appreciate that this probably means that pulses became more expensive.

At this point it may seem that the story has ended: the poor suffered a worsening diet and must have been worse off than before. Yet it is not as simple as that. The effective demand that the poor have over pulses, for example, depends not only on their price. If the poor are purchasing their food in the market-place, clearly their money income matters. What do these incomes depend upon? One crucial thing must be employment. What matters to agricultural labourers is whether the green revolution increased their employment or decreased it. Did the increase keep up with the rate of population growth, for instance? Did it make the demand for labour more seasonal and less reliable? We return to these questions when we discuss decisions about family formation. For the moment let us say that initially, at least, the demand for labour seems to have increased in the region. Later, increased mechanization made the situation less favourable.

So far we have been discussing the effect of the green revolution on the poor mainly through theorizing. What sort of evidence would one look for to see if they really suffered or not? We have already described how a poor nutritional intake, especially for children, can interact with disease and lead to death. Let us then look at mortality among children.

Table 2.2. Indices for output of cereals and pulses and for total population, India 1950–80 (1950 = 100)

	1950	1955	1960	1965	1970	1975	1980
Cereals	100	132	163	147	228	255	280
Pulses	100	131	151	118	141	155	126
Population[a]	100	—	120	—	150	—	188

[a] Population figures apply to 1951, 1961, 1971, and 1981.

Source: Government of India, Annual Statistical Abstract.

BOX 2.1. INDEX NUMBERS

According to the decennial censuses, the population of India (in millions) has grown as follows:

1951	1961	1971	1981	1991
364	439	548	685	844

By setting 1951 = 100, we can form an index of relative population size as follows:

For 1961: $(439/364) \times 100 = 120.$

For 1971: $(548/364) \times 100 = 150.$

For 1981: $(685/364) \times 100 = 188.$

For 1991: $(844/364) \times 100 = 232.$

The indexed population becomes therefore:

1951	1961	1971	1981	1991
100	120	150	188	232

Whether the actual numbers or this index are used, the growth rates remain the same. The reader can calculate these. Indices enable one to see percentage changes very easily. The population of 1951 doubled at some point between 1981 and 1991. The reader can check the doubling time exactly by first calculating the annual growth between 1951 and 1991 (see Box 1.1). Note that multiplying throughout by 100 is optional; one can also set 1951 = 1.0.

Indices are also useful for comparing changes in two different quantities, for example food and population, as in Table 2.2.

This is easier to suggest than to do. From where would we get the figures? Recording of births and deaths in rural areas is poor. However, social surveys have been carried out that provide some information on present and past mortality. Fortunately demographers can attempt to reconstruct infant mortality rates from the past to the present from these survey data. But, even if we showed that infant mortality had been rising or falling over the period, what conclusions could we draw? If the rate went down, would that support the argument that the poor did well out of the green revolution? What about other parts of the Indian subcontinent where the green revolution hardly occurred—suppose infant mortality went down there too? We really need some comparisons, some controls (to use the technical jargon), and some micro-studies that distinguish different classes of people and different possible causes of mortality change.

The evidence shows that the infant mortality rate did fall in the Indian

Fig. 2.2. Pattern of age and sex-specific mortality rates

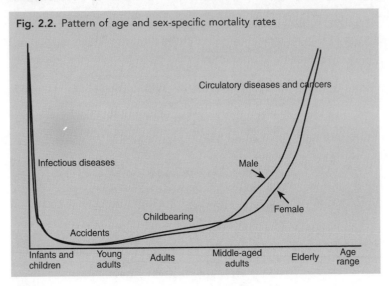

Punjab between 1960 and 1984, but it fell more or less as fast in other states of India. Even the landless experienced a fall in infant mortality. However, the surveys also show that the infant mortality did not fall as far for the landless as it did for the landed farmers' children. There remains a gap between them.

At this point you might ask what we are measuring with the *infant mortality rate*. Figure 2.2 shows what we mean by *age-specific mortality rates*, and Figure 2.3 shows (using data from an Asian city) how they relate to underlying diseases, some of which have a strong link with nutrition. Box 2.2 shows how to calculate these rates.

Nutrition and the urban migrant

Many countries of the developing world are urbanizing rapidly. (This process is discussed further in Part V of this book.) Thus it is becoming increasingly important to ask what is the effect on individuals and their families of living in towns and cities. How is their nutritional status likely to change from living in an urban rather than a rural environment?

Besides buying food, the urban household has to make other important, even vital, expenditures. One of these is for shelter. This may cost very little in rural areas, especially if the household pays no rent. Rural incomes for poor, landless labourers, for example, might just suffice to buy enough calories and to provide the upkeep of a small thatched hut. This is illustrated

Fig. 2.3. Profile of diseases by age recorded in Indian cities

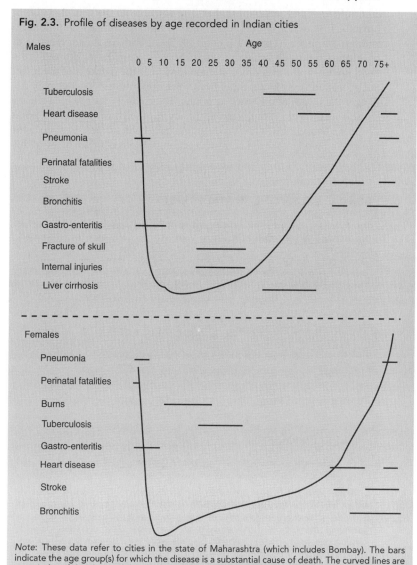

Note: These data refer to cities in the state of Maharashtra (which includes Bombay). The bars indicate the age group(s) for which the disease is a substantial cause of death. The curved lines are a reminder of the shape of the age-specific mortality schedule.

in Figure 2.4 by point A. On migration to a large urban area the household faces a changed situation. The cost of shelter is now very high. Typically, rent must be paid even to occupy a hut in a slum. Those who construct their own dwelling often pay rent to a local slumlord or a bribe to the police to prevent their home being demolished. Some households cannot afford both sufficient food and sufficient shelter. The outcome for the household is not obvious. It may not be the best choice to opt for sufficient food and do without the shelter (Figure 2.4, point B). Doing without shelter may mean squatting temporarily in a damp area close to a polluted river and below the flood line or on the margins of a main road near the outskirts of the town. Such locations may be far away from work opportunities or they may endanger the health of the working adults. Thus, paying for minimal shelter may be necessary to earn the money to buy any food at all (Figure 2.4, point C). Urban households in this predicament have been studied. They do compromise on food intake in order to meet compulsions of urban living of this kind.

BOX 2.2. AGE-SPECIFIC MORTALITY RATES

The following table for Taiwanese males gives the approximate number of deaths by age recorded in a single year in the 1960s and the estimated population at risk of death during the same year. Ages are grouped in ten-year groups, except for the first five years of life. These are of particular interest to demographers and are reported in two narrower groups: less than 1 year and 1–4 years.

Table A

Age group	Deaths	Population
<1	8,695	255,000
1–4	5,822	766,000
5–14	1,986	1,806,000
15–24	1,783	849,000
25–34	2,517	868,000
35–44	3,611	737,000
45–54	5,121	507,000
55–64	6,934	273,000
65–74	6,365	103,000
75+	7,106	45,000

Those aged less than one year are known as infants. Those aged 1–4 years are known as children (though this term is also used for the entire age group 0–4 years). Demographers define age groups such as 5–9 years to mean 'including the fifth birthday and up to the tenth'. This corresponds with common parlance. People say that they are aged 9 even when they are a few days away from their tenth birthday.

To calculate *age-specific mortality rates* divide the population in each age group by the corresponding deaths. For example, the 1–4 mortality rate is:

$5,822 \div 766,000 = 0.0076.$

This is usually then multiplied by 1,000 to give a rate of 7.6 per thousand. For example, the 5–14 mortality rate is:

$1,986 \div 1,806,000 \times 1,000 = 1.1$ per thousand.

BOX 2.2. continued

Similar calculations yield the following complete table:

Table B

Age group	Mortality rates per 1,000
<1	34.1
1–4	7.6
5–14	1.1
15–24	2.1
25–34	2.9
35–44	4.9
45–54	10.1
55–64	25.4
65–74	61.8
75+	157.9

The rate for 75+ is an average for all ages above 75 years. At some very high age the rate must become 1,000 per thousand (i.e., at the age at which the oldest person dies).

In this table the death rate for infants is calculated like the others. The census data are used for the denominator. This is *not* the infant mortality rate as usually defined and calculated. The *infant mortality rate* is:

$$\frac{\text{Number of infant deaths in a year}}{\text{Number of births during that year}} \times 1,000.$$

One advantage of this measure is that it can be calculated for any year from vital registration records without having to make estimates from the census. It is not, however, an exact measure of the probability of dying in infancy in a particular year. This is because some of the deaths in a year occur to infants born the previous year and some of the births in a year result in infant deaths the following year.

Another example might be that of fuel. In some rural areas this can be gathered from the jungle almost free of cost (free at least of cash cost, though family labour effort is involved). In urban areas fuel has to be bought. It tends to be very expensive. Wood is very costly in most cities and, while soft coal is sometimes cheap, its smoke may lead to bronchitis and tuberculosis. Kerosene is sometimes affordable but many accidents are caused by small stoves in the cramped conditions of urban slums.

These problems affect all poor urban residents, not only recent migrants. A study in the slums of a city in Bangladesh found that 64 per cent of the poorest quarter of households had become indebted simply to cover the cost of food and these other essential expenditures.[3]

Other problems of adjustment to urban living conditions occur because the migrant finds him or herself in a new social environment. She or he is

Fig. 2.4. Nutritional implications of rural-to-urban migration: the case of shelter

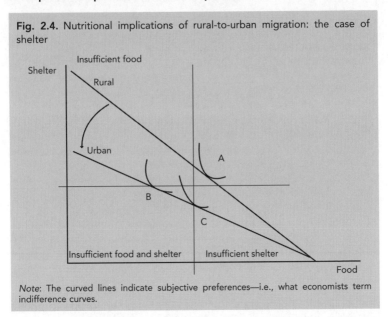

Note: The curved lines indicate subjective preferences—i.e., what economists term indifference curves.

much more conscious of a large middle class living close by and sees life-styles that she or he wants to emulate. The activities of the advertising industry can serve only to encourage this. For example, for the first time in his or her life, the migrant is confronted with exciting new foods that represent an alternative to rice. These are heavily advertised and are consumed by the rich and thought therefore to be good. (Economists term this the demonstration effect.) They are also very expensive. A whole range of such foods and beverages exists, including packaged sugary biscuits, fizzy drinks, and canned or powdered baby milk. We call all such foods junk food and assume that they provide only a small percentage of the calories that can be obtained from a similar expenditure on rice. In the migrant's village, junk food was probably virtually unavailable. The labourer consumed only rice and obtained just enough calories that way. Junk food is more available in the city and costs a little less: transport costs are lower and the possibility of bulk supplies for collective consumption lowers unit costs. The migrant begins to buy it and consumes less rice. Powerful advertising and a seductive taste (enhanced by additives such as sugar and salt) encourage the migrant to substitute ever more junk food for rice. The household's calorie intake decreases. Maybe the husband enjoys both junk food and sufficient rice, while his wife has to make do with less money to feed herself and the children. Suppose that the price of junk food rises (as the producer seeks to exercise his monopoly power, for example). The consumer may now be 'hooked' on it and refuse to give any up: he may now feel that a bottle of fizzy drink a day is his right and his status symbol. Even fewer calories are consumed by the family.

We mentioned the use of baby foods like tinned or packaged milk in the above paragraph. This is probably the most outstanding deleterious demonstration effect of urban living. Breast milk, which is the usual food for infants in rural areas, is of enormous nutritional value and extremely cost-effective. It contains antibodies against common diseases, it is rich in vitamins and minerals (especially if the mother herself is well fed), and it contains all the calories most babies need for the first four to six months of life without any further supplementation. (Only a small minority of mothers cannot supply enough milk.) Nevertheless, middle-class mothers in many countries have taken to bottle-feeding their infants with cow's milk or milk products. From the late nineteenth century, the baby food manufacturing companies tried hard to promote their wares, though nowadays such advertising is much restricted. Poor migrants still often wish to imitate the practice of bottle-feeding. Yet, powdered or tinned milk is very costly in comparison with the calories it provides (in the poorest countries absorbing up to 50 per cent of the daily earnings). Therefore, poor mothers often dilute it with water to make it go further. In the environment of urban slums this is a particularly bad idea. The available water is often heavily contaminated and fuel is too costly for it to be boiled first. For the same reason, the bottle cannot be properly cleaned or the nipple sterilized. The result is the widespread transmission of disease plus inadequate nutritional intake. It is the single factor to which rising infant mortality has been attributed in some cities. In the 1980s, studies in urban Malaysia found that 11 per cent of the élite and 30 per cent of the poor breast-fed their children for six months. In rural Malaysia, 65 per cent did so. Such differences can be found all over the world. A study in Papua New Guinea found that the risk of severe malnutrition in bottle-fed children was seven times greater than in those who were breast-fed. Similarly, the risk of mortality among children in Brazil was seven times higher among children who were breast-fed for less than six months than among those who were breast-fed for longer.

These examples of reactions to the urban environment might suggest that the problem of malnutrition arises because people do not always know how best to look after themselves. There is some truth in this for all classes of society: overeating by the rich illustrates this well. However, there is plenty of evidence that the poor can adapt quickly to new forms of diet if the opportunity allows. A study in a city in Peru showed how households changed their consumption pattern to maintain their desired intake of protein-rich foods as relative prices changed. As meat became more and more expensive over a ten-year period, people changed from taking 70 per cent of their proteins from meat to obtaining the same amount from protein-rich vegetables like beans. It is often poverty, deriving from the insecurities of urban employment and the deleterious physical environ-

Table 2.3. Mean kilocalorie intake per consumer unit per day from survey data in India

Consumer group	Range of means[a]
Urban	
High income	2,000–3,085
Middle income	1,880–2,715
Low income	1,760–2,665
Industrial labour	1,900–2,510
Slum dwellers	1,760–2,290
Rural	
More than 10 acres	2,375–3,100
5–10 acres	2,100–2,860
Landless	1,865–2,310
Harijans	1,600–2,460

[a] Range of means for the various cities and rural areas sampled.

Source: K. S. J. Rao, 'Urban nutrition in India—1', *Bulletin of the Nutrition Foundation of India*, 6: 4 (1985).

ment, due in part to the failure of the State to organize sanitation programmes, that causes malnutrition. It is not always ignorance.

Again we have been looking at arguments and case studies. Yet are the urban poor really worse off in terms of food intake or mortality than their rural counterparts? This is a complex question. We take it up in more detail later in this book. For the moment we restrict ourselves to looking at surveys of calorie consumption for India in the late 1970s. (See Table 2.3.) These suggest that the poorest of the urban poor may get no more to eat than the poorest of the rural poor (despite the plentiful supply of a good variety of food to urban areas). This is consistent with the picture just outlined.

Family formation and household resources

In the adjustment models outlined in Chapter 1, we referred to couples delaying marriage or childbearing in response to a worsening economic situation such as a local food shortage resulting from increasing population pressure on the land. When new techniques of production were introduced and wages and productivity returned to their former level, family formation proceeded apace once more. The assumption is that family formation always responds to changes in income and the assets that produce that income. For instance, an increase in income may result from more land being cultivated by the household or from the introduction of better tools of cultivation or even machines (like pumps to improve irrigation). Once these have been acquired, families can afford to have more children, that is to increase their fertility (which is the demographer's term for live births).

Do decisions necessarily occur in that order? Suppose that it is traditional to marry early and bear children: it is a moral duty in life to create human assets in this way. Human beings mature to become the agricultural work-force and income (in kind or in wages) flows from the product of that labour. Managing the household assets in a way that provides the complementary capital or land for that labour to work might be necessary. The process would be one of adjusting one's household resources to meet the results of family formation, rather than the other way round. To use the technical terms, maybe families regard fertility as parametric and other household resources as variable. This way of looking at things seems odd to those economists who have been brought up in the Western neo-classical tradi-tion of thinking in which fertility is the variable factor and other assets are parametric. In the modernizing world, having a video-recorder in the house may seem imperative, even if the family has to cut down on children to afford one. At other times and in other places, families might have different priorities, however.

In the 1920s, a Russian economist, Chayanov, proposed a theory of household resource adjustment and family formation that has many of the characteristics of modern Western (or neo-classical) economics but as-sumes that the household economy is adjusted in response to family forma-tion and not the other way round. To follow his argument clearly, look at Table 2.4, which was drawn up originally by Chayanov himself. The num-bers in the table refer to consumer units (as in Table 2.1). An adult man is standardized at 1.0 and children are taken to consume less than that (though the scale is different from that used in the earlier table). An adult woman's consumption needs are shown as 0.8, which we have argued is too little if the woman is pregnant or nursing. Observe how this family is formed year after year, with the original couple eventually rearing nine children with intervals between births of three years. The total consumption needs that this leads to are shown in the column headed 'Consumers'. There is another column for the production potential of that family. It is again stand-ardized with the adult male at 1.0. As illustrated in Figure 2.5, Chayanov calculated a consumer: worker ratio by dividing the one index into the other. This is a slightly odd thing to do. We suggested earlier that adult production potential is generally well above consumption requirements. (Otherwise there would be no surplus for the young and the old, not to mention non-agricultural workers, to consume.) However, Chayanov's ratio indicates the relative change in household production and consumption reasonably well. Figure 2.5 shows how this ratio changes over the family's life history. The consumption burden rises to a peak and then declines when the older sons and daughters enter the labour force.

Table 2.4. Family formation and consumption/production indices in Chayanov's scheme

Years	Index of married couple's consumption	Index of children's consumption									Total	
		1	2	3	4	5	6	7	8	9	Consumers	Producers
1	1.8	—	—	—	—	—	—	—	—	—	1.8	1.8
2	1.8	0.1	—	—	—	—	—	—	—	—	1.9	1.8
3	1.8	0.3	—	—	—	—	—	—	—	—	2.1	1.8
4	1.8	0.3	—	—	—	—	—	—	—	—	2.1	1.8
5	1.8	0.3	0.1	—	—	—	—	—	—	—	2.2	1.8
6	1.8	0.3	0.3	—	—	—	—	—	—	—	2.4	1.8
7	1.8	0.3	0.3	—	—	—	—	—	—	—	2.4	1.8
8	1.8	0.3	0.3	0.1	—	—	—	—	—	—	2.5	1.8
9	1.8	0.5	0.3	0.3	—	—	—	—	—	—	2.9	1.8
10	1.8	0.5	0.3	0.3	—	—	—	—	—	—	2.9	1.8
11	1.8	0.5	0.3	0.3	0.1	—	—	—	—	—	3.0	1.8
12	1.8	0.5	0.5	0.3	0.3	—	—	—	—	—	3.4	1.8
13	1.8	0.5	0.5	0.3	0.3	—	—	—	—	—	3.4	1.8
14	1.8	0.5	0.5	0.3	0.3	0.1	—	—	—	—	3.5	1.8
15	1.8	0.7	0.5	0.5	0.3	0.3	—	—	—	—	4.1	2.5
16	1.8	0.7	0.5	0.5	0.3	0.3	—	—	—	—	4.1	2.5
17	1.8	0.7	0.5	0.5	0.3	0.3	0.1	—	—	—	4.2	2.5
18	1.8	0.7	0.7	0.5	0.5	0.3	0.3	—	—	—	4.8	3.2
19	1.8	0.7	0.7	0.5	0.5	0.3	0.3	—	—	—	4.8	3.2
20	1.8	0.9	0.7	0.5	0.5	0.3	0.3	0.1	—	—	5.1	3.4
21	1.8	0.9	0.7	0.7	0.5	0.5	0.3	0.3	—	—	5.7	4.1
22	1.8	0.9	0.7	0.7	0.5	0.5	0.3	0.3	—	—	5.7	4.1
23	1.8	0.9	0.9	0.7	0.5	0.5	0.3	0.3	0.1	—	6.0	4.3
24	1.8	0.9	0.9	0.7	0.7	0.5	0.5	0.3	0.3	—	6.6	5.0
25	1.8	0.9	0.9	0.7	0.7	0.5	0.5	0.3	0.3	—	6.6	5.0
26	1.8	0.9	0.9	0.9	0.7	0.5	0.5	0.3	0.3	0.1	6.9	5.2

Source: A. V. Chayanov, (1925), *The Theory of the Peasant Economy*, ed. D. Thorner (University of Wisconsin Press, Madison, WI, 1986).

Fig. 2.5. Consumer/worker profiles by years of a family's existence

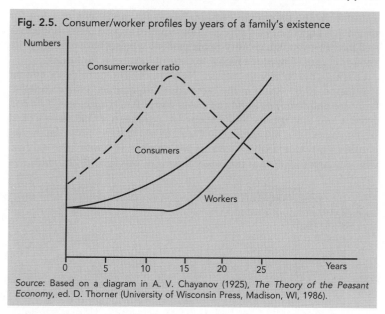

Source: Based on a diagram in A. V. Chayanov (1925), *The Theory of the Peasant Economy*, ed. D. Thorner (University of Wisconsin Press, Madison, WI, 1986).

The important point of this model for our purposes is that it takes the family formation process as given. Chayanov then asks how the family will put its growing labour force to productive use. He suggests that, as the new members become of working age, the household will rent more land for them to work on. So the farm itself will become bigger; it will accumulate assets in response to the growing family. Chayanov was describing what he believed had been happening to peasant households in nineteenth-century Russia. Eventually the farm would be divided. Exactly when this would occur would depend on the individual family's circumstances. One could imagine the original parents dying and married sons leaving the family unit, though in Russia this tended not to occur early in the life cycle of the family. Some readers may feel that this model has curious features, especially in relation to their own experience of analysing farming households. These would be worth thinking through.

Furthermore, one might like to consider how feasible this theory is on purely logical grounds. What would Malthus's objection to it have been, for example? A first thought might be that this theory would only work if plenty of land was available for households to rent as they grew. A little more reflection would suggest, however, that if some families were growing while others were dividing, a certain amount of land swapping—hiring in and hiring out—could occur. To return to Malthus's point, while the population as a whole is growing there is a net requirement for more land for this process to work. Therefore the theory can only apply where unused land is available. In the nineteenth century, Russia was something of a frontier region. It is arguable that such conditions applied in parts of Asia and Africa well into the twentieth century. Some modern scholars have examined the applicability of Chayanov's theory to parts of Indonesia, for instance.

Chayanov did not simply theorize. He also looked at the evidence of what had happened in Russia in the recent past. He examined the records on farm size and family size and calculated correlation coefficients. If he had fitted a line through his observations on a graph, it would have looked something like that in Figure 2.6(a). Does the fact that there is a relationship between the two mean that Chayanov was right? Does it mean that Malthus, who saw larger families as the cause of poverty, was wrong? Chayanov was

Fig. 2.6. Relationship between the family's characteristics and farm size, nineteenth-century Russia
(a) *FAMILY SIZE*
(b) *FAMILY AGE*

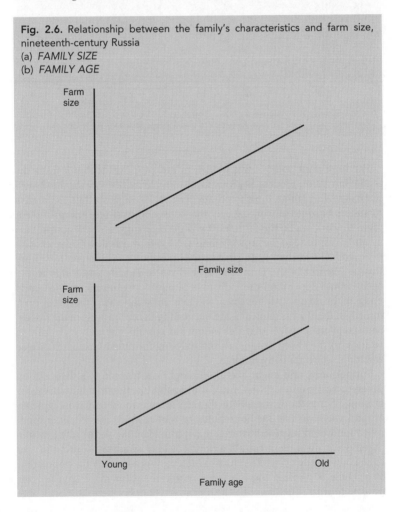

clear-headed enough to see that this relationship was not sufficient to reject the Malthusian law.

The problem is that the evidence is static; it does not tell us what is happening to the farms over time. Households may remain small because of their limited farm resources. Maybe they would have liked a large family, but either some form of prudential restraint (late marriage) or some positive check (high infant mortality) prevented them. Chayanov went on to argue that, if this were the case, many small farms would consist of ageing parents and a few grown-up surviving sons or daughters (the rest having died). If most of these small households contain a few young children, their parents are clearly only starting to build their families and may go on to have more children and create a larger farm. In this case, Chayanov's interpretation is the more plausible one and the Malthusian one less likely. To test this further proposition, Chayanov examined the household data again. What he found this time is presented as a linear relationship in Figure 2.6(b). Here we plot farm size against the youthfulness of the household. It seems that younger households dwell on smaller farms and that Chayanov's interpretation is supported.

Chayanov wanted to explore his dynamic theory of the evolution of farm size further by looking at data over time. For this purpose he drew up a matrix of farm size mobility. From this he could see whether small farms really became large and whether large farms became small again, as the sown area of land was reduced when the household eventually divided. Looking at Table 2.5, we should first consider how this matrix would look if, contrary to Chayanov's belief, small farms did not evolve into large farms and large farms always remained large. There would be large percentages (100 per cent in the extreme) along the diagonal, and small percentages (zero in the extreme) everywhere else in the matrix. In fact, after 29 years, only a few of the farms were the same size as initially (shown in bold).

Table 2.5. Chayanov's table of sown area in 1911 by sown area in 1882 (%)

Area sown in 1882[a]	Area sown in 1911[a]					
	0–3	3–6	6–9	9–12	>12	Total
0–3	**28.2**	47.0	20.0	2.4	2.4	100.0
3–6	21.8	**47.5**	24.4	8.2	2.4	100.0
6–9	16.2	37.0	**26.8**	11.3	2.4	100.0
9–12	9.6	35.8	26.1	**12.4**	16.1	100.0
>12	3.5	30.5	28.5	15.6	**21.9**	100.0

[a] Area in *desyatinas*.

Source: A. V. Chayanov, (1925), *The Theory of the Peasant Economy*, ed. D. Thorner (University of Wisconsin Press, Madison, WI, 1986).

Principles of Population and Development

This process by which farm size is determined by family formation is known technically as demographic differentiation. It contrasts with social differentiation, which is the Marxist understanding of how things change. Indeed, Lenin strongly disagreed with Chayanov's interpretation of what had been happening in nineteenth-century Russia, and his writings were discredited. As we noted, the neo-classical school has revived interest today in what he had to say.

We have alluded to social differentiation when discussing the development of capitalism in European agriculture. Farmers sought to acquire large acreages of land under their own ownership. In the process, they often turned tenant farmers into landless agricultural labourers. Farmers with small holdings and their families, who had often become indebted to large farmers, were easily bought out (or simply evicted). Thus, the different sizes of farms that could be found in nineteenth-century Russia, for example, were believed by the Marxists to be an indicator of the development of capitalism. Lenin was eager to show that capitalist farming had already developed in Russia before the Revolution and that the family farm was an unviable mode of production that had failed to survive. After the Revolution the capitalist farm had been replaced by a more efficient and equitable system in Lenin's view—large-scale collective farms managed by the State.

By contrast, Chayanov believed that the distribution of farm sizes was an indicator of the demographic process that we have just described. He thought that pre-Revolution farmers in Russia were continuing to farm according to the principles of household production. They were not seeking to maximize profits but simply to balance the amount of hard work every member did with the need to ensure an adequate subsistence consumption for all the members. In fact he claimed that 90 per cent of Russian farms did not use any hired agricultural labourers. He thought that the system of family farming was a viable one and had not been challenged by the development of capitalism as Lenin claimed. Therefore, it could continue to operate efficiently and equitably for all time. The implication was that there was no need for capitalism, nor for a socialist revolution.

This intellectual debate has taken us far from the principal subject-matter of this chapter. The debate continues today, however. The empirical evidence used in it has shifted from Russia to places like Indonesia and India, where a growing literature on the subject exists. It is not without practical importance. After all, the surplus food grain production that has made it possible to feed a rapidly growing urban population, while produced using green revolution technology, seems in crucial cases like India to have come predominantly from farms managed according to capitalistic principles. In contrast, China managed to feed its growing population with collectivized agriculture. However, as we shall see, famine and malnutrition have not been banished by these new modes of production in either country.

Improved agricultural technology and fertility

To understand the modern neo-classical approach to the question of household resource management, we turn to a particular, but highly relevant, case. What is the impact of the green revolution on family formation? By the green revolution we refer to a whole package of new agricultural technology, including new breeds of high-yielding seeds, manufactured inputs like chemical fertilizer, and increased use of irrigation. We outline several areas over which a discussion on this topic should range. The reader can easily add to the debate from his or her own experience or analytical perspective: the subject is still alive and has not yet become stale.

Improved health and survival

The increase in labour productivity that results from the introduction of new seeds and new methods of cultivation may improve the purchasing power and consumption of the poor. We have already discussed the conditions in which this occurs. If the result is an improvement in child survival (a fall in child and infant mortality), one might expect farm households to respond in one of two different ways. If they had always wanted more children than conditions had permitted, then they would continue to have as many children as they could and be delighted that more of them survived than before. This is the case in parts of Africa, where infant mortality is still very high and where, even when it has fallen, high fertility resulting in a large family size is still economically valuable. On the other hand, if households were already achieving the numbers and sex composition of children that they wanted, say two boys surviving until after their father retired from the most arduous aspects of farm work, then improved survival might change the desired total number of live births or *total fertility* (see Box 2.3). How could it achieve this?

In an extreme case, if only two-thirds of newly born children are likely to survive to the age of 15, three births produce only two survivors. If survival improved to 100 per cent, one needs only two births for two survivors. So fertility (in the technical sense of live births) could fall in response to reductions in mortality. Still, surely the matter is more complicated than this? The actual improvement in survival will be from 67 per cent to 85 per cent or something similar and not to 100 per cent. Also, the probability of having a boy is only about one-half. Moreover, who is going to gamble that the average demographic improvement will be enjoyed by their family? How does one know that the survival rate of children has improved anyway?

It seems plausible that eventually, as a result of a great many hit-or-miss decisions, people as a whole will respond to improved survival by reducing their number of births. Nevertheless, it may take time for the relationship between infant mortality change and fertility change to become established. Statisticians have spent much computer time trying to work out what really happens at the aggregate level of the population. While they claim that the response of fertility to mortality change is not very great, existing statistical models may not capture the complete social process very well.

BOX 2.3. AGE-SPECIFIC FERTILITY RATES

The following data are from Taiwan in the 1960s. They show the number of women by age and the number of births that they had in total during a single year. Of course, not all the women in each age group contributed to this number of births. Indeed, many women in the youngest age group were still single.

Table A

Age group	Annual births	No. of women
15–19	24,144	503,000
20–24	118,910	470,000
25–29	143,190	430,000
30–34	96,390	378,000
35–39	54,925	325,000
40–44	21,014	266,000
45–49	2,717	209,000

To obtain age-specific rates, repeat the procedure outlined for age-specific mortality in Box 2.2. Divide the births by the number of women and then multiply by 1,000. For example, the *age-specific fertility rate* per thousand for women aged 15–19 years is:

$$24,144 \div 503,000 \times 1,000 = 48 \text{ per thousand.}$$

The age-specific rates are calculated and presented below. Note that, if they were plotted on a graph with rates on the vertical axis and age on the horizontal axis, they would trace an 'n' shape (see, for example, Figure 7.4).

Table B

Age group	Age-specific fertility rates per 1,000
15–19	48
20–24	253
25–29	333
30–34	255
35–49	169
40–44	79
45–49	13

BOX 2.3. continued

Deriving a simple summary measure from these rates is possible if one stops regarding the women as a population counted at one point in time. Assume instead that these rates refer to a group of 1,000 women who have their fifteenth birthday on the same day. If none of them dies, each year between their fifteenth and twentieth birthdays they will produce forty-eight babies on average. Over the five years they give birth to 240 children. Again assuming no mortality, the same 1,000 women will progress through the next five years, producing an average of 253 babies annually and so on. By the time that these 1,000 women have ended their childbearing life they will have been responsible for (1,150 × 5) births altogether. This is the sum of the age-specific fertility rates column multiplied by five and equals 5,750.

Presenting this number as the ratio of live births to women is usual, so we divide by 1,000 to get 5.7. In other words, an average woman, if she survived through to her fiftieth birthday would have had just under six live births. This measure is known as the *total fertility rate* (TFR). It is an intuitively appealing summary measure of fertility because it is similar to the notion of the average number of children in the typical family (although this also reflects mortality).

Demographers interested in the reproduction of populations calculate a further measure: the *gross rate of reproduction* (GRR). This is the equivalent of the total fertility rate for female births only (i.e., the TFR divided by just over two). Finally, because we have assumed no mortality so far, we have overestimated the ability of a population to reproduce itself. Some women die before completing their childbearing years and some of their daughters die before reaching the age when they too can become mothers. The effect of mortality is netted out by the *net rate of reproduction* (NRR). To calculate this, one adjusts (i.e., multiplies) each age-specific fertility rate (ASFR) by the probability of survival from birth to that age group. To summarize the relationships:

$$TFR = \sum ASFR(a),$$

$$GRR = TFR \div \left[1 + SRAB(m{:}f)\right], \text{ and}$$

$$NRR = \sum ASFR_f(a) \times p_f(a),$$

where:

a = age in single years,
SRAB = the sex ratio at birth,
m = male,
f = female (with subscripts indicating measures that refer to girls only),
$p(a)$ = the proportion surviving from birth to age a.

All rates are assumed to be per person, not per thousand. The sex ratio at birth is usually about 1.05 male births to each female birth. Note that if ages are grouped, it is necessary to multiply each age-specific fertility rate by the number of years in the age interval. (If each interval is the same width, just multiply the total by the number of years in the intervals.) Using the figures for Taiwan given earlier:

$$TFR = 1,150 \times 5 \div 1,000 = 5.75 \text{ and}$$

$$GRR = 5.75 \div 2.05 = 2.80.$$

BOX 2.3. continued

(The net reproduction rate cannot be calculated without survival data. To calculate these requires some demography that is described in Box 9.3.)

One important conclusion arises. For a population to reproduce itself it is necessary that an average woman produces one daughter who survives to become a mother of a woman in the next generation and so on. To succeed in this, an average mother must bear a little more than one daughter to allow for mortality. Looking at this another way, 1,000 women need to produce more than 1,000 female babies (say 1,200) so that at least 1,000 survive to become mothers themselves and produce a further 1,000 female babies. For a population to reproduce itself exactly the net reproduction rate must equal one. Some East Asian countries are concerned because this is no longer the case: their net reproduction rate has fallen below unity.

Rising aspirations

If the benefits of the improvements in productivity stemming from the green revolution are distributed widely, many rural households will experience a tangible improvement in their incomes for perhaps the first time in their lives or the history of their households. The evidence usually suggests this for at least those who manage farms of a moderate or large size. How will this affect their desire for children? If children can be regarded as a household good, not purchasable in the market-place presumably but costing money to feed, clothe, shelter, and school, then a higher income makes children more affordable. As was argued earlier, if households wanted more children but felt themselves constrained by their limited household budgets, then they might respond to their higher incomes by having more children. This is what economists call the income effect.

Typically, other things are changing when the green revolution gets under way. For instance, with increased prosperity a market for consumer durables begins to open up, as traders discover an opportunity to sell to these agricultural communities. At first, wrist watches, radios, and bicycles, then later television sets, video-recorders, and motor bikes catch the eye of the potentially upwardly mobile farmer. If sons or brothers migrate to the cities for a time, or overseas to the Gulf or beyond, the demonstration effect adds to the temptation to buy. In the prosperous green revolution areas of India and Pakistan there has been much migration of this kind. The world and its possibilities are opened up suddenly. Other ways of spending one's money than on the rearing of children develop. Tractors rather than large families become a status symbol. Households begin to opt for smaller families; fertility declines. This is what economists call the substitution effect.

Increasing aspirations of this kind have been documented by those familiar with rural households subject to this changing situation. Even in countries where Islamic values favouring large families still predominate, like Pakistan, the phenomena of rising aspirations for material goods and incipient fertility decline among the better off can be perceived today.

Increased demand for labour

The green revolution has complex implications for rural employment. During the earlier stages, the process is characterized by the adoption of new high-yielding seeds, an increased need for irrigation (and hence pump sets), heavy inputs of chemical fertilizer, pesticide and herbicide (or at least an intensification of weeding by hand), and the compression of two or three crop cycles into a single year. All this can be very labour-intensive. Therefore the demand for labour increases. (The demand curve shifts upwards, in economic terminology.) Rising labour productivity and rising yields are obtained without substituting capital for labour. The demand for both goes up. This might seem to make children, as labour power, more attractive. Just as Chayanov envisaged the family using extra labour to take in more land, this could involve families using additional labour by purchasing 'labour-using' equipment such as pump sets, quick-ripening seeds suitable for multiple cropping, and chemical sprays (carried on the back).

Some qualifications of this view are needed. The green revolution increases the seasonal intensity of agricultural production. For instance, planting and harvesting the new crops is not spread over the whole year (any more than it was before). Much of it has to be done in the same short season as before. This means that much more labour is needed, concentrated in a very short period. Family labour is not the ideal solution to this, as there is little for the family to do for the rest of the year. Hiring in labour, as and when it is needed, is the obvious solution. This would not seem to encourage landowning households to have more children. It might encourage landless households of agricultural labourers to do so. Marx's expectation of an emerging pool of rural unemployed may be falsified. For, although landless labourers might be created by the process of land accumulation, there would be more jobs for them.

A further issue arises here, however. In some parts of the world, labour migrates over a long distance at times of peak agricultural demand. Thus, the local labour market in green revolution areas quickly becomes saturated. Local labour has to compete with in-migrant labour. The incentive to grow your own labour, so to speak, is much reduced. This has happened in northern India, where labourers from Bihar and eastern Uttar Pradesh migrate to the Punjab seasonally. Besides, capitalist farmers often prefer migrant labour to that which is born locally. It increases their bargaining power and makes hiring and, especially, firing easier. Resident labour forces feel more secure and are likely to strike harder bargains.

The later stages of the green revolution usually involve the use of tractors for hauling equipment like ploughs, rakes, and sprays and even combine harvesters for cutting the crop. These reduce the demand for labour (that is, they are 'labour-displacing' items of capital equipment). Sometimes they are introduced in economies where labour is fairly cheap in terms of wages paid; equipment is thought to be more reliable and less troublesome than labour (especially when large work-forces are involved, as on the largest farms). Capital is substituted for labour after all and children will not be of potential future value as labour in agriculture.

In summary, during the green revolution the local demand for labour may rise (for some classes at least) and then fall. Moreover, in deciding to have a child today, one creates fully developed labour power only for tomorrow—which means in ten to fifteen years' time. When rapid economic change is taking place, the labour market requirements may have changed by then.

Returns to education

With increasing mobility and contact with the world outside the village, peasant households become acutely aware of the value of education for their children. This is surely nowadays the key to getting on in the world. Government jobs, which are prized highly in Asia because they are normally both secure and well paid, usually require secondary school certificates as minimum entry requirements. Some economists argue that basic literacy is becoming increasingly important for the use and understanding of the green revolution technology. Indeed some studies have shown that more literate farmers get higher yields on their farms. However, in the minds of the peasant household, the desire for an educated son may have more to do with employment opportunities outside agriculture, and even overseas. Similarly, having an educated daughter may make her more suitably mar-riageable when standards of male education are going up. Whatever the process, educating children is a costly business. You have to buy them new clothes and even books and they cannot easily work on the farm while they are students. (Moreover, in some places, if you want your children to have a reasonable education, you have to send them to a private school or hire private tutors to supplement the school education, as is frequently done in South Korea for example. Fees become a costly item in the household budget.) In practice, one observes rural families opting to have fewer but more highly educated children, rather than greater numbers. Quality is substituted for quantity. This also induces a fertility decline.

Employment of women

The burden of looking after children falls principally on the mother in most societies. In agricultural economies women often do much of the field work as well, such as weeding and harvesting. With the introduction of new tech-nologies in agriculture, men often begin to take a leading role, operating the equipment that performs tasks formerly undertaken by women (or even children). This may be because men feel it is now more prestigious to do so (since machinery is involved), rather than because they have any superior technical knowledge. Also, in some cultures it is regarded as a mark of a man's low economic and social status in society if he has to keep his womenfolk employed in manual jobs. So, with rising incomes and new technologies, women may stop working in the fields and be confined to the household. Would one expect fertility to rise or fall as a result? The answer is not clear. Childbearing and rearing are compatible with rural agricultural labour but it is certainly a strain to have to do both jobs at once.

On the other hand, if the status of women improves because of greater access to education, aspirations to work outside the home in skilled or semi-skilled jobs may be fulfilled. If women aspire successfully to become upwardly mobile in this way (i.e., they break away from male attempts to control their lives), they will almost certainly wait longer before getting married. Moreover, they will often regard the more professional jobs that they are now doing as incompatible with continuous childbearing and rearing. So one might expect fertility to go down.

This brief discussion does not exhaust all the points that might be made. The reader is referred to the writings of Eva Mueller for further discussion on the impact of technological change in agriculture on human fertility.

Up to now we have referred rather casually to fertility decline. We indicated earlier that demographers are referring to live births when they use the technical term fertility. Clearly fertility may change because marriage is delayed, which means that fertility rates at the younger ages fall. On the other hand, fertility may change because women stop childbearing earlier than before, when they have already three children in their thirties, rather than on completing a family of six children in their forties. This means that fertility rates at older ages fall. To distinguish these developments we need to measure fertility according to the age of the mother: these measures are called *age-specific fertility rates* by demographers. Box 2.3 explains how these rates are calculated.

Notes

1. There are a few exceptions to this, such as diets based on staple foods that simply do not contain enough protein for everyone. Cassava is the classic case.
2. This is measured as a percentage of total calories.
3. These examples show how economists or politicians concerned about malnutrition have to think beyond food itself. Food subsidies may help, but sometimes a more appropriate policy might be rent controls, encouraging a freer market in fuel supplies, or promoting new technologies for the more efficient use of fuels. (There are superior and cheap designs of stoves that are little known and little used.) Similarly, as many diseases lead to malabsorption of food, the provision of clean drinking water can improve nutrition.

Part II

Population in the Perspective of Time

3 | The Changing Balance of Births and Deaths

The traditional pre-transition model

The demographic transition is a term used to describe the process whereby whole populations progress from the experience of high birth and high death rates to low birth and low death rates. Death rates usually decline first and birth rates follow. The complete process nowadays takes perhaps thirty to fifty years to complete. Since the natural growth rate of a population is the excess of its birth rate over its death rate, the period of transition is characterized by increased growth rates. This concept is probably familiar to most readers. It is illustrated graphically in Figure 3.1. What exactly do we mean by birth and death rates? This is explained in Box 3.1. Roughly speaking, demographers define the birth rate as annual births divided by total population, and the death rate as annual deaths divided by the same.

Virtually all Asian countries have entered the demographic transition. While a few have not progressed very far (these are mainly in South Asia), some have virtually completed the transition (these are all in East Asia). The two most populous countries, India and China, are in the course of transition. Fertility is declining in India, while in China the transition is nearly complete. Mortality has fallen quite a long way in most of Africa but fertility transition has only begun in a few countries. Most of Europe passed through the transition between the last quarter of the eighteenth century and the first quarter of the twentieth century, the whole process taking nearly a century to complete (although the decline in the birth rates alone usually took only half that time).

In this chapter we are going to focus on the pre-transition stage of the model. This is not a matter of irrelevant history. Understanding the pre-transition period makes us wary of what the post-transition period (which is very much our present or future) might have in store. The story will also reveal the curious cultural bias embedded in the assumptions of some demographers. This should help to inform our own analysis.

Demographers formerly assumed that the pre-transition period was characterized by universally high birth rates and death rates. These cancelled each other out in the sense that the long-run growth rate was close to zero. This picture extended back over the centuries. It helped to explain why the

Fig. 3.1. The demographic transition model

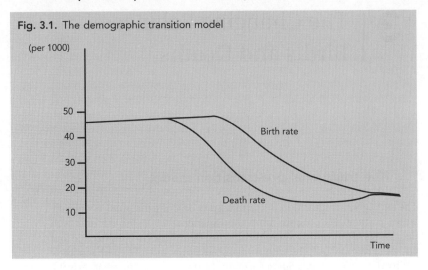

world's population, despite the fact that people had been around for millennia, was still quite sparse until the present century. We have already seen how the force of a geometric increase, sustained over a long enough period, eventually becomes very substantial in terms of absolute numbers. If the population grows at only 1 per cent per year, it doubles every seventy years: at that rate of increase, even if we started with only two people a few thousand years back, there would have been many times the actual population of the world by the turn of the twentieth century (as the reader may easily check). So long-run growth must have been virtually zero. However, most demographers accepted that death rates must have fluctuated year by year, as bad harvests and epidemics brought peaks and good years brought troughs in the death rates. Some historians accepted that there might have been compensating peaks and troughs in birth rates also. This has been confirmed by modern demographic analysis for countries as diverse as England and India.[1]

For some time such demography was really a matter of guesswork. No one knew of any nationally compiled records of births or deaths. Historians did know, however, that in some countries births and deaths had been registered quite well locally. Some examples of these registers had been analysed in the same way that Chayanov analysed data on a few districts in late nineteenth century Russia. A notable example was Wrigley's study of a small number of villages in England (in the county of Devon).

Historians, however, had long been aware that age at marriage differed in different societies in the past. One would expect therefore that birth rates would differ too. In the 1960s, the American demographer Coale initiated a

BOX 3.1. BIRTH AND DEATH RATES

Birth rates and death rates (known as vital rates) are calculated from data provided by vital registration systems and from national census data. Vital statistics (for births and deaths) should be registered on a continuous basis but censuses are usually held only once in ten years. Thus, projection is necessary to supply inter-censal population totals (see Box 10.1). As pointed out elsewhere in this book, vital events are often poorly registered. In many developing countries the result is a serious undercount of births and deaths. The calculation and reporting of unadjusted birth and death rates from such inadequate registers are pointless.

More advanced techniques than those included in this book provide ways of estimating births and deaths from defective data. For our purposes, we assume that more or less complete registration data are available and define the relevant rates:

$$\text{Birth rate } (b) = \frac{\text{Total number of births in a period of time}}{\text{Total population counted at the mid-point of that peroid}}.$$

$$\text{Death rate } (d) = \frac{\text{Total number of deaths in a period of time}}{\text{Total population counted at the mid-point of that peroid}}.$$

In both cases multiplying by 1,000 to give a rate per thousand is customary. The *rate of natural increase* measures the speed at which population size changes because the number of births and deaths differs:

$$r = b - d.$$

The rate of natural increase differs from the growth rate of the population because the latter measure is also affected by migration. The birth rate, death rate, and rate of natural increase are often referred to as 'crude'. The reason for this will become apparent later.

major project to analyse the demography of Europe at the beginning of the European transition province by province. He constructed an index of marriage from the contemporary statistics, in which populations that marry young score close to one and those that marry late (or where marriage was not universal) score close to zero. The technicalities need not bother us here. The results were plotted on a map of Europe, province by province (Figure 3.2). Some fairly striking patterns emerge. Coale was particularly interested in a division first detected by Hajnal and referred to as the St Petersburg–Trieste line. In essence, marriage patterns differed between Western and Eastern Europe (with a few clear exceptions in France and Spain).

To sociologists and historians this would come as no surprise. The reader

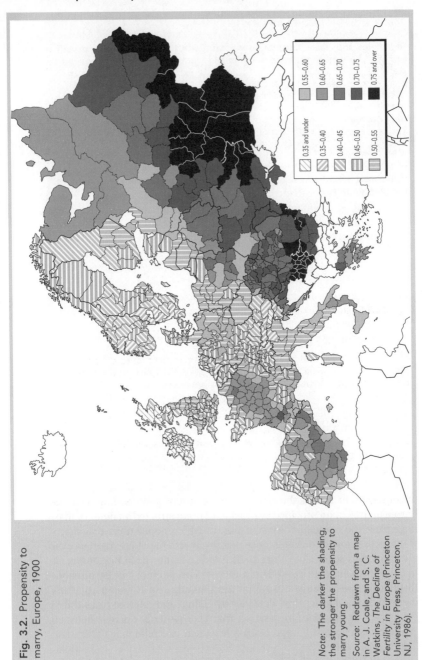

Fig. 3.2. Propensity to marry, Europe, 1900

Note: The darker the shading, the stronger the propensity to marry young.

Source: Redrawn from a map in A. J. Coale, and S. C. Watkins, *The Decline of Fertility in Europe* (Princeton University Press, Princeton, NJ, 1986).

will recall from our discussion of Chayanov's observations that the Russian peasant household married young. This was economically possible because the married sons tended to stay on the family farm for some years (accumulating leased land if necessary). Current resources were shared within the joint household. A split did not occur until some major event such as the death of the original parents. By contrast, in much of Western Europe, the young sons did not marry until they were personally rich enough to set up a household of their own.

The first really comprehensive study of long-term demographic changes did not come until the 1970s. Such comprehensive empirical studies became feasible only with the development of high-speed computers. In 1981 Wrigley and Schofield published a reconstruction of the population history of England and Wales that covered a span of four hundred years. The most striking finding to emerge from this study for our understanding of the demographic transition is clearly illustrated in Figure 3.3.

Look at the gross rate of reproduction. (This measure of fertility is explained in Box 2.3.) Prior to the demographic transition (which began in England in the late eighteenth century, when the death rate first began to fall without reversal towards its currently low level), fertility was not fluctuating around a high level equilibrium as most demographers had suggested. Instead we observe fairly lengthy cycles, or long swings, in fertility. Fertility fell from the late sixteenth century to the late seventeenth century, rose from then until the early nineteenth century and fell somewhat thereafter until a sharp decline set in from the 1870s. Similarly, mortality was found to have gone through fairly extended periods of rise and fall. These long-term changes occurred in addition to the year-by-year fluctuations due to epidemics and famine.

As I have suggested, there is some cultural bias, or ethnocentricity, in the assumptions made by many demographers. For, despite the evidence that Europe was characterized by substantial differentials in fertility across regions and that at least one Western country had experienced long-run changes in birth and death rates before the demographic transition, it was felt that Asia must have been more homogeneous and must have fitted the pre-transition stage of the demographic transition model better. The picture of high and unchanging birth and death rates was still accepted widely for the world to the east and south-east of Russia and for Africa.

A population with unchanging birth rates and unchanging death rates has certain properties that demographers can use when trying to reconstruct patchy data of uncertain quality. Clearly if these two rates do not change, then neither will the growth rate (barring migration). A growth rate that never changes is referred to as *a stable growth rate*. It may be 2 per cent a year, 4 per cent a year, or 0 per cent a year. It is the constancy that defines it as stable. If the growth rate is constant at zero, then the population is called a stationary population. One should not confuse stationarity with stability—these are technical terms used distinctively by demographers. The as-

Fig. 3.3. Long swings in the gross rate of reproduction and the average age at death, England and Wales, sixteenth century to nineteenth century

(a) *GROSS REPRODUCTION RATE*

(b) *AVERAGE AGE AT DEATH*

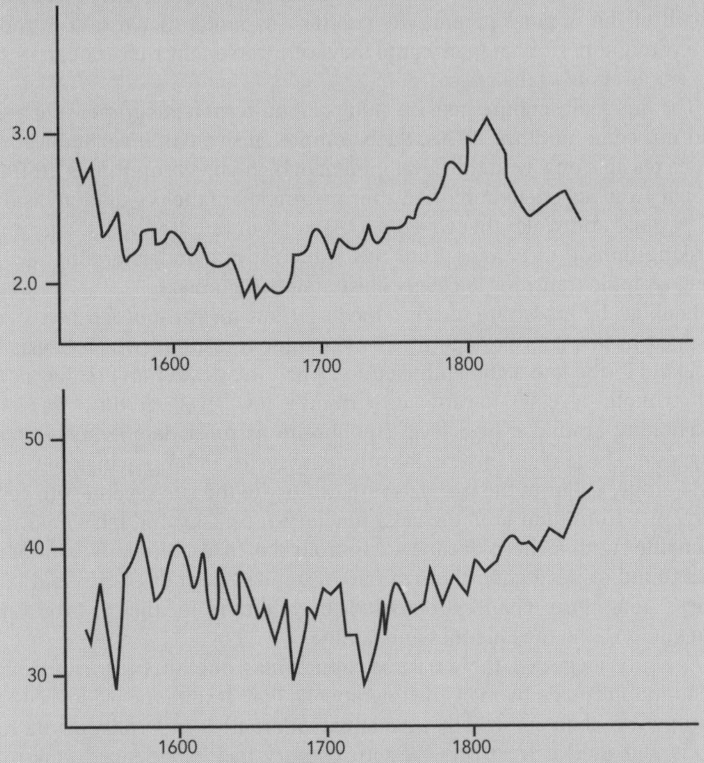

Source: Based on a figure in E. A. Wrigley, and R. S. Schofield, *The Population History of England 1541–1871: a Reconstruction* (Edward Arnold, London, 1981).

sumption of pre-transition stability is widespread. We have already shown that this is a questionable assumption for Europe; we shall now show that it is questionable for Asia also.[2]

Characteristics of pre-transition demography of Asia

It takes historical demographers a long time to compile statistics on demographic events like births, deaths, and marriages from local data and correct them for errors and omissions. Most demographic analysis has not gone beyond using census counts of the total population and calculating the growth rates in between. This fails to allow for the incompleteness of coverage of each census but probably gives results of the right order of magnitude over long periods of time. Various estimates for countries in Asia suggest that population growth rates were generally low, in the sense that they fell well below 2 per cent a year before the demographic transition (when they increased, as we have indicated, to 2 per cent or more). But they were not always zero. Generally there seem to have been periods of rise and fall. Look for instance at the case of China in Figure 3.4. During the Sung dynasty and later during the Ming, there were periods of sustained population growth. The reader can calculate that for the two centuries between 1400 and 1600

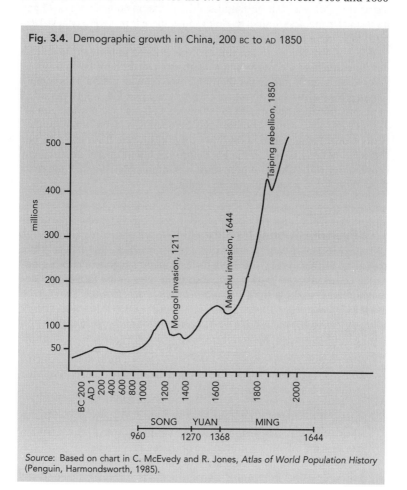

Fig. 3.4. Demographic growth in China, 200 BC to AD 1850

Source: Based on chart in C. McEvedy and R. Jones, *Atlas of World Population History* (Penguin, Harmondsworth, 1985).

the annual average growth, although it was positive, remained rather close to zero by modern standards. More striking, though perhaps controversial, is the evidence of growth in South-East Asia, with Java and the Philippines enjoying growth from the eighteenth century to the nineteenth century and Siam (now Thailand), Burma, and the then Malaya growing well into the nineteenth. In South-East Asia the growth rate seems to have risen to 1.5 per cent a year over long periods, which in demographic terms is well above zero. We are on firmer ground with data from Japan: there is no doubt that the population grew substantially from the late nineteenth century until the Second World War, though the reader may feel that part of the period is during the demographic transition. We return to the details later.

Can we say anything about the components of those growth rates? The old assumption was that birth and death rates were equal at about 45 per thousand. In fact, as we shall go on to show, there is reason to believe that birth rates were a little lower much of the time, at say 40 per thousand. Hence, it is not difficult to imagine birth rates rising to between 45 and 50 per thousand over a century, while death rates might have fallen in some cases to between 30 and 35 per thousand over a similar period. This combination gives rise to a growth rate of 1.5 per cent a year following a period of near zero growth. I find it hard to believe that all the long upward growth swings could have come about through the operation of one of the components alone. For instance, a decline in the death rate from 40 to 25 per thousand seems unlikely in the era before sanitation reform or sustained economic growth (which is not to say it was impossible). We shall return to these thoughts in a later chapter on health.

Pre-transitional fertility

We can go further in breaking down the explanation of growth into components. Let us proceed (backwards) from birth rates to the factors that demographers describe as the *proximate determinants of fertility*.[3] They can be listed as follows:

- marriage;
- fecundity (i.e., the physical ability to bear children);
- post-partum amenorrhoea (i.e., the period after a birth during which a woman is unable to conceive: this period may be lengthened somewhat by the practice of breast-feeding);
- coital frequency;
- contraception (although breast-feeding has a temporary contraceptive effect after birth, it is seldom practised for that purpose—the intention is to feed the infant); contraceptive practices adopted before the development of 'scientific' methods during the last fifty years include withdrawal or *coitus interruptus*, barrier methods such as early condoms

and diaphragms, and timing intercourse to avoid the most fertile period in the woman's monthly cycle;

- abortion;
- I am inclined to add infanticide, since this is a way of limiting family size; demographically speaking, however, it is not a component of fertility but a live birth followed by an infant death.

Proximate and underlying determinants of fertility change

Marriage

Chapter 1 discussed how ages at marriage may reflect short-run incentives to delay family formation until the effects of a disaster like a war, epidemic, or famine wear off. There is also evidence, however, that marriage ages rose or fell over longer periods. We have referred to the growth of the population of the Philippines in the nineteenth century. Studies of the data from a particular parish from 1810 through to 1870 indicate that the average age at which women married for the first time declined by 2.5 years over the sixty-year period. This could have had the effect of raising the total fertility rate by one child, a substantial addition which, in turn, could raise the birth rate from about 40 to 45 per thousand.

Another good example of changes in ages at marriage is Japan. Look at Table 3.1, which shows the proportion of women married by age in a Japanese village during the nineteenth century. What observations can we make? Japan is striking in having a very slow pace of marriage formation, with a substantial proportion of women never getting married at all at certain periods in the country's pre-transition past. As a result, the birth rate in this village remained less than 30 per thousand throughout this period.

Table 3.1. Age-specific proportions of women married in a Japanese community (%)

Age	1775	1794	1810	1825	1837	1844	1863
15–19	7.7	4.5	0.0	0.0	6.1	13.0	2.6
20–24	38.5	20.0	32.0	44.4	53.6	38.2	47.6
25–29	81.3	84.2	66.7	70.6	75.0	70.8	62.1
30–34	92.9	82.6	84.6	96.1	91.7	78.9	64.0
35–39	93.3	100.0	72.7	77.8	94.1	84.2	88.2
40–44	83.3	90.0	73.6	93.3	72.4	73.3	87.5

Source: S. B. Hanley and K. Yamamura, *Economic and Demographic Change in Pre-Industrial Japan, 1600–1868* (Princeton University Press, Princeton, NJ, 1977).

e birth rate in Japan

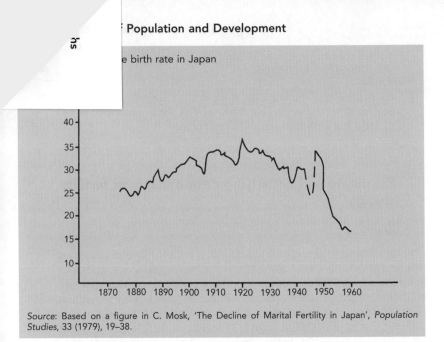

40 ·
35 ·
30 ·
25 ·
20 ·
15 ·
10 ·

1870 1880 1890 1900 1910 1920 1930 1940 1950 1960

Source: Based on a figure in C. Mosk, 'The Decline of Marital Fertility in Japan', *Population Studies*, 33 (1979), 19–38.

One can see from Figure 3.5 that from the late nineteenth century there was a gradual rise in the birth rate from quite a low level (around 25 per thousand). There is a strong correlation between the reduction in ages at marriage and the rise in the birth rate in Japan. Japan was the first clear exception to their assumptions about the pre-transition period to be discovered by demographers. Even then, they were inclined to regard Japan as an exception among Asian countries. I suspect that the more we learn about other regions of Asia, the more exceptions will be discovered and the less plausible the traditional model will seem.

Why were birth rates and the proportions married so low in Japan and why did they rise over the half century preceding the 1920s? Some scholars have argued that the so-called substitution effect, whereby families seek lower fertility so as to enjoy other material benefits in life instead, had already begun to operate in nineteenth-century Japan. This was due partly to considerable mobility of the population, with many of the young men spending a period in the towns in government service. Upward social mobility could be achieved more easily with smaller families and lower household expenditures. The demonstration effect of consumer lifestyles in these towns may have begun to take hold (compare what was said in Chapter 2 about the effect of the green revolution in South Asia much later). Writers in the Malthusian tradition of thinking are inclined to look more on the dismal side and see delayed marriage and suppressed child bearing as an indicator of bad times. Hence, when the economy began to expand after the Meiji restoration in 1868, people found their incomes rising and their budget constraints less binding and increased their pace of family formation.

Other work on the Japanese population compares different regions and different classes of society. Morris and Smith carried out an analysis of a low-caste Japanese village, engaged in wage labour. He found very high birth rates at times during the eighteenth and nineteenth centuries, but also very severe fluctuations in birth rates. These may well have been a response to famine. The poorest sectors of the community are unlikely to aspire to upward social mobility and their physical mobility was much more limited. Another scholar, Hayami, has shown that it was in the more prosperous eastern region of Japan (where raw silk production rather than subsistence agriculture dominated) that the birth rate rose from the 1880s onwards.

A further factor to consider when studying high mortality societies is that widowhood makes a substantial contribution to suppressed fertility, since it constitutes a permanent separation of spouses. Furthermore, remarriage is quite rare in some societies. Dyson carried out an analysis of birth rates using relatively complete registration statistics for one of the provinces of colonial India, Berar, which is now in eastern Maharashtra. It covered the period from the late nineteenth century to the end of the colonial period in the 1940s. He found that the birth rate averaged around forty per thousand until the early years of the twentieth century, after which it rose to around fifty per thousand before falling back to forty per thousand by 1940 (Figure

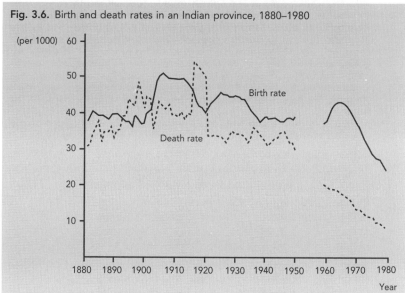

Fig. 3.6. Birth and death rates in an Indian province, 1880–1980

Source: T. Dyson, 'The Historical Demography of Berar, 1881–1980', in *India's Historical Demography*, T. Dyson, ed. (Curzon, London, 1989).

3.6). This is a clear illustration of the fact that there were major swings in birth rates before the demographic transition (which only starts in the post-colonial period) and that birth rates were not universally high. Dyson suggests that one reason for this history was the high level of widowhood and difficulty of remarriage, especially for Hindu women. Initially falling mortality may have precipitated rising birth rates for this reason.

Among the data used in this discussion are statistics on the proportion ever married of the population by age. It would be useful to have a summary measure of these, such as the average age at marriage. Box 3.2 shows how to calculate marriage rates and a measure of the average age at first marriage, known by demographers as the *singulate mean age of marriage*.

Fecundity and post-partum amenorrhoea

There is almost no evidence about fecundity in pre-transitional populations. Indeed, there is little modern evidence either. It has been noted, however, that during acute food shortages usually well-nourished

---

BOX 3.2. MEASURES OF MARRIAGE

One of the most important determinants of fertility in populations where contraception is not practised is how many of the adult population are married. Defining marriage is difficult. In some societies statistics about legal marriages underestimate the proportion of the population cohabiting in stable conjugal unions. Setting aside these difficulties, one of the more appealing statistics that summarizes marriage patterns is the average age at first marriage. To calculate this one has to know the proportions of women (or men) who have ever married. Note that their current marital status may be currently married, divorced, widowed, or separated. The complement of this ever-married proportion by age is clearly the proportion single by age, which is those who have never married as a proportion of everyone of that sex in the age group.

We illustrate the idea with data from an Indian census giving the total number of women and the number who remain single according to age.

Table A

Age group	Single women	Total women
10–14	31,678	33,562
15–19	15,237	39,229
20–24	4,289	64,968
25–29	1,328	69,117
30–34	542	48,568
35–39	331	34,009
40–44	142	22,672
45–49	104	20,780
50–54	50	12,468

BOX 3.2. continued

To get the proportion that is single, divide the single women by the total in each age group. For women aged 10–14 years:

$$31,678 \div 33,562 = 0.944.$$

For those aged 15–19:

$$15,237 \div 39,229 = 0.388,$$

and so on.

Imagine 1,000 women going through life from birth. During the first ten years of their lives they acquire a history of ten years spent single each (or an aggregate total of 10 × 1,000 years spent single). However, this group of women do not each acquire another five years of single life between 10 and 14 years of age. In this society, some of them marry in this age group. The Indian data show that 944 of each 1,000 remained single, however. So, by age 15, the complete group accumulates (1,000 × 10) + (944 × 5) years of single life in total. By the age group 15–19 years another 556 women are married, leaving 388 still single. Thus, we add another (388 × 5) years of single life and so on.

This procedure allows us to calculate the total years spent single by age for a cohort of 1,000 women:

Table B

Age group	Proportion single	Years of single life per 1,000
0–9	1.0	10,000
10–14	0.944	4,720
15–19	0.388	1,924
20–24	0.066	330
25–29	0.019	95
30–34	0.011	55
35–39	0.010	50
40–44	0.006	30
45–49	0.005	25
50–54	0.004	20

In total, these 1,000 women experience 17,229 years of single life by age 50. An average woman experiences $17,229 \div 1,000 = 17.2$ years of being single.

It appears that virtually nobody marries in India beyond age 50. One can calculate an average age at first marriage for those women who marry by removing from the calculation the few who remain single throughout their life. The latter are estimated as the average number still single between 45 and 55. Expressed as a proportion of the age group this becomes:

$$0.005 + 0.004 = 0.0045.$$

These forever-single women experienced (0.0045 × 1000 × 50) years of single life by age 50. Subtract these from the total years spent single:

$$17,229 - 225 = 17,004 \text{ (or 17.0 per woman)}.$$

Finally, divide by the number of women in the cohort who marry eventually:

$$1,000 - 1,000 \times 0.0045 = 995.5.$$

BOX 3.2. continued

Thus, the complete calculation of the average number of years lived as single among women who eventually marry is:

$$\frac{17{,}229 - 225}{1{,}000 - 4.5} = 17.08.$$

This measure of years spent single is identical to the mean age at marriage. More precisely, it is the mean age at first marriage among the single who are destined to get married. The formula for the *singulate mean age at marriage* (SMAM) is:

$$\text{SMAM} = \frac{S + \sum_{a=S}^{W} S(a) - W \times S(W)}{1 - S(W)}$$

where:

S = first age at which marriage takes place,
$S(a)$ = proportions never married at age a,
W = last age at which first marriages take place,
$S(W)$ = proportion never married at age W.

Note that if the data refer to age groups one must multiply each $S(a)$ by the number of years in the age interval.

One limitation of this summary measure is that it does not distinguish between populations that have many women or men that never marry and those that do not. It does not necessarily follow from an early mean age at first marriage that there is universal marriage, nor from a late mean age at marriage that a large proportion go unmarried. As an indicator of the impact of marriage on fertility, therefore, the singulate mean age of marriage may be incomplete.

women suffer interruptions in their menstrual cycles. Historians of South-East Asia have concluded that famine was largely absent from the region in the nineteenth century and have argued that the population may have become gradually better nourished from the eighteenth century to the nineteenth century, with attendant improvements in the ability of women to conceive and bear children. A similar argument has been made for Japan from the 1880s. In this case there are a few data from the village studies to which we referred earlier relating to the period of relatively suppressed fertility. Look at Table 3.2 and consider the implications of the large number of years that apparently elapsed between births. There is more than one possible explanation, but one of them is that women were taking a long time to conceive because of their poor nutritional status. The reader might like to consider the alternative explanations. But one thing that must be stressed is

Table 3.2. Birth intervals in a Japanese community, 1773–1801

Birth interval	Years between births
First to second	4.20
Second to third	4.09
Third to fourth	4.12
Fourth to fifth	3.71
Fifth to sixth	3.82
Average	4.11

Source: S. B. Hanley and K. Yamamura, *Economic and Demographic Change in Pre-Industrial Japan, 1600–1868* (Princeton University Press, Princeton, NJ, 1977).

that only very serious nutritional deprivation is likely to suppress fecundity and hence fertility in this way. After all, many modern populations have high fertility even though the calorie intake of the majority of the population is low enough to render them vulnerable to disease and maternal mortality.

In modern Asia and Africa, changes in the practice of breast-feeding have an important effect on fertility. Reduced breast-feeding occurs as people migrate to the cities. If modern contraceptives are not used, fertility goes up. This has occurred in present-day Pakistan and Kenya. Historians have suggested that changes in economic behaviour may have affected breast-feeding in the past also. Hunter-gatherer populations need to breast-feed their children for prolonged periods because there are few suitable weaning foods available; agricultural populations sometimes can grow foods that are more suitable for infants. It may also be the case that women take a more active part in settled agricultural production and that this may lead to more interrupted breast-feeding. It is only lengthy and regular suckling that prolongs the infertile period after birth. We discuss the incompatibility of women's work with childbearing in Chapter 7. In the context of the discussion so far, we note that some scholars of South-East Asia have suggested that this part of the world ceased to be a frontier economy in the course of the late eighteenth and early nineteenth centuries. Agricultural activity became more settled and more intensive. During the colonial period in Indonesia the people of Java were tied to the land by the need to cultivate cash crops for export alongside subsistence crops (a thesis developed by Geertz). Perhaps these developments indirectly account for the fertility rise in some South-East Asian countries in the pre-transition period. The contrast with Japan is instructive. As population grew in Indonesia it had to be absorbed within the agricultural sector. In Japan, a considerable sector of the population could transfer to industry and commerce in the urban areas.

Coital frequency

Again no quantitative data exist on people's sexual habits in the past, though modern-day demographers often make enquiries on this subject of the contemporary population in sample surveys. Studies in historical Europe have shown that birth rates have strong seasonal patterns that can be related to the separation of spouses during seasonal migrations for work. The same is found today in populations where such migration is common, for example in Southern Africa. In fact, in every country on earth for which there exist data on births according to the month of the year, a seasonal pattern shows up. There are several possible reasons for this. One important factor is that marriage ceremonies tend to be undertaken after the harvest. Festivals and homecomings all tend to congregate at the time of plenty, when the harvest has been gathered. Holidays and festivals throughout the world tend to provoke conceptions (both intentional and unintentional) and the birth rate peaks nine months later (see, for example, Figure 3.7).

If seasonal migration becomes less important, this should reduce the seasonality of births. In addition, if seasonal separation had been prolonged, there could be an increase in birth rates annually resulting from

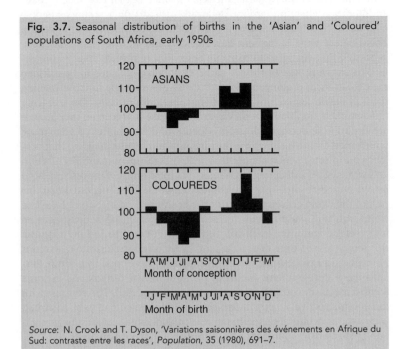

Fig. 3.7. Seasonal distribution of births in the 'Asian' and 'Coloured' populations of South Africa, early 1950s

Source: N. Crook and T. Dyson, 'Variations saisonnières des événements en Afrique du Sud: contraste entre les races', *Population*, 35 (1980), 691–7.

the change. One would not expect a great difference at the population level, however, as the reunion of spouses annually should enable most couples to reproduce as much as they want to. Nevertheless it has been suggested that reduced migration to the frontiers as the population became more settled may have contributed to the rise in South-East Asian fertility.

Contraception, abortion, and infanticide

We discuss these three factors together because they all represent deliberate attempts to space or limit the number of children that are reared beyond the first few days of life. Whereas changes in breast-feeding practice or even changes in ages of marriage are not necessarily intended for the purpose of family planning, the principal purpose of contraception, abortion, or infanticide is just that. As with sexual behaviour, demographers have little or no idea of how commonly contraception within marriage was adopted in pre-transitional populations. We do know, however, from historical studies in Western Europe that pre-modern contraception can be quite effective at the level of the population. For instance, the fertility transition in England was largely achieved through *coitus interruptus*. Similarly, the Roman Catholic country of Malta achieved quite low rates of fertility by adopting the only method of birth control approved by the church, rhythm. These methods are very unreliable from the individual point of view. Nevertheless, they can substantially reduce the birth rate of the population if used by a large proportion of cohabiting couples in the reproductive ages.

We know that abortion was an important way of limiting births in Japan. It was not legal, however, and abortifacients were marketed clandestinely until after the Second World War. The effect of legalizing abortion was dramatic: a rapid decline in fertility followed: look at the birth rate after 1948 in Figure 3.5. By contrast, it is possible that the Spanish colonial authorities, by prohibiting abortion in the Philippines, contributed to the rise in the birth rate there. Until recently, this country had one of the highest fertility rates in Asia. As far as infanticide is concerned, Japan was also a country where this method of control was adopted widely. We observed earlier that long birth intervals occurred in Japanese villages in the mid-nineteenth century. It was suggested that these intervals might have something to do with poor conception rates. They may also represent births averted through abortion or subsequently eliminated through infanticide and not recorded as live births at all. People are even more eager to conceal infanticide than induced abortions. There is, however, some tell-tale evidence in the case of infanticide. In a society that favours male over female children, infanticide is often sex selective. Sex ratios at birth (male to female) are nearly always just more than one (1.04, say). In these Japanese villages, they are substantially higher. This is unlikely to be biologically determined or a statistical accident.

Pre-transition mortality

Demographers have tended to neglect fertility change in the explanation of rising and falling growth rates in the past. That is why we started here with an examination of fertility. But there is no doubt that mortality change also contributed to growth-rate fluctuations, especially those in the short term but also some of the longer-term swings.

Diseases move with people but they also have a momentum of their own. It is often easier to see why new diseases (or new strains of existing diseases) appear in a country than to explain why they decline and disappear. In India mortality from a number of diseases rose towards the end of the nineteenth century and did not decline again until the 1920s: the impact on overall death rates can be seen from Figure 3.6. The cause of the rise was undoubtedly the introduction of bubonic plague into India through the commercial ports (especially Bombay) in the 1890s and the introduction of Far-Eastern varieties of influenza at the beginning of the century with devastating results.

Once a disease has 'settled' in a country, it is described as endemic. When it strikes in waves it is referred to as epidemic. Epidemics often characterize the earlier stages of the introduction of a disease: at that time, serious diseases may be fatal for most of those infected. During the endemic phase immunity is established and many diseases, like measles or chicken pox, become diseases of childhood in the process of which immunity is acquired for the rest of life. Some scholars suggest that South-East Asia entered the endemic phase for many diseases early in the nineteenth century. This may have contributed to the increase in the population growth rate via a lowered death rate.

It is important not to regard the State as passive in the face of disease. For instance, even before the major control campaigns that occurred from the 1930s onwards in much of Asia (and heralded the onset of the demographic transition), there were vaccination campaigns to reduce smallpox. These were apparently quite successful in South-East Asia and Japan, as they may have been in England before the twentieth century. Even malaria was partly controlled in late nineteenth-century Japan through the administration of appropriate curative drugs.

Nevertheless, the interaction between disease and nutrition is crucial to any understanding of pre-transition mortality regimes. Here again the State was involved more widely than is usually appreciated. We return to this point when we examine famine. Some scholars believe that colonial regimes were fairly effective at reducing the incidence of famine. The building of railways in India and, to a lesser extent, China allowed the quick transfer of food to deficit regions where local shortfalls in consumption occurred. Others have argued that the opening up of local economies to trade meant that food tended to flow out of them in search of higher prices (which could often be obtained in the cities and centres of military establishment). Colonial governments were aware of this problem. Albeit late in the day the government of India devised mechanisms to combat the increasing incidence of famine in the late nineteenth century, such as maintaining the effective demand by local populations by giving them work for pay and thereby attracting food into deficit localities.

In order to understand the State's involvement in increasing food supplies and in maintaining local demand, one needs to remember one central demographic point. Over most of the historical period there was a potential shortage of labour. Nowadays, owing to the sharp increase in growth rates during the demographic transition, we find this difficult to grasp. But fast rates of growth belong to recent history. For centuries populations were growing too slowly to provide the labour needed for large-scale public works. Without such works, which include the building of dams and canals, the clearing of jungle, and the terracing of hills, there can be only limited increase in food supplies and certainly no surplus generated. Hence, it is no exaggeration to say that periods of prosperity were periods of population growth. Of course the State was often eager to increase the health and growth rates of the population not in order to expand the food supply *per se*, but to build palaces and temples and to provide for the army. But this also requires the generation of a food surplus. This was of equal concern to feudal and colonial regimes and was ultimately a way of transferring consumption towards the rulers themselves.

The Chinese experience

We illustrate some of these points with a brief review of the Chinese demographic experience prior to the transition. Look again at Figure 3.4. Apart from the periods of long-run growth to which we have already referred, there are abrupt downturns. The first period of substantial demographic growth begins with a crisis that does not feature on this chart (which only picks up long-run tendencies). In AD 1012, soon after the start of the Song dynasty (960–1270), a severe drought was experienced in the increasingly colonized region of the Yangtze. The response by the State was interesting. New varieties of seeds were distributed to the farmers. These were quick ripening, which meant that, as long as there were initial rains, a crop could be harvested even if the weather subsequently deteriorated with drought or flood. These seeds came from Indo-China. This is a good example of the Boserupian principle of induced innovation. Clearly the existence of these varieties was already known; they did not have to be bred specially. But it required an emergency threatening the survival of the population to induce the adoption of this technology for raising food output. Interestingly, the emperor distributed not only the seeds but also some literature on their use, much in the way that extension workers in agriculture do today. This innovation clearly helped to prevent periodic collapse in output (and consumption) per head.

During the Song dynasty the population began to grow, increasing by as much as 0.5 per cent a year in the eleventh century. At the same time it moved its focus from the wheat-growing areas of the north to the Yangtze valley and to new frontiers in the south-east of China towards present-day Guangzhou (Canton). Then, in 1211, its progress was set back dramatically by the Mongol invasion from the north. This demographic disaster, which shows up as about two centuries of demographic decline following two centuries of unprecedented growth, might be interpreted as a Malthusian positive check.[4] However, the Chinese population was not outstripping its resource availability: as we have just seen, the population was moving into new and sparsely occupied land and developing new agricultural techniques. On a more global scale, it might be argued that the movement of the Mongols towards the south was a response to their own population pressure and that, as they could only move into already well-populated areas, the consequent strife and carnage were indeed a Malthusian positive check (on them and their neighbours). This is to stretch the Malthusian model a long way.

It was not until 1400 or so that the Chinese population recovered from the invasion from the north. During the Ming dynasty (1368–1644) there was a new upward swing in demographic growth, which was sustained at 0.35 per cent a year over two centuries. This required the creation of new sources of food supply on a grand scale and there is evidence of a substantial increase in the number of irrigation projects in already settled areas of north, east, and central China (see Table 3.3). Such infrastructural works could not have been undertaken without the increase in labour, especially young labour,

Table 3.3. Water control projects in China

| Region | Century (AD) | | | | | | | | |
	Before 10th	10–12th	13th	14th	15th	16th	17th	18th	19th
North-west	6	12	1	2	9	28	6	78	92
North	43	40	30	53	65	200	84	168	32
East	168	315	93	448	157	314	291	128	9
Central	50	62	21	52	91	365	85	116	131
South-east	27	353	43	106	101	88	53	115	34
South-west	19	10	6	5	31	83	61	195	95
Total	313	792	194	666	452	1,074	580	818	394

Source: D. H. Perkins, *Agricultural Development in China, 1368–1968* (Edinburgh University Press, Edinburgh, 1969).

that such demographic growth entailed, and the subsequent increase in population density. This was a characteristic of major agricultural expansion that Malthus (whose focus was on the short-run) seems to have missed totally, but of which the contemporary Chinese emperors were no doubt aware, as indeed was the later communist leader Mao Zedong.

The next serious setback to demographic expansion was the Manchu invasion in 1644, again from the north. This was followed by the fastest growth ever at 0.68 per cent a year, well ahead of the near-zero growth rates sometimes assumed for the pre-transition period.[5] It is possible to think of the increase occurring from a combination of a birth rate of 45 per thousand and a death rate of 35. Without the invasions, that might have been the trend rate of growth for centuries. It is also clear, however, that increasing and substantial efforts were being made to feed the people without which mortality would have been higher. D. Perkins suggests, on the basis of economic models applied to admittedly hazardous data, that yields per acre may have gone up by 50 per cent between 1400 and 1800. We can note from Table 3.3 that irrigation projects multiplied considerably faster than the population in the fifteenth and sixteenth centuries and were concentrated in those regions of the country that were already well populated.

The nineteenth century witnessed the first major population movement into south-west China, the region of present-day Yunnan. The opening up of the new frontiers in the hilly regions was achieved at a cost, however. Increased frequency of flooding was observed at the time and a Chinese geographer commented that the incipient erosion was the cause, and that this in turn could be blamed on the need to accommodate population growth. This sounds more like a modern version of the Malthusian story; but at the end of the previous century the Chinese demographer Hung Liang-Chi also commented on the ease with which population growth could outstrip food supplies. He suggested, however, that as a solution the State exhort the peasantry to improve agricultural productivity.

In 1834 there was a serious flood in Jiangxu province. Again the government was jolted into activity and distributed the fastest ripening rice yet to the affected peasants. These innovations seem to follow disasters (as is so often the case) but the Boserupian mechanism (liberally interpreted) can be seen at work.

The final check to demographic growth occurred in 1851, the Taiping rebellion. This was an uprising of former tenants who had been driven from their land. Scholars who seek to explain all these major upheavals in demographic terms would argue that population pressure was the root cause. Through famine and sickness many small peasant farmers had been driven into debt. Unable to recover their loans, the landowners drove these tenant farmers from their land and seized it as compensation. However, other scholars would point to the failure of these landowners to invest in or to maintain the irrigation infrastructure, hence constraining the growth of food output. After all, Japan managed to obtain increasing agricultural yields from the mid-nineteenth century onwards, introducing chemical fertilizers from the 1880s. This interpretation would suggest that class structure and the mode of production in the Chinese countryside was the root cause. The reader will recognize that these contrasting interpretations illustrate the Malthusian and Marxist theories respectively.

From the late nineteenth century, major improvements in the transportation system were made. This helped offset other developments that may have been making famine more likely, such as increased erosion. The railways facilitated the distribution of food for relief and the steamship allowed the growth of northern cities like Tianjin and Beijing. Though such technological breakthroughs give the potential to avoid disasters that arise from lack of food in deficit areas, the commitment of the State must go further than this to ensure there is no starvation. We will see this more clearly when we discuss modern famines in China and elsewhere in Chapter 5.

The relationship between economic and population growth

Looking at the relationship between China's population and its food supply over a very long period raises the more general question of how population and economic growth relate to one another. To examine this theoretical question, we turn to a very simple but insightful economic growth model proposed by Harrod.[6] He argues that the growth of an economy depends on how much people save for investment, and how productive that investment turns out to be. Put more technically, in terms familiar to the economist, the growth rate of the domestic product equals the average savings rate times the incremental output-to-capital ratio. This is a particularly meaningful proposition in the steady state, where the growth rate is unchanging (which means that, since the incremental output-to-capital ratio is assumed to be unchanging, the savings rate must be constant too).

The meaning of the savings rate is fairly well known: remember that it can be divided between private household, private company, and State saving. In the very long-run picture being discussed here, most saving and investment will have been done by private households and the State. A farming household, by contributing to the building of a dam to trap water for irrigation purposes, will have been using its labour to create an investment for the future (whereas alternatively it could have hired that labour out to help harvest a food grain crop on someone else's estate, which would then have been consumed).

The meaning of the incremental output-to-capital ratio is less easy to grasp. But, to illustrate by giving an example, if the dam took ten men one year to build, we could think of the capital embodied in that dam as worth ten person-years of food production. If the creation of the dam enabled each of the ten households to produce one additional tenth of a labourer's product each year because of the better crop yield that resulted from irrigation, then the total addition to output would be one person-year's production of food (continued forever, or until the collapse of the dam). The ratio of the additional capital thus valued to the additional output thus valued is 10:1. The incremental output-to-capital ratio is 0.1.

Over the long term you might expect some changes in technology to change the output-to-capital ratio. But, to keep the model simple, technical or organizational change that raises the economic growth rate is simply added to the formula and the output-to-capital ratio is assumed to remain constant. Capital is not envisaged as embodying the technical change therefore. Hence, for example, the long-term growth rate of the Chinese economy may have been less than half of 1 per cent a year, say 0.35 per cent. Suppose the savings rate was 3 per cent. This rate multiplied by an incremental output-to-capital ratio comes to $0.03 \times 0.1 = 0.3$ per cent. The extra 0.5 per cent must have come from technical innovations like the use of new varieties of seeds.

No doubt during prosperous eras, when the population was usually in upswing (as during the Ming dynasty), economic growth rates were better than these suggested averages. Perhaps a growth rate of 1 per cent a year was achieved. To obtain this, savings rates may have been jacked up (to 10 per cent), as participation of the State in major irrigation works enabled it to force surplus labour out of the peasantry. Or, maybe there were more technical innovations—such as the distribution of further new strains of seed. Or, perhaps, some other characteristics of production changed, which brings in the role of population growth once more. While it took huge amounts of labour to build large irrigation works, this strategy may have been more efficient than building lots of small dams, at least when new lands were opened up. In this case, we have economies of scale. This means that the incremental output-to-capital ratio should no longer be taken as fixed, but must have gone up (from 0.1 to 0.33, say, giving a 1 per cent growth rate) without any increase in the savings rate and without any technical breakthrough. Most probably some combination of all of these developments occurred.

We have referred to the concept of steady-state population growth, known as a stable growth. If fertility and mortality stay the same, then a constant population growth rate is assured for ever. It can be proved that if the total population is growing at a constant rate, then each age group must be growing at a constant rate. This implies that the ratio of the number of people in any age group to the total population remains constant (see Box 3.3). Hence, for example, 45 per cent of the population maybe in the under-14 age group, 51 per cent in the working-age group, and 4 per cent aged above 60. In a stable population these percentages remain the same year after year. It is worth noting a parallel here with economic growth. When that is steady, a constant proportion of income is saved. When population growth is steady, a constant proportion of the population is young.

Similar parallels occur if something changes to disrupt the steady state. In the case of the population, if the fertility rate goes up (perhaps because wars stop, couples reunite, or, with more food available, fecundity improves), the population growth rate also goes up. Therefore, so does the growth rate of the child population and, after fifteen years, the growth rate of the working-

---

BOX 3.3. PROPERTIES OF THE STABLE POPULATION

A *stable population* is one with a growth rate that has been constant indefinitely. For most practical purposes this can occur only in a population that is closed to migration and we assume this in what follows. We continue to refer to the 'growth rate', although it is identical to the rate of natural increase in such closed populations.

The growth rate may be constant at any level. For example:

- A population whose growth rate has been constant at 3 per cent a year indefinitely is a stable population.
- A population whose growth rate has been constant at −1 per cent a year for a long time is stable.
- A population whose growth has been zero forever is also stable. In this special case it is also *stationary*.

These examples make it clear that in demography the concept of stability is a theoretical one. It has nothing to do with economic or ecological sustainability. The technical definition differs from the popular (or at least non-demographic) idea that only a stationary population is stable.

The necessary conditions for a stable population to exist are:

- The age-specific mortality rates remain constant in all age groups over time.
- The age-specific fertility rates remain constant in all age groups over time.
- No migration takes place. (Theoretically migration can occur in a stable population provided the age-specific migration rates are of a very unusual kind: the reader is left to work out how this can occur for himself or herself.)

This complete set of conditions is sufficient. A little calculus shows that, if these conditions are fulfilled, not only is the overall growth rate constant but also the age composition of the stable population is unchanging, implying that the rate of growth is the same at every age.

We discuss the dynamics of stability later (in Chapter 9). Here it should be noted that:

- Even if the necessary and sufficient conditions are established, the stable population does not result instantaneously. It may take 100 years to reach the stable state.
- Whatever the initial conditions, if they remain unchanged the population converges on the stable state eventually.

BOX 3.3. continued

These points are all illustrated in the projection for Zambia that follows. The age-specific fertility and mortality rates are kept constant from 1990 to 2090. As the total fertility rate is 6.8 children per woman (see Box 2.3), the population grows rapidly. If you calculate the growth rate (see Box 1.1) in each later decade of the projection, you will find that it stabilizes at 3.5 per cent. Note the contrast between the dramatic growth in the population's size and the lack of change in the age structure. The population is virtually stable by the middle of the next century: indeed it is not very far from being stable even in 1990, which means that not much change in fertility and mortality can have occurred in the recent past.

Table A

Year	Total population	Under 15 years (%)	Over 65 years (%)
1990	7,911,850	47.67	2.68
2000	11,086,681	47.69	2.58
2010	15,669,026	47.79	2.43
2020	22,209,278	48.05	2.30
2030	31,494,859	48.00	2.23
2040	44,711,173	48.03	2.22
2050	63,480,309	48.05	2.23
2060	90,119,504	48.04	2.23
2070	127,952,925	48.05	2.22
2080	181,682,555	48.05	2.22
2090	257,964,474	48.05	2.22

Source: United Nations' Assessment Data, 1984.

A more dramatic illustration of convergence on a stable age distribution from a very different age distribution is provided in Table 9.1.

age population. Moreover, if fertility goes up, with more births coming in at the lower end of the population pyramid, the proportion of young people increases also (see Box 7.1). In the economy, if the savings propensity of the people or government goes up, then the average savings rate goes up and with it investment. The economic growth rate increases as a result.

Here we come to a very important point in pre-transition demographic history. An increase in economic growth is only possible if there is labour available to do the work—build the dams and harvest the crops, for example. In times of very slow population growth, there would be slow growth of gross domestic product. Economic growth could only occur once population growth picked up and the additional births matured into men and women able to enter the labour force. Thus, the Harrod growth model has an upper constraint: the rate of growth of the labour force. So, here we see a clear relationship between population and economic growth. But of greater concern is the growth in gross domestic product per head. That, as we have argued, may depend on two population-related factors: first, the availability of surplus labour which can be engaged in investment programmes and, secondly, the achievement of crucial densities of labour on the land to reap economies of scale from large infrastructural works.

On the other hand, it could be that any increase in births also has some effect on the savings rate. For example, we have seen from the Chayanovian model that households face a squeeze as the number of children rises in the interval before any of them mature to become producers. This could mean that household savings are reduced when population is growing faster and young people represent a larger proportion of the total. But do not forget that the State may maintain saving and investment in such circumstances by forcing the peasantry to starve (as occurred in Stalin's Russia).

Some economists have argued that, although the State may continue to save and invest when population growth increases, the output-to-capital ratio may fall. This occurs if the State invests in projects that do not contribute immediately to output. Dams can improve yields in food production as soon as they are finished, which in our earlier example was within a year. In contrast, projects like school building do not improve economic growth until the children begin to join the labour force. The outcome depends on whether the State and individuals do invest in a different set of things when the population begins to grow. To what extent do households extend their dwellings to accommodate a growing family instead of building productive things like dams and to what extent do they squeeze their children into their existing accommodation? Does the State start building schools instead of irrigation works or does it simply increase the size of existing classes? These are questions of politics and power. Their answers cannot be predicted from economic theory alone.

Enough has been said to show that the relationship between economic and population growth is problematic. We should return to one point that is not controversial. Other things being equal, if the population is growing faster than domestic product or income, then income per head must be falling. If the labour force is growing faster than capital, then the number of tools (or other capital equipment) per member of the labour force must be going down. To compensate one has to increase the economic growth rate, for example by pushing up the saving rate. This is more of a problem in the modern era, when population growth rates have become very fast. Over the long pre-transition period, any increase in population was probably welcomed because it made it possible to raise the rate of economic growth more than enough to compensate for the problem just described. In the past, the net effect was almost certainly that prosperity, or potential income per head, rose during periods of population growth. Unfortunately, what had been accumulated was often lost in wars and invasions that brought the progress of the economy and the growth of the population to a halt.

Notes

1. To a minor degree this follows from any change in the death rate because of the consequent changes in age structure. The effect is far greater if conceptions are reduced during a famine or epidemic.

2. The properties of the stable population (which are described later in this chapter in Box 3.3) have helped demographers considerably in the reconstruction of demographic trends from local records. It enables them to detect errors and omissions and make the corrections required. Stable population analysis can even be used to estimate recent fertility and mortality levels in populations that have entered the demographic transition. The definition of a stable population might suggest that this would give misleading answers but, so long as fertility and mortality do not change very abruptly, such analysis remains useful. How to undertake the reconstructions to which we refer is the subject of more advanced texts than this.

3. The link between fertility rates, such as the total fertility rate or gross rate of reproduction, and the birth rate is discussed in Box 6.1.

4. There is a slight mystery about such a prolonged period of zero growth. It has been suggested that further unrecorded natural disasters may have occurred.

5. The Chinese demographic transition is generally described as starting with the 1949 revolution when the death rate fell dramatically for the first time.

6. In the modern world, human capital development and international trade are crucial to this relationship. We return to this in Chapter 10.

4 | The Environmental Impact of Population

A population growing in a limited environment can approach the ultimate carrying capacity of that environment in several possible ways. It can adjust smoothly to an equilibrium below the environmental limit by means of a gradual decrease in growth rate. It can overshoot the limit and then die back again. Or it can overshoot the limit and in the process decrease the ultimate carrying capacity by consuming some necessary nonrenewable resource. For instance, deer or goats, when natural enemies are absent, often overgraze their range and cause erosion or destruction of the vegetation.

These words come from the book, *The Limits to Growth*, first published in 1972 as a report for the Club of Rome's project on the predicament of mankind. It represents a view widely held then and now regarding the relationship between population growth and the environment (see Figure 4.1). It is recognizably Malthusian, although the limits to growth are no longer just those of food, but include all non-renewable resources as well. Such resources may prove a more binding constraint than food production for, by definition, there is no growth, neither arithmetic nor geometric, in a truly non-renewable resource. Its use, therefore, must ultimately cease to grow altogether. The most appropriate check envisaged was the slowing down of population growth through a decline in the birth rate. The alternative was clearly similar to the Malthusian positive check.

We now make several assertions by way of critique of this position. The rest of the chapter will elaborate on these. First, it is not true to say that population growth, size, and density have always been chief among the causes of environmental degradation. Slowing population growth would therefore not be sufficient to prevent such degradation—much more would have to be done besides. Indeed, in many cases slowing population growth would have no impact on the environmental problem at all. In other words, such a policy is unnecessary because the problem will occur in any case. Nor is this a modern problem, or potential problem. Environments were being ruined long before the current acceleration of population growth. Equally, there are fragile environments that have survived high population densities and growth rates successfully. To focus the argument on population exclusively is to concentrate on the wrong piece of a complex puzzle.

Fig. 4.1. Three alternative scenarios of future population and resources suggested by the Club of Rome

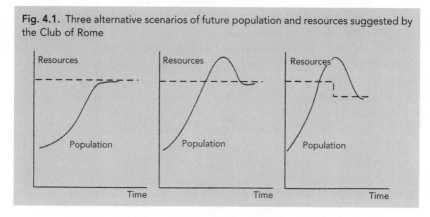

Technology, inequality, and the environment

To see why population cannot be counted chief among the causes of environmental degradation, one has only to consider the role of technology in conjunction with high levels of productive capacity. Rich countries, and rich people in poor countries, can damage the earth out of all proportion to their numbers. Keyfitz, a demographer, highlighted transport technologies in this respect in the 1970s. He pointed out that one-third of the world's oil production was being used to fuel automobiles. The growth in the number of automobiles would continue even if the population could stop growing tomorrow: it is still growing in the Western economies where population growth has stopped. There is enormous scope for increases in the number of automobiles as the world's poorer populations become richer. If the technology remained the same, many areas of the world could seriously pollute their atmospheres. Some mortality can already be attributed to air pollution; conceivably it could soar above present levels.

The damage done by existing technologies is somewhat dependent on location, as the following example readily illustrates. As people travel, they spread pollution around. Some locations are particularly vulnerable to pollution damage. In these cases, quite small populations can increase their own mortality rapidly. Take for example a coastal city, like Bombay, built on the flat land between the sea and the coastal hills. During the day the prevailing wind from the sea stacks up the polluted air against the hills. At night, during much of the year, a slight breeze off the land ensures that the polluted air drifts back over the city again (Figure 4.2). Although most of the population of Bombay is quite poor, the city's twelve million inhabitants use enough energy to create unacceptable pollution levels. Automobile use is limited to a minority. If just half the present population, six rather than twelve million, lived in Bombay at a standard of living that allowed most of

Fig. 4.2. Wind currents and pollution in a coastal city (Bombay in western India)

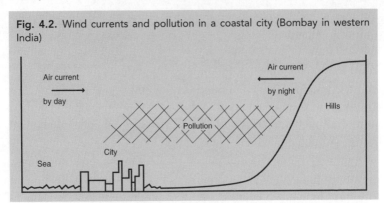

them to own cars, the level of pollution would be far worse. While less mortality would arise from malnutrition and its interaction with disease in an affluent Bombay, the net effect might be to increase mortality. This example is as doom laden as those in the scenario depicted by the Club of Rome but serves to illustrate the importance of technology and location and to shift the focus away from population alone.

The foregoing discussion implies that environmental damage is tied up closely with inequality in the ownership of world resources. But, not only may the rich damage their environment (and everyone else's) because they are rich, the poor may damage their environment because they are poor. This is not wilful damage but damage through compulsion. For example, if the rural poor need fuel and are unable to afford whatever is available in the market, they have no other recourse than to plunder the surrounding countryside for whatever brushwood they can gather. Without fuel, households cannot cook, sterilize water, or, in some climates, keep sufficiently warm and dry. The result of such deprivation is an elevated risk of mortality. When premature death is just round the corner, people cannot be expected to concern themselves about the future of the environment; they will satisfy their immediate needs, even if this destroys their environment within their own lifetimes. To use the jargon of the economist, in certain circumstances the poor have very high discount rates. However, this does not mean that the poor always have high discount rates for, provided they have enough to survive on, they usually show considerable concern for the future—their old age and the future of their children. As we shall see, their low discount rates can be translated into a very enlightened approach to environmental preservation.

Inequality may result from the rich buying out the poor or simply forcing them off the land. We discussed this process in relation to the development of capitalist farming in Chapter 1. The commercialization of cropping for international markets may speed this process up, with devastating effects.

The population that becomes marginalized has to intensify its use of the marginal land to which it is driven. The speed of change allows no time for development of ways to protect the environment: the poor are compelled again to extract what they can in order to survive. Meanwhile, large commercial organizations farm what had been the land of the poor: the gains from such enterprises may eventually, but will not necessarily, lead to improved earning opportunities for all. But the immediate impact can be severe on the poor and severe on the environment too. Moreover, the commercial organizations may also damage the land that they have acquired; they may cut down more trees than they plant or allow more soil to blow away than they enrich through fertilizer. If this is how they behave, it suggests that commercial organizations do not care much about the future: that is to say, they may have high discount rates also. Perhaps of greater importance, they do not always suffer from the damage that they do. If fertilizer finds its way into the river, it is people who live downstream that suffer most. If trees are cut down too quickly, there may be serious climatic implications. These issues need not worry the owners of the enterprise too much as they are rich enough to lay claim to whatever food there may be around in time of drought or flood.

Theory and practice of environmental regulation

The argument that is being advanced is that we need to regulate damaging economic activity. In practice, many societies have devised means of so doing. One can think of a very simple model that illustrates this. Consider a square kilometre of scrubland with a fragile soil. We call this a common property resource as it is 'owned' by the community in general. Two herdsmen, A and B, feed their goats on half the area each and we suppose that the herds are small enough to ensure that the fertility of the land is preserved year in and year out (Figure 4.3). If the herdsmen have open access to this common resource, however, there is no reason why they should restrain their herds to each half of the land. Herdsman A could breed more goats and graze them on part of B's scrubland. The result would be that the strip of land that is being grazed simultaneously by both parties ceases to yield enough grass to feed the goats as adequately as before. Herdsman A has increased his total profits from goat-herding (though his profit margin per goat may have gone down) but B has taken a cut in overall profit because A has reduced the productivity of one of B's factors of production, namely land. In the jargon of the economist, A is imposing an external diseconomy on B.[1]

It can be seen that part of the problem lies in a lack of mutual trust between the two herdsmen. After all, A might have been prepared to graze his additional goats on his own half of the property if he had known that B,

Fig. 4.3. Scheme of grazing on open-access land

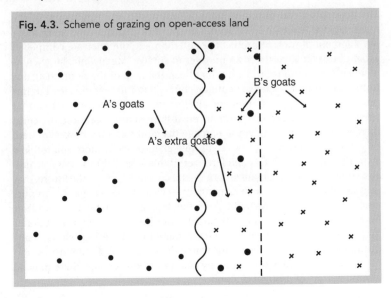

when faced with the same possibilities of increasing profits, would do the same. He was not prepared to take that step as he knew that B would not necessarily co-operate and do the same. Herdsman B would no doubt argue in the same way on this point. Somehow they have to agree as to the optimal increase in the number of goats that enables them both to carry on goat-farming with equal profitability and to stick to the agreement. If there is no way of enforcing the agreement, then the situation may even arise where A and B find that they have allowed their herds to increase to the extent that some of their goats are undernourished. It is therefore essential that there be regulated, not open, access to this public property resource. In the extreme case, where land was limitless, both parties could increase their herds and take in new virgin land for the purpose. Unregulated access would not pose any problem. Of course, bringing the land into private ownership with a fence dividing A from B would also be a solution, but an expensive and perhaps impractical one if the land area is large and the farmers are poor.

A rather similar problem arises over the preservation of the environment from one generation to the next and, indeed, from one day to the next. The two goat farmers might, by their increased grazing, reduce not only the adequacy of nutrition of each other's herd. They might also reduce the fertility of the land. In that case they would need to agree on the size of herd, and each herdsman's share of it, that could be sustained by the local pasture. It might turn out that Herdsman B cared much more about the future than Herdsman A. In this case the need for regulated access is even stronger: Herdsman A would always be prepared to break the rules and expand his herd so long as it was profitable today to do so. He would not bother about tomorrow so much.

Similarly, we can think of the future generation as rather like another herdsman, Herdsman C. Suppose that today the only herdsman is A. If he increases his herd he may still be able to make a profit, but suppose the quality of the land he can bequeath to C is much reduced thereby. He is imposing an externality on C. One needs a protector of society, present and future, to make the rules in this case, and to restrict A's expansion. It is rather as though Herdsman A is bargaining with Herdsman C, as he had been before with Herdsman B, the only difference being that Herdsman C is not yet born (or, at least, not yet grown up).

In all these models the crucial consideration is the rules that people make for the use of their resources. If the pasture is sufficiently fragile, rules are needed even when the population of herdsmen is rather small. While there are some very robust environments where rules need not be made even when the population has become quite large, it is certainly the case that rules need to be made sooner or later. Population growth (and with it a growth in the animal herds) merely makes it more likely that rules are needed sooner rather than later.

In practice, many societies have devised rules to preserve their environments. For example, Jodha lists the following indicators of longstanding attempts to regulate the use of common property resources in India: the existence of evenly scattered watering points for animals, to reduce the concentration of damage done by too great a concentration of animals; the deliberate rotation of grazing around different watering points; the periodic closure of parts of the common property resource area; and the periodic restriction of entry of animals to parts of the common area. These practices were enforced by the posting of watchmen and the creation of a village enclosure in which animals violating the regulations could be impounded. Furthermore, there was a widespread levy of a grazing tax on common land and a forced contribution of labour for desilting ponds. The enforcement of these regulations depended largely on the authority of the local landowner. Jodha argues that land reforms in the 1950s reduced this degree of environmental protection. Much of the common land was placed in private ownership and came under the plough, considerably reducing the common property resources available for grazing. This probably led to overuse for, although the need for regulation was even stronger than before, the impoverished herders were compelled to squeeze a livelihood out of a diminishing resource. To survive, they destroyed their future livelihood. Additionally, the power of the local landowner was transferred to quasi-democratic local bodies. They were less inclined to collect taxes and exercise the authoritarian powers of the landowner and, in any case, most of the representatives now had private land. It would appear that the new administrative systems failed to create effective local management of the environment; jobs that used to be done by the community were taken over by the central government, often much less effectively.

One could argue that the need for land reform was made more pressing by growth of the population. But, even before such growth, inequality in landholding had been high and redistribution was thought necessary in the interests of equity. The use of public property resources in this distribution was undoubtedly made all the more essential by the growth of population subsistence needs in advance of any rise in agricultural productivity. This particular example indicates the effect of institutional change resulting from the establishment of the independent state. However, similar examples can be given to illustrate the effects of colonialism on institutional change. One of the effects of colonial peacemaking in Africa, for example, was to weaken the political authority of the chiefs. They, like the Indian landlords, had previously had the power to enforce conservation measures in pasture lands, a role the colonial authorities were less interested in taking upon themselves.[2]

Concern for and damage to the environment is certainly nothing new. There are, for example, many classical Chinese texts that emphasize the need to protect flora and fauna. Yet, over the generations, the destruction of trees has led to serious soil erosion in the foothills of north and western China. Nowadays, in addition, trees are destroyed by acid rain from the emissions of power stations. On the other hand, in densely populated Japan, according to scholars who have worked on this problem, three centuries of careful management of village commons has resulted in their preservation.

It was pointed out earlier that environments are often overexploited for commercial gain. This might not appear to be very sensible, as presumably a business operation does not want to drive itself out of business by ruining its resources. But the matter is not so simple. Business managers (and shareholders) do look to the future, but they also apply a discount rate: profits in fifty years' time are much less attractive than profits tomorrow. Whereas village communities, or even governments, may feel obliged to ensure the welfare of future generations, business organizations usually do not. Gradually but inexorably, therefore, they tend to run down their stock: the forest disappears. Furthermore, businesses are not necessarily concerned, as we have said, about the harm that their activity does to the lives of others. That is why the State, in response to its citizens' demands, is so essential an actor in the regulation of economic activity, even when the resources in question are privately owned.

In order to arrive at some estimate of how much land, water, or even air is being overused and where the greatest abuses lie, the concept of 'carrying capacity' has been used. This refers to the number of people that a particular area of land and its associated biomass can support continually. But the concept is a slippery one. To begin with, technological change can substantially increase or decrease the carrying capacity of a given locality. Carrying capacity is a very static concept, while the ecology of rural areas has changed with time. As Boserup has argued, forests have given way to arable land and fallowing has become progressively shorter with the more intensive use of manure, in order to accommodate a growing population. Many of these more intensively farmed lands have been able to sustain a higher carrying capacity as a result. On the other hand, quite fragile soils supporting low population densities have been rendered useless by inappropriate technology. Deserts of sand or saline soil were once populated and probably in some cases, given the right technology, could be populated again.

A more serious problem with the carrying capacity concept is that it fails to allow for trade. The herdsmen discussed previously may live on poor agricultural land, which is none the less suitable for grazing animals. Even if these lands are grazed conservatively, only small populations could be supported if people had to live off the milk and flesh of their animals. As soon as this population begins to trade, however, it is possible to exchange milk for grain grown elsewhere on richer soils. The herders should be able to buy more grain for their milk than they could grow themselves on their marginal land.[3] In a sense, therefore, the local carrying capacity of the land is raised by trade. This again demonstrates the static nature of the usual concept of carrying capacity and many similar concepts of self-sufficiency. On the other hand, trade may lead to damage to the environment. For example, agricultural land of superior quality may be damaged by the increased use that trading opportunities encourage.

The economic logic of international trade enables the richer nations of the world to protect their immediate environments. One interpretation of the comparative success of Western countries in the control of air and water pollution would emphasize that they no longer have growing populations pressing harder on the carrying capacity of their land area. In addition, they gain from trade with poorer countries that are still polluting their environments seriously. Indeed, imports or financial flows into the rich countries may be related directly to environmentally damaging activity elsewhere in the world. For example, exports of wood products from countries that still have forests are only as high as they are because the products are cheap. This is only the case because the exporting countries are failing to regulate the exploitation of the forests (whether on private or public lands).

Japan is faced with potential environmental problems as a result of rapid industrialization on a small land area over a short period of time. One could argue that Japan has reached its carrying capacity. Population growth has now slowed and is heading towards zero, but incomes continue to rise. One solution is for Japan to carry out its industrial processing overseas. Much new industrial plant has now been set up in South-East Asia: not only are labour costs lower, but pollution restrictions are less severe. The latter may be because air is an uncongested resource at the moment. Or it may be simply that legislation is less binding. In a sense, the Japanese economy is exporting its pollution overseas. Neither the prices of its imports, nor the size of its dividends from these operations, reflect this fact. Thus, it is imposing an external diseconomy on the host country. The horrific disaster at Bhopal in India reminds us what this can mean in human terms.

To put the argument in a nutshell, economic growth and the manner in which it is managed are responsible for environmental degradation. Management is probably made more difficult by rapid population growth, as some of the earlier examples illustrate. But, as the growth rate slows, which it has already begun to do throughout most of the world, the problem does not go away. In the long run, we are all Malthusians. We cannot envisage sustainable life on this planet with an infinite population size, nor can we easily envisage colonizing space. Focusing too closely on population size and growth, however, when trying to explain or reverse trends in poverty, food insufficiency, or natural resource destruction, causes us to miss some essential factors. For, without major changes in the management of resources and the technologies we use, economic growth is unsustainable even with zero population growth.

In Chapter 3 we indicated that in many countries of Asia and Africa fertility had begun to fall, meaning that the number of births per woman was declining. Couples who in the past would have had families of five or six children are now terminating childbearing with the third or fourth child. In some countries, such as China, the total fertility rate is as low as two, which means, if we ignore mortality, that each couple is replacing itself exactly. In a stable population of this kind, natural increase would therefore be zero. The age composition would be static, as in all stable populations, and there would be zero growth in each age group. Generation after generation, each age group would replace itself exactly (see again Box 3.3).

However, zero population growth does not occur immediately when fertility reaches replacement level, a fact not always appreciated by non-demographers. The reason for the delay is called *demographic momentum* by demographers. In the past, when fertility was high (say, six live births per woman), the number of female births (i.e., girl babies) was increasing rapidly (at 3 per cent each year, say). As these daughters grew up and (ignoring mortality) became mothers, the number of mothers also increased at 3 per cent a year. These are the women who are giving birth today. Even if they reduce the number of children they have to two births each (which in the long run would give zero population growth), for the present the number of births will go on increasing each year. This is because the number of mothers is still increasing (as a result of the growth in past births). Only when each mother has just two births and the number of mothers also stops growing will the growth of births fall to zero. It usually takes several decades for the number of mothers to stop growing and population growth to cease. We illustrate this in Box 4.1 and Figure 4.4.

BOX 4.1. DEMOGRAPHIC MOMENTUM

If the proportion of women of childbearing age in the population is high, a relatively large number of births will occur. Thus, as indicated in the text, the impact of recent age-specific fertility decline on the birth rate will be offset by the growing number of women in the childbearing ages.

This can be illustrated by projecting a population forward through a period of rapid fertility decline. For example, Figure 4.4 shows the impact of an abrupt fall in the total fertility rate in Zambia to two children in 1990. Notice two things:

- The number of births rebounds after the initial sharp decline in fertility, rising to a peak after about twenty years before declining again.
- The age structure of the population retains a high proportion of women in the childbearing ages during and after the period of fertility decline.

As a result, although in the long run a total fertility rate of 2.0 in Zambia without any reduction in mortality would produce population decline, it takes nearly fifty years for this to occur. Boxes 6.1 and 9.4 discuss more fully how age composition affects birth and death rates and how to correct for this.

Another way of looking at this is to realize that the proportion of young people, aged less than 40, say, in a fast-growing population is larger than in a stationary population. (We referred to this fact in Chapter 3 and demonstrate it more clearly in Chapter 7, Figure 7.2.) Hence, there is a relatively large proportion of potential mothers in the population. The past increase from year to year in the number of births means that the number of women of childbearing age will continue to grow rapidly for at least a generation after fertility begins to decline. While the relative size of this group of women remains larger than in the stationary population, the number of births will increase each year even if fertility falls to replacement level. Thus, the age structure of a high-fertility population has an inbuilt momentum for further growth.

Case study of West Africa

Mention of West Africa, and particularly of the Sahelian region, conjures up images of a fragile physical environment where recurrent droughts in recent years have laid claim to thousands of lives. However, damage to this environment extends back hundreds of years. As with more modern examples, damage often occurred when technologies changed or when trade with richer nations was opened up. By the fifteenth century, trade across the Sahara required 12,000 camels each year. One of the products that was much sought after was charcoal. Another was gum arabic, which was used in the developing European textile industry: this was obtained from the acacia trees of Senegal. Both these requirements for trade led to the felling of the Senegalese forests and the exposure of land to wind and water, the effects of which can be witnessed today. It is not clear that any adverse climatic effects of such behaviour are particularly recent either. There are records of five-year droughts affecting the Niger Bend in the

Fig. 4.4. Demographic momentum following fertility decline, simulation for Zambia

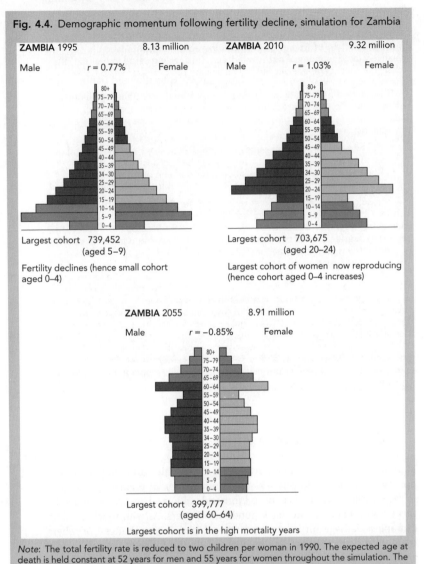

ZAMBIA 1995   8.13 million

Male   r = 0.77%   Female

Largest cohort   739,452
            (aged 5–9)

Fertility declines (hence small cohort
aged 0–4)

ZAMBIA 2010   9.32 million

Male   r = 1.03%   Female

Largest cohort   703,675
            (aged 20–24)

Largest cohort of women now reproducing
(hence cohort aged 0–4 increases)

ZAMBIA 2055   8.91 million

Male   r = –0.85%   Female

Largest cohort   399,777
            (aged 60–64)

Largest cohort is in the high mortality years

Note: The total fertility rate is reduced to two children per woman in 1990. The expected age at death is held constant at 52 years for men and 55 years for women throughout the simulation. The projection methods used for this simulation are explained in Box 10.1.

eighteenth century, and the 1913 drought is widely believed to be the worst in memory.

Many studies in the region demonstrate that lack of population growth held back economic progress. There was not the labour available to bring about agrarian change in directions that might have increased the sustainability of land use. Gleave has examined changing agrarian practices in the 1960s and shows that increasing population pressure led to a transition from shifting cultivation to more permanent settlement systems. This involved changing to techniques that tended to preserve the fertility of the soil such as manuring, which is what Boserup argued would happen. It is possible to adapt her thesis to the environmental problem: it may be necessary for populations to press heavily on their natural resources before they have the incentive, or the necessary labour, to preserve them. Otherwise, one can simply migrate to escape the consequences of over-exploitation.

Clearly political boundaries will dictate how this works in practice. Some writers have argued that the densely populated area around Kano in Nigeria is a success story in the adoption and management of intensive land use patterns, with the city providing manure and a market that can sustain a local population of 500 per square kilometre. There are others who would argue otherwise. They believe that increased urbanization in West Africa has led to degradation of the rural areas. Forests have been felled to provide fuel and, as villages are incorporated in an urban sprawl, wells become overused and salinity results. In rural areas, moreover, traditional fallow systems are disrupted when population grows. Far from devising methods of soil preservation, fertilizing is achieved by annual burning of stubble. This damages trees. If landscapes are open, there is a tendency eventually for soil treated thus to blow away.

So, there are different interpretations of what is occurring in West Africa and how far population growth and density have helped or hindered progress towards sustainability. It is clear that complacency will not do. Even if people learn to manage their environments eventually, they may have to go through a catastrophe and period of 'die back' as envisaged by the Club of Rome before they do so (just as a natural disaster seems to have been the prerequisite of technical change in ancient Chinese agriculture). It is clearly imperative that ways of establishing good environmental management practice are devised, or learned from others who practise them, and that their interaction with population growth (for that growth will continue even if fertility falls tomorrow) is thoroughly understood.

Notes

1. Technically speaking the private marginal cost of A's enterprise is now below the marginal social cost (i.e., accounting for the impact on B).
2. The argument so far might seem to justify authoritarian regimes. But there is no theoretical reason why democratically elected governments (whether local or national) should not pass and enforce the necessary legislation, if they are persuaded of the urgency of the public problem in comparison with the private interests that they may partly represent.
3. Economists will recognize the beginnings of a theory of comparative advantage here. They will also be able to add to the story the following observation to com-

plete it. Traders, as we have noted, may bring their superior food grains from a part of the country that is blessed with soil that is of good quality and well watered. On those lands it may be possible to keep animals as well as growing high-quality food grains, in both cases using less labour and land than in the rough lands of the herders. If the productivity of herders is higher than that of agriculturalists in the rough grazing lands, however, and the productivity of agriculturalists is higher than that of herders on the good-quality lands, both communities will gain from trading with each other.

Part III

Political Economy, Famine, and Disease Control

5 | Famine and the Prevention of Mass Mortality

Introduction

Much has been written on famine, and some of the conclusions reached appear paradoxical. One of the most striking contentions in the literature is that famine, which is defined as mass starvation, can occur without there being a massive shortage of food. In fact this assertion can be put even more strongly by saying that famine can occur even during a record harvest of food grains. It is, however, often the case that famine is triggered by a shortfall, particularly a localized shortfall, in the production of some commodity or other (which may or may not be food).

Equally surprising to some would be the claim that, even if there is a huge shortfall of food in some region or other, famine need not follow: indeed there are examples of such massive deficits occurring (a 50 per cent shortfall in an area with a population of 50 million for example) but not being accompanied by mass starvation. Intervention of an appropriate kind by the State, in conjunction with the private sector, can prevent famine nowadays. Maybe it always could have. What amounts to an appropriate intervention may not have as much to do with food, however, as with employment and disease control. This brings us to another surprising and perhaps controversial conclusion reached by some students of famine: in a 'famine' most people die of disease, not of starvation.

The Bengal famine of 1943

The economist Amartya Sen initiated the recent debate on famine by taking as an illustration the series of events that led to the great Bengal Famine of 1943, when India was still under British rule and the Second World War was in progress. Although this may seem like a roll of distant thunder from a bygone storm, the principles of the discussion have led to much debate on the feasibility of avoiding more recent disasters of this kind in Africa and elsewhere.

The basic outline of events was as follows. The 1942 autumn harvest was down only 3 per cent on the previous years. Then, in October, a cyclone and a fungus disease damaged the crop that was due to be harvested in December (which was the most important crop of the year in Bengal). The result was a harvest shortfall of 17 per cent. An intervention that might have been expected would have been to import rice into Bengal from Burma across the Bay of Bengal (as Burma was part of the British Empire at that time). However, the Japanese had taken Rangoon, the capital of Burma, cutting off this possibility. The price of rice nearly doubled between December 1941 and December 1942; it had more than doubled again by May 1943.

Distress was evident from December 1942 when the first protests were organized by the community, and migrants began to enter the city of Calcutta in search of relief. By June 1943 the city was packed with destitute people, but the only relief was the opening of some charity kitchens. By December 1943 mortality was at its peak (see Figure 5.1). All in all, Sen estimates that there must have been about three million deaths in excess of what was normal. A cruel but not unusual irony is that the harvests of autumn and winter 1943 were perfectly adequate.

Two further and related facts need to be noted. Britain was at war in Europe and East Asia and India was crucial to the war effort. In Calcutta as many factories as possible had been turned over to the manufacture of munitions; indeed this gave rise to a local economic boom. At the same time, the arrival of the Japanese in Burma had resulted in everything possi-

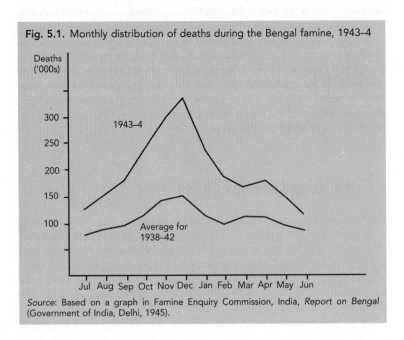

Fig. 5.1. Monthly distribution of deaths during the Bengal famine, 1943–4

Source: Based on a graph in Famine Enquiry Commission, India, *Report on Bengal* (Government of India, Delhi, 1945).

ble being done to prevent them from getting a toehold on the east Indian coast: all small Indian fishing craft were confiscated and sunk.

The British put the following simple explanation of the famine on record: 'the serious shortage in total supply of rice available for consumption in Bengal as compared with the total supply normally available'. Sen makes the following points of interpretation by way of critique.

First, the shortfall in food availability (that is including wheat imports) was non-existent: in fact availability in 1943 (calculated as a three-year average ending at that date, when disastrous levels of mortality were occurring) was a little higher than the three-year average ending in 1941. Allowing for population growth during the two years would make very little difference to availability per head. There was therefore no shortage of food in Bengal.

Secondly, by looking at those social or occupational groups that were worst affected we can trace the processes that led to the famine. The occupations among which destitution increased most were those of agricultural labour and fishing. The former were affected most directly by the small harvest shortfall because their main livelihood at that time of year is helping with the harvest. When the harvest is smaller than usual, there is no need to hire in extra hands. The fishermen also lost their source of income when their boats were taken away. Examining affected occupations in greater detail reveals some curiosities: for instance workers in 'semi-luxury services' like hair-cutting also fell disproportionately into destitution. The process is best understood in terms of the employment multiplier familiar to economists—only here the process is working in reverse. In the first place an exogenous shock is received: work is taken away from all those connected most closely with the harvest (and from the fishermen). They therefore earn no income and have no claim (or entitlement) to food. They have neither cash nor rights over food through payment in kind, for they have done no work. Then the second round of the multiplier comes into effect. These people cannot purchase the services of others; they cease to obtain anything that is not absolutely necessary, for instance minor luxuries like a hair cut, household items like utensils, or simple (and nutritionally desirable) additions to their basic meal such as vegetables and pickles. All these items are processed, manufactured, transported, or marketed by other workers, who accordingly see a cut in their own incomes. They in turn react by cutting back on their purchases. At the margins, people are thrown out of work and hence lose their claims on food. Some starve. Others share a meagre portion of calories within their households: young children will become malnourished, become vulnerable to disease, and perhaps die.

There were of course exacerbating factors in 1943, which have sometimes been forgotten in discussions of this famine. The expansion of the war effort meant that wages were allowed to rise for those involved in munitions production in Calcutta: this was done as an incentive to hard work and to ensure a healthy work-force. The effective demand of these industrial workers resulted in prices of food rising in Calcutta. This must have attracted food out of the countryside and into the city. At the same time, the British failed to shift food into Bengal until it was too late. This encouraged speculative hoarding by traders. The British government was not concentrating on the affairs of Bengal; its prime concern was not to lose the war.

Sen, in refuting the claim of the British Famine Enquiry cited above, alleges that the British Raj 'was disastrously wrong in its theory of famines'. However, a glance back into history reveals that this had not always been the case and casts doubt on whether it can have been the case in 1943. For example, when severe droughts afflicted much of western India in 1876, the British administrators, especially local ones like the district collectors, knew exactly what was needed to prevent mass starvation. If destitution resulted from loss of employment (in processing the harvest), then the solution was an injection of autonomous demand (to use the Keynesian expression before its time) through creating public employment. This was quite clear from correspondence between the District Collector of Poona, the Governor of Bombay, and the Government in Simla (its summer residence). The only argument was about what kind of public employment to provide: the Government did not want to spend too much money if the financial return on the investment was uncertain. Here are three extracts from the correspondence.

[from the Assistant Collector to the Collector of Poona] To summarise this long report I consider that in Bhimthadi and Indapur two thirds of the kharif crop are gone and the remainder stands a fair chance of being lost. Should this prove to be the case, the local fund and provincial works, together with any aid the Railway, Forest, and Irrigation Departments may be able to give us, will keep the labouring classes from starving through September, and if heavy rain falls through that month the rabi crop will probably be secure, and no special steps need be taken. If however there is little or no rain in September, it will be necessary to obtain funds from Government, and also to urge the departments named above to help us to the best of their ability.

[from the Governor of Bombay to the Government of India in Simla] The small works spoken of in your letter have been sanctioned and are nearly done. We are unanimously of the opinion that the works on the Dhond and Munmar Railway must be commenced at once.

[from the Government of India to the Governor of Bombay] The Government of India regret that the distress in three of your districts is so great, but do not think it right to authorise the commencement of so expensive a work as the railway in question, the expediency of constructing which in preference to other important lines has not yet been determined, merely to meet a temporary, though serious, emergency.

Then as now, the major problem was the lack of purchasing power, or other entitlement to food, of landless agricultural labourers who were hired and fired as and when needed. The peasant proprietor could eat the reduced amount of food he produced (and harvested himself). The sharecropping tenant retained some claim to food, even if the total was diminished. If there was no food at all, the owner-cultivating peasant, and perhaps the sharecropper, could sell what assets they had (including land) to buy food on the market. The large landowner would only have to sell a little to get all he needed.

A harvest shortfall that puts labourers out of work need not be that of a food grain harvest. A cash-crop shortfall would have the same effect: without appropriate public intervention there would have been a famine in Bangladesh in 1984 when the jute crop was diseased and failed. The problems are worse if the shortfall is concentrated locally, which happens when a particular crop is concentrated locally. Otherwise, if employment collapses only in one small sector, it may be possible to accommodate the unemployed elsewhere in the local economy. In a monoculture this is not possible. Work sharing is no longer a solution: there is open unemployment and the unemployed starve. It is even conceivable that famines could occur if some mining or industrial complex employing thousands of local people were shut down. Certainly there have been reports of starvation in India when large coal mines in underdeveloped areas have closed suddenly.

Famine in China, 1959–61

Perhaps the most important insight to be gained from Sen's interpretation of the Bengal famine, and indeed from the correspondence of the early administrators during previous famines, is that the crucial immediate problem is the loss of purchasing power by a specific sector of the population. From 1953 to 1958 the Chinese planners accorded priority to industrial production. At the same time they pressed ahead with the collectivization of agriculture, whereby peasants contributed their labour to large communal farms (with as many as 5,000 households per farm). From these, the State purchased between one-fifth and one-third of the grain. Most of this was stored locally. The overall output of food kept up with the growth in population during this period. However, the planners were dissatisfied with the increase in industrial output. In 1958 Mao Zedong announced an initiative which was known as the Great Leap Forward. Additional labour was pressed into heavy industry and withdrawn from agriculture to make this possible. Transport was dedicated to moving industrial supplies around the country.

As a result, food grain output fell to about 15 per cent below the average in 1959. Then a series of exogenous problems occurred. In 1960 there was a serious drought causing a loss of about 25 per cent of the crop. In 1961 floods reduced the output yet again by about the same amount.[1] Output did not return to normal until 1964. There was a massive famine. In 1960 the death rate more than doubled (to 25 per thousand). It was 50 per cent above average in 1959 and 1961 according to the official records released much later. While the relative increase in mortality (i.e., a doubling of the death rate) looks rather similar to the experience of the Bengal famine, the population affected was vast. Estimates put the Bengal death toll at between two and four million. There were between fifteen and thirty million deaths in China, depending on whose data you believe.[2]

Can this catastrophe best be understood in terms of a failure of purchasing power? One's first impression might be that there was quite a serious shortfall in food availability from natural causes, which constituted the major problem. A closer look at Figure 5.2 indicates that deaths began to increase substantially in 1959. This cannot have resulted from harvest failure the following year. In fact there is good reason to call this crisis a 'man-made' famine also (a view held subsequently by several Chinese scholars). The shortage of agricultural labour from 1958, that resulted from the competing demand for labour from industry, meant that some of the crops that came to fruition could not be harvested. Furthermore, as grain was stored in a decentralized fashion, considerable logistical problems arose in getting food from surplus to deficit areas. These were compounded by the lack of transport vehicles, particularly railway wagons, which had been requisitioned to carry steel rather than grain. So, the food was in the wrong place and the strategy of the Great Leap Forward made it impossible to rectify the problem. These might be regarded as special circumstances, similar to those of the wartime economy in Bengal. But the crisis was certainly exacerbated by the distribution of purchasing power. The Chinese system of

Fig. 5.2. Birth and death rates in China during the period of the famine, 1959–62

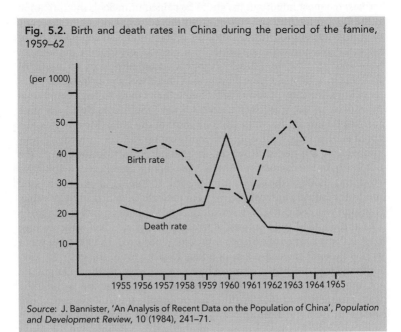

Source: J. Bannister, 'An Analysis of Recent Data on the Population of China', *Population and Development Review*, 10 (1984), 241–71.

awarding 'work points' as claims on food and other purchases is similar in some crucial ways to payment in cash. By awarding increased work points for increases in industrial worker productivity, the State increased the purchasing power of workers in heavy industries like iron and steel production, exactly as the British had done by paying workers in the munitions factories extra wages. Industrial workers' demand for what had become a diminishing quantity of food went up. As industry was a priority, that demand was met by the State, which increased its procurement to do so. Hence, there was insufficient food to fulfil the guaranteed minimum ration for the rest of the population: many of the agricultural workers' claims were not met. The guaranteed minimum, which the State had provided for everyone previously, turned out not to be a true entitlement.

It is clear that, however we interpret the disaster, it did not occur just as a result of the production shortfall. Indeed, as we go on to show, with appropriate management even such a large production deficit need not cause starvation. In the past, both communist and capitalist governments have failed at times to implement interventions that could have saved countless lives.

Famine control

Much has been written recently on the question of famine control—that is to say, strategies to prevent mass starvation when a substantial decline in purchasing power occurs, whether or not this is triggered by a major shortfall in domestic food production. Such strategies should be distinguished from those required to prevent such events occurring in the first place. The latter are one of the central concerns of long-term economic development whereas the subject of current interest is the ability to cope with emergencies (accepting, for the current argument, that they are sometimes bound to occur).

The cornerstone of an appropriate strategy is seen by Sen and his followers to be the institutionalizing of public works. There is no better way of reversing a sudden decline in purchasing power and its negative employment multiplier effect than to be able immediately to step up the level of demand for labour. This is the role of the State, and the requirements are detailed in a book by Dreze and Sen called *Hunger and Public Action*. As we have seen, the idea is as old as the hills but the technical (and not unimportant) details of the effectiveness of such a plan have not been discussed fully until more recently.

Dreze illustrates the operation of such a scheme with reference to the successful containment of famine in the Indian state of Maharashtra between 1972 and 1973. He contrasts this with the less successful containment of famine in Bihar in 1965 and 1966. Both states experienced a massive shortfall in food production: in each case a little more than 50 per cent. 'Success' is a relative term in this field. The demographic evidence is very sketchy but is consistent with there having been a 20 to 30 per cent increase in deaths (peaking in 1967) following the major shortfall of food production in Bihar in 1966. By contrast, in Maharashtra after a similar shortfall, deaths increased by only 10 to 20 per cent. More reliable and significant data from surveys relate to the reduction in food intake. In Bihar, landless labourers suffered a 40 per cent decrease in cereal intake whereas, in Maharashtra, the deficit was spread more evenly across all social classes with agricultural labourers suffering approximately a 20 per cent decrease. Dreze accounts for this difference by the far more successful implementation of a public works programme in Maharashtra than in Bihar. Both states had a population of around fifty million, but in Maharashtra five million people were employed on public works at the height of the crisis. In Bihar the maximum was half a million. It can also be shown that the districts in Maharashtra that were worst affected by the drought had the highest employment on public works, which is to say the programme was well targeted.

For such a response by the State to work well, several conditions have to be fulfilled. To begin with, as we have seen from the previous case studies, giving people claims on food is useless if the food cannot be provided. In the case of Bihar much of the necessary food had to be imported—it came through American aid. Delays in the declaration of famine (not declared until April 1967, almost a year after the monsoons failed) meant that it nearly arrived too late. Furthermore, the distribution had to be handled by the government: this was partly because the food had to be distributed largely to people who had no work and hence had no direct claim on food to which the market system could respond. Food was distributed to children at school, for instance, but that proved futile where schools had been closed because of the crisis. The logistics of a State-administered distribution scheme are problematic. Where a reasonable market and private transport network exists, arguably one should use it. That means putting cash in people's pockets, so that they can attract the necessary food in their direction. This is what was done in Maharashtra, and the food came into the state through private traders. Actually, this was illegal. Interstate grain movements have been prohibited since colonial days for fear that deficits might simply be transferred to neighbouring regions. In practice this had ceased to be a serious problem by the 1970s, probably because a good transport network meant that food grains could move fairly freely throughout the country, evening out the deficit throughout.

One of the advantages of a scheme of food or cash for work is that only the truly needy are attracted to participate. There is little danger of attracting labour away from productive work elsewhere. Of course, to ensure this does not happen, the wages paid have to be sufficiently low to be unattractive to those already employed (while being sufficiently high to ensure that those in the scheme command sufficient food to meet their calorie requirements).

By paying only the labourers, however, one is assuming that other members of their family will get food from them. As we argued in Chapter 2, this does not always follow. In fact, in Maharashtra, while a substantial number of women were employed on the relief works, in some cases they may have been left behind in the village. It was with this consideration in mind that the programme in Bihar tried to target children directly. But, where school or clinic attendance is rare, significant sectors of the population get missed by schemes that use such facilities as distribution centres. Usually the poorest, and hence the most needy, suffer most. The Bihar programme is sometimes claimed to have been a success because it initiated a fortified food-for-children programme in the state. This cannot have been extended very far. The child mortality data suggest that the overall record in Maharashtra was probably better regarding child welfare than in Bihar.

The speedy declaration of famine is clearly important. Many governments are reluctant to declare a famine for political reasons. Lack of credibility inevitably follows admission of a food shortage. For this reason neither did the British declare the Bengal famine, nor the Chinese the Great Leap Forward famine. More recently, the Ethiopian Government failed to declare a famine in 1983–4. However, early warning systems can have disadvantages in a market economy. In Maharashtra, the most powerful claims on water, a public resource allocated by the State, come from large capitalist sugar farmers who sell their produce in the market. If a shortage is feared, they increase their claims rapidly, thus removing whatever water there is from subsistence farming. Conceivably this could create a 'man-made' drought.

Is the system of providing public employment for relief an appropriate one in every situation? In densely populated India, it is possible to initiate public works within easy reach of most villages. There are roads to be repaired and irrigation canals to be dug. In many parts of Africa, such as the Ethiopian highlands, agriculture is more extensive and people are scattered over vast areas. Travelling long distances leads to weakness and ill-health: by the time people arrive at relief works or camps they are exhausted and sick. It is then impossible to give them work to do and food has to be distributed directly by the State. Even in Maharashtra there has been much criticism of the inappropriateness of the public works scheme. In practice, most people were employed on road mending or building. This required the breaking of stones in the summer heat, which is not a helpful activity for weakened bodies. Indeed it considerably raises their calorific needs.

As we have indicated before, bodies weakened by poor nutrition and excessive stress or labour are particularly vulnerable to disease. Furthermore, the close proximity of large numbers of such people at a relief camp or public works site aids the transmission of disease. The temporary nature of such establishments usually means also that sanitary facilities are minimal. We will discuss the implications of all this for a successful emergency strategy when we have looked at the demography of famine in greater detail.

The demography of famine

Demographers have analysed the mortality data for the Bengal famine in some detail. As we have noted already, the worst mortality occurred about twelve months after the worst harvest. Why should that be? The obvious answer is that, if the shortfall has not been too serious, food does not begin to run out until shortly before the next harvest. This may be the case for those who can store their own grain. For the rest the effect must work through the market mechanism—the lowest wages and highest prices come simultaneously late in the year. Thus, from May 1943 there was a fairly sharp rise in the price of rice and the real wage index remained at one-third of its 1941 level for three months. The malnutrition that resulted from the lack of calories that this entailed for the poorer agricultural labourers (and subsequently the rural service-sector workers and craftsmen as the demand for their services dried up) would precipitate more serious and prolonged episodes of disease. In a normal year the peak season for illness in Bengal is December: the 1943 peak also occurred in December but was double its normal magnitude (see Figure 5.1).

How do we know what the level of mortality was? There is a death registration system in most countries. Responsibility for maintaining the record in rural areas is usually left to the village headman or watchman. Some administrations have taken great care to see that this system works but usually it is far from complete. Moreover, during a crisis such as a famine the record may be even less complete than usual: there are other things to worry about than keeping apparently useless records of who dies. Besides, people leave their villages in times of distress, seeking sustenance elsewhere—often in the major cities. If they die on the road, who will record their death? Although we believe that there was under-registration affecting the reported level of mortality, we can still look at the pattern of mortality during famines like the Bengal famine. Table 5.1 displays the cause of death statistics. There is no column labelled 'starvation'. This partly reflects the fact that half-starved people usually die of some identifiable disease. In a normal year in a poor country 10 per cent of children may be severely malnourished but those of them who die do so from infectious disease before they starve. Even in a famine, this remains true. This does not mean that such children have not died as a result of the famine, for without a food shortage their chances of survival would have been much higher. In the case of Bengal we can see that fevers of all kinds including malaria were much elevated in both 1943 and 1944. Cholera also peaked in 1943. In fact, both malaria and cholera can be said to have reached epidemic proportions during and after the famine. In contrast, some other diseases did not peak during the crisis. It is not fully understood why this should be but some diseases kill very quickly after infection while others take longer. Cholera moves very fast indeed. A large

Table 5.1. Registered deaths by cause in West Bengal, 1941–6

Date	Dysentery, diarrhoea & enteric fever	Cholera	Malaria	Other fever	Smallpox	TB	Other respiratory	Total
1941	25,321	15,612	85,505	109,912	9,286	7,989	34,345	384,220
1942	23,234	11,427	85,078	97,764	1,023	6,734	32,847	347,886
1943	41,067	58,230	168,592	159,398	2,261	6,830	35,140	624,266
1944	36,040	20,128	166,897	176,824	19,198	7,318	37,052	577,375
1945	24,463	8,315	123,834	122,549	23,974	6,951	33,839	448,600
1946	25,651	9,774	102,339	121,391	4,971	7,227	31,926	414,687

Source: Census of India, 1951.

proportion of the population might have died of tuberculosis had not cholera carried them off first.

No doubt many cholera deaths occurred in the appallingly insanitary conditions of Calcutta, where thousands of people had taken refuge from the famine. This reminds us of another problem of famine management. The people who are on the move in search of food or work are most likely to be the young men. The demographer, Tim Dyson, has shown that in many famines a disproportionate increase in young male mortality occurs. Of course the absolute number of victims from among children and old people is usually greater, but that is also the case in a normal year. Famine simply exaggerates the normal tendency to neglect the very young and the very old, perhaps especially the infant girls in some societies. Indeed, female infanticide was reported during the great Chinese famine. But the unusual characteristic of many famines that have been studied is the elevated mortality among young adult men.

Great famines leave a spectacular imprint on the age structure of populations, as can be seen from the age-sex pyramids drawn from data recorded in some provinces worst affected by the great Chinese famine (see Figure 5.3). The data are from the 1982 Census; the 'hollow' occurs around age 20, indicating a substantial reduction in the number of children surviving from birth twenty years earlier. This not only reflects mortality. More important, it reflects the fact that there were substantially fewer births during those famine years.

Chapters 1 and 2 mentioned that households respond to harvest failure by postponing marriages or births. This temporary control over fertility can be seen in operation during the Chinese famine. Figure 5.4 shows that many marriages entered into in 1957 were not followed up by first births one year later, which is the usual practice in China. A substantial number of first births were delayed for four to five years, that is, until the famine and its after-effects were fully over. Many famines have been characterized by a dip

Fig. 5.3. Population pyramid for Henan Province, China, 1982

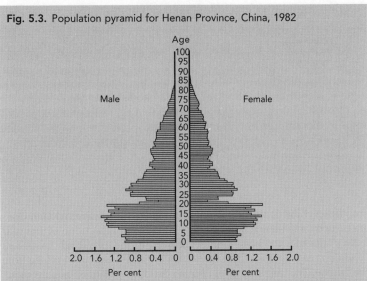

Source: Based on a figure in P. Kane, *Famine in China 1959–61: Demographic and Social Implications* (Macmillan, Basingstoke, 1988).

Fig. 5.4. Per cent distribution of intervals between marriage and first birth, marriage cohorts of 1957 and 1970, China

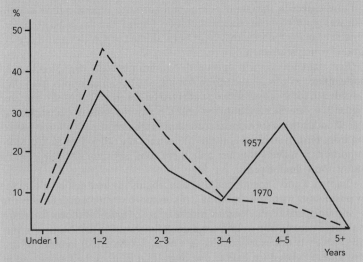

Source: P. Kane, *Famine in China 1959–61: Demographic and Social Implications* (Macmillan, Basingstoke, 1988).

in fertility as well as a rise in mortality. As in wartime, the dip is often made up subsequently by a temporary increase in the birth rate above the trend (see Figure 5.2).

This discussion of mortality in famines indicates additional conditions that need to be fulfilled for an intervention strategy to succeed. Once people have arrived at centres of food distribution, medicines for disease control are as important as food. In Ethiopia, for example, the dispersed nature of the population has made it difficult to distribute food except through centralized relief centres. Eighty per cent of Ethiopians live more than half a day's walk from a road. In Wollo, the region of famine in 1973 and 1984, there are only two main roads. Transporting food off the roads results in the breakdown of vehicles. Furthermore, war in the country hampered trade, so that local shortages caused huge price rises. In spring 1984 there were clear signs of impending famine following the failure of the rains in the previous year. People were on the move and selling their cattle and even their houses to obtain some claim on food. Though it was not until autumn of that year that an adequate food commitment was made, a considerable volume of food aid did eventually reach relief camps. There would seem to be little alternative to getting food to the people in this way. But, as the director of one of the major charities put it, 'overcrowding into unhygienic camps caused more people to die of infectious diseases than from hunger'. Conceivably in such a situation much of the food could be wasted. For example, as well as food, preventive interventions are needed against cholera and dehydration salts for the treatment of all diarrhoeal diseases. In the African highlands, cold weather at night is often a further problem. Blankets and warm clothing are needed. It is clear that the strategies that work in one economy cannot be replicated exactly in another: substantial modifications are necessary. Overall, a successful famine intervention strategy requires far more than simply food. But what is an appropriate combination of food relief, relief work, and health services depends on the country in question.

Till now, the discussion has concentrated on mortality, nutrition, and food crises. One theme that has emerged is that nutrition can be tackled at various levels. Some responsibilities lie within the household, some within the local community, and some at the level of the State. This is partly because so many different factors affect nutrition, including disease, the capacity to pay for food, and the status of women and children within the household. Hence a successful nutrition strategy involves employment strategies to ensure the capacity of households to pay for food; investments in water supply; vaccination campaigns and other such measures to ensure that people are healthy enough to absorb the food they get; and even programmes to enhance the education and status of women. In some cases the involvement of the State may not be necessary, or at least not sufficient, to improve nutritional status. Usually, however, it is necessary. And in the case of famine, Dreze and Sen have argued that the State *can* always intervene to prevent high mortality. There are cases where it has done so with success in the past.

Notes

1. One might query how exogenous these events really were. As indicated earlier, it has for centuries been by considerable irrigation works that the Chinese population has been fed. After 1949, a sharp fall in mortality gave rise to an unprecedented growth in population. To meet the demand for energy and food, the Chinese began a major programme of irrigation works intended to use the waters of the Huang He (the Yellow River) more effectively. The idea was too ambitious (given the technology of the day) and severe problems of silting were to occur subsequently. The risk of flooding was probably increased greatly by this programme.
2. Famine is a highly sensitive issue and at the time no mortality was reported. After Mao's death his detractors were happy to release official estimates of about fifteen million dead. American demographers tend to be sceptical of the accuracy of Chinese death statistics (not just during the famine). Computer models have been used to attempt a correction for underestimation: the result is to double the number of deaths attributed to the famine.

6 | The Political Economy of Health

All improvements to health and mortality cannot be attributed to nutritional improvement, important though this may be. Indeed the quite abrupt and apparently irreversible decline in mortality at the start of the demographic transition (see Figure 3.1) probably had other causes. We argue in this chapter that the State has played a crucial role in mortality decline. To some extent the colonial state was active in the pre-independence era. This often makes it difficult to date the start of the demographic transition with precision (see Figure 6.1). However, the major changes usually occurred after independence. The question arises why a colonial or capitalist state should wish to become involved in this aspect of welfare.

Health interventions under colonialism and neo-colonialism

The first concern of an imperial administration is the preservation of the army, for the army is the last resort in checking rebellion and ensuring the safe continuation of trade. It is no accident therefore that colonial sanitary reports often start with an assessment of military welfare. It may come as a surprise to learn that the main enemy of the British army overseas was disease: far more soldiers died that way than in military engagements. As a result of living in an unfamiliar climate with the company of a host of parasites, bacteria, and viruses, the mortality of soldiers in some locations was five times what it would have been had they remained in Britain. Some of the diseases responsible (like yellow fever) did not exist in Britain. Hence the visitors had no immunity. Others (like the diarrhoeal diseases, especially cholera) were less prevalent. Only a few diseases (like tuberculosis) were less of a threat in the colonies, perhaps because air pollution and poor nutrition were relatively unimportant problems for the army overseas.[1] Crude death rates for the expatriate adult male population were sustained at levels of fifty per thousand in parts of India in the first half of the nineteenth century. This was an extremely costly way to run an empire.

When the first annual report of the Bengal sanitary commission was

Fig. 6.1. Mortality decline, 1930–70, illustrated by Sri Lanka, Taiwan, Egypt, and the Indian province of Bombay

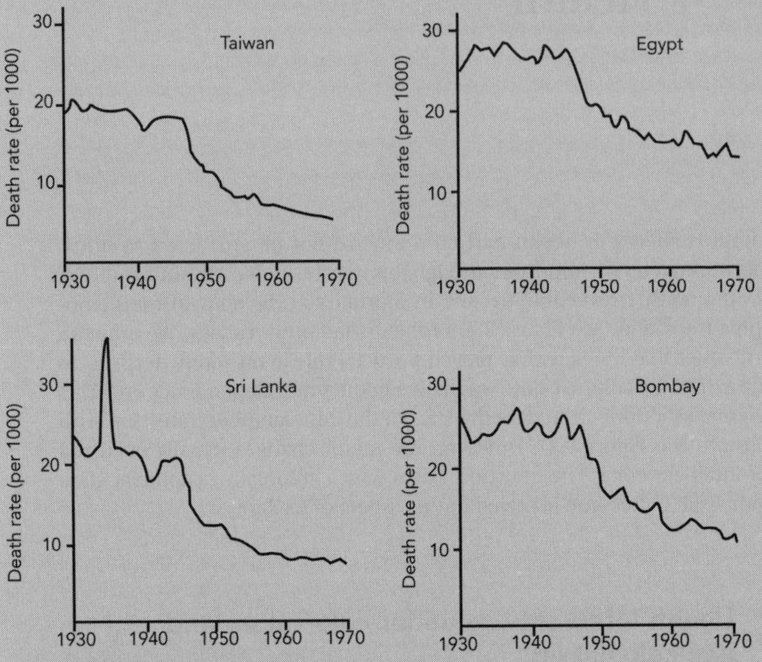

Source: T. Dyson, 'Future LDC Demographic Research: Some Thoughts on Data, Methods, Theory', in *La Demographie en perspective, visages futurs des sciences de la population* (Université Catholique, Louvain-la-Neuve, 1985).

produced in 1865, paragraphs 1 to 12 dealt with the army. It was not until paragraph 18 that attention was turned to the sanitary condition of Calcutta, which had 'grown so rapidly into an immense city without sufficient care being taken to secure cleanliness and proper ventilation'. It was appreciated that to secure the health of the army some improvements had to be made to the overall sanitary environment. The report of ten years later makes an assessment of the position in the poorest housing in Calcutta, the 'bustees', or 'villages' as the British called them:

The villages are all, or nearly all, after one type, consisting of a collection of huts of different sizes, which have been constructed from time to time without any plan or arrangement, generally surrounded by filthy drains, and having only tortuous narrow foot paths for access to the interior; and many of them having slimy stagnant ponds, full of putrid vegetable and animal matter in a state of decomposition.

This description would be quite apt if applied to many urban localities in Asia or Africa today. It still applies to parts of Calcutta. The report goes on to address the crucial problem: it is not difficult to devise a programme of sanitary improvement such as the excavation and realignment of the ditches and the construction of public toilets, but,

The question then arises, who is to pay for this costly reform? . . . The land on which each village is built belongs to proprietors who lease out plots of land to tenants . . . As the Municipality can hardly be expected to expend any very large amount on improving private property, the owners must bear the chief burden of the cost, as to impose on tenants, who live from hand to mouth, much pecuniary responsibility would simply be impossible.

Of course, it was unusual for the landowners to see much advantage to themselves in costly sanitary reform of this kind. So little got done. When major epidemics occurred or were feared, however, the colonial government started programmes of an emergency nature, not involving construction works. For example, when the plague arrived in Bombay in 1896 the health authorities began to disinfect houses (to kill the plague-carrying fleas that infested the rats of this maritime city). Similarly, mass inoculations against cholera were carried out at the beginning of the twentieth century when a large population of pilgrims descended upon a holy town for a religious festival. The result of these piecemeal and halting activities cannot have been very substantial. Any decline in overall mortality that occurred before the colonies obtained independence was slight and may have occurred for reasons other than those just described. There was, however, a notable decline in the mortality of the army (see Figure 6.2).[2]

The independence of many countries in South and South-East Asia followed the end of the Second World War. It might have been expected that the Western world would take no more interest in the health of the region. This was not so. Although the independent governments of the new states undertook their own health programmes, they were assisted by organizations funded by the Western world. While the motives of many of those involved with this form of aid were no doubt altruistic, such intervention was also in the interests of the Western capitalist nations. There were two reasons for this. In the immediate post-War period the United States of America, in particular, was deeply concerned about the rise of communism in East Asia and its possible implications for the political stability of South-East Asia (the 'domino effect' as it was called). The United States envisaged a need for a military presence in the region. Like the British before them, they were concerned to improve the environment for the operation of their troops. Intervening to improve health also yielded longer-term benefits. United States trade and business were expanding in the region. It was recognized that good health improves the productivity not only of expatriates engaged in business but of the local working class as well. In case this argument sounds like the exaggerated claim of a radical political economist, we quote the following assertion of a consultant from the Rockefeller Foundation: 'Dr Russell pointed out that a malaria eradication

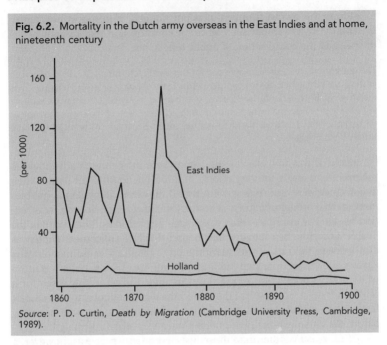

Fig. 6.2. Mortality in the Dutch army overseas in the East Indies and at home, nineteenth century

Source: P. D. Curtin, *Death by Migration* (Cambridge University Press, Cambridge, 1989).

program was a dramatic undertaking that would penetrate into the homes of people and would benefit the US politically and financially.' Thus, the United States sponsored the World Health Organization's major programme to eradicate malaria from Asia. The programme was pursued less enthusiastically in Africa, where the United States had fewer commercial interests.

Why was malaria selected as the primary target? First, it was a major contributor to overall mortality in the region. For instance it accounted for between 10 and 20 per cent of all deaths in Sri Lanka. Once the programme became established a dramatic and (until now) unreversed decline in mortality occurred in many countries.[3] The word 'campaign' gives a clue to another reason for the decision to tackle this disease. The programme for its elimination could be conducted like a military operation, both in terms of its administration and in the field. (This is an interpretation developed by D. Banerji.) The objective was to eliminate mosquitoes carrying the parasite that causes the disease. This was attempted by spraying large areas of its habitation with a chemical that was fatal to the insect, DDT. The strategy was not unlike that of bombing an enemy in the jungle. Indeed, some of it was carried out from the air. Unfortunately, the chemical harms human beings and other animals as well. More efficient ways of conducting the campaign were devised, including the spraying of the interiors of dwellings.

This minimizes environmental damage by reducing the quantity of chemicals that get into the food chain while targeting mosquitoes that are likely to be malarious. Programmes to distribute prophylactic drugs were also started. This control strategy worked well in Asia because it was cheap and unobtrusive. In contrast to efforts to control diarrhoeal disease, the problem of who should pay for major improvements to infrastructure on private land did not arise.

Malaria was not the only disease tackled in mass campaigns of this sort during the 1940s and 1950s. The programme to eradicate smallpox was also conceived on a grand scale with serious State and international involvement. The thrust of the campaign was prevention through vaccination. Vaccinating the whole population was not necessary. The procedure adopted was to identify groups of people—inhabitants of particular villages for instance—who were most at risk of contracting the disease. This was done in Bangladesh, for example, by collecting reports of outbreaks of the disease and then vaccinating everyone in the village concerned. There was even a reward for anyone who identified a smallpox case. Remember that the technology to eradicate smallpox had been known to man for hundreds of years in China and in Europe. Even in England, where inoculation was replaced by safer vaccines by the end of the eighteenth century, for a long time the State only became involved in vaccination campaigns intermittently, usually when a major epidemic occurred. Thus the onslaught against this disease was slow to begin even in the West, although it was ultimately completely successful. The problem is not one of technology, but of political will and State responsibility. Thus, in a study of the mortality transition in Europe, Mercer has argued that State involvement was crucial to the initiation of the mortality transition as the anti-smallpox programme improved the population's health sufficiently to lead indirectly to reductions in several other diseases. (In 1800, smallpox accounted for about 20 per cent of all mortality in England.)

It is not only capitalist states that have perceived the benefit and relatively low cost involved in attacking certain diseases. We discuss the Chinese programme to eradicate schistosomiasis in the next section.

The economics of disease control

The owners of industry have always been aware that the productivity of their work-force depends on its health. This will not necessarily motivate industrialists to improve the health of their workers if there is plenty of labour in reserve to hire when someone falls ill or dies. Marxist writers and economic historians used to draw attention to the deplorable working and living conditions of the working class, especially miners and plantation workers. However, as industrial production becomes more sophisticated and requires the technical training of part of the work-force, industrialists' attitude to health issues changes. It becomes important to them that they should not lose this more highly trained component of labour, since hiring replacements will involve costly training all over again. That is why some industrialists build housing for their employees and set up their own medical facilities. They also keep careful records of sickness in their staff: even States whose record on human rights has been poor (for example apartheid South Africa) take a particular interest in the health of their key work-force (for instance in the mines) because of its effect on efficiency and profits. In general, the standard of health-promoting facilities offered rises as the work-force becomes more highly qualified. For example, the amount of such provision in India in the 1950s tended to rise as one proceeded from mining and plantation industries, through the lighter manufacturing industries like textiles, up to the most sophisticated manufacturing—or at least that most highly valued by the State—such as steel-making and heavy engineering.

Is efficiency in agriculture also a reason for State intervention in health? Until the 1950s there were always pockets of labour shortage, even in densely populated Asia. This implies that labourers who were lost through ill health could not always be replaced. On the whole, however, State or capitalist farms did not find the efficiency argument sufficiently compelling to invest in health. Besides, most agriculture was not carried out in commercial farms operating on profit-maximizing principles. From about the mid-twentieth century, the more rapid development of capitalism in agriculture has been a factor in the increasing incidence of landlessness (see Chapter 1) and the appearance of surplus labour that capitalist farmers can hire or fire at will. Since the 1950s, population growth has been another factor in the rapid growth of labour supply. A strict cost-benefit calculation of the gains from malaria eradication in rural areas might show no benefit at the margin, therefore. The financial benefit from reducing the days off sick of a labourer who is surplus to needs is zero. When large tracts of the countryside are infested with some disease-bearing parasite, however, it is likely that many of the labour force are working below capacity. There may not be as much surplus labour as meets the eye. If the existing labour force were physically able to work more hours, production would readily increase. This was claimed to be the case in China in the 1950s, when large acreages of land were affected by the water-snail that carries the liver-fluke responsible for the disease called schistosomiasis.

In the infected regions, like the Yangtze river basin, between 20 per cent and 40 per cent of the labour force was estimated to have the debilitating disease. Mao Zedong instigated a campaign to clear out the snails by digging them up from the watercourses and burying them (causing their suffocation). It was one of those technically straightforward programmes that needed state commitment and military-style organization. The opportunity cost of the campaign was low, though only as far as the massive labour requirement could be slotted in with seasonal demands for agricultural work. By the 1950s, sufficient labour was becoming available to provide a work-force of the critical size needed for this public health programme. The result was fairly successful and, in those areas where the snail and its fluke were virtually eradicated, agricultural production is said to have risen by one-third.

Most mortality in Asia and Africa today is caused by the wide variety of diseases that affect the digestive tract, generally known as the diarrhoeal diseases, and a variety of conditions that affect the chest, known as the respiratory diseases. These two groups of diseases thrive in particular environmental conditions. The diarrhoeal diseases generally spread fast where water is easily contaminated with faecal matter (and they thrive in ill-nourished bodies). Clearly, this is where insufficient water is available to absorb or wash away wastes. The respiratory diseases are more likely to take root in people whose chest and lungs have been subjected to serious air pollution (including, but not only, that created by smoking). Clearly this is where the atmosphere is unable to absorb or blow away wastes, whether in dwellings, factories, or industrial and commercial towns. The economic problem is that preventive remedies are very costly. The provision of good-quality drainage, sewerage, and fresh water supplies often require considerable resources. For example, getting water to isolated villages may involve considerable public works. Equally, providing adequate drainage or sewerage for heavily built-up areas may require laying of concrete pipes well below the surface and entail rebuilding of dwellings above the surface to enable the operations to take place.

More recently, low-cost materials and methods have been developed: for example, bamboo piping where bamboo is plentiful and aqua privies, which are toilets where the waste is rendered harmless by bacterial action in pits immediately below the ground. However, such methods require careful maintenance to be effective: it is not only the initial or capital cost that is an issue. Measuring the economic benefit of improving health for a large number of people is difficult if they are not employed in one specific factory. Moreover, in societies where curative medicine is not provided for everyone at public expense, reckoning up the economic benefit of reduced expenditure on hospital care when people fall sick is not easy. For all these reasons, the capitalist State has been slow to approach the problem of ill health from the diarrhoeal diseases. However, political pressures other than those from industrial capitalists exist and have led to sanitary reform, as we shall now see.

If a factory pumps toxic waste into a stream that runs through the city, hutment dwellers who live closer to the stream may suffer ill effects. If they work not in the factory but as self-employed traders, there may be no economic motive for the factory or the capitalist State to become concerned. Unless the hutment dwellers represent an important source of votes for the government, they also have little direct political power to enforce reform.

However, if the stream runs on into the neighbouring countryside and kills cattle on commercial farms, a powerful sector of the capitalist economy will be motivated to challenge the factory owners. This was one major factor that led to improvements in factory-pollution controls in nineteenth-century Britain.

Similar stories could be told regarding air pollution. Recently in India one company threatened to sue another one for emitting carbon-laden smoke that caused electrical faults to occur in its switches. Rather than go to court, the offending company modified its smoke stacks to reduce the pollution. Economists refer to this sort of activity as an externality—one firm creates a nuisance that helps or hinders another firm without any transaction taking place.[4] A common solution is that one party demands compensation and the other party decides to eliminate the nuisance at its own cost as this is cheaper than paying the compensation. Indirectly, nearby residents benefit also: hutment dwellers are no longer endangered by the smoke.

It is possible also for consumers to impose an externality on other consumers through their economic activity. If I throw the paper wrapping from my take-away meal on to the road, the litter blows past the homes of local residents: its smell attracts flies, which spread disease. When the residents fall sick, I have imposed a cost upon them but I do not pay. If this happens in middle-class areas whose inhabitants have some political influence, pressure is usually brought to bear on the local authority to provide litter bins or to sweep the streets. As the authority can collect higher taxes or charges in such areas, it may be willing to make this kind of expenditure. Encouraging people to adopt hygienic rules of behaviour is pointless if the basic infrastructural requirements like litter bins or public toilets are not provided.

Political parties in multi-party States often represent particular interests regarding environmental pollution. In nineteenth-century Britain a conflict existed in some cities between the so-called 'clean' party, which represented the interests of consumers and industrialists who were suffering from the type of externalities described above, and the more narrowly focused 'economic' party (also called the 'dirty' party by its critics) that intended to win votes simply by keeping taxes low. Similarly in Third World cities today one can see instances of vote-catching when political parties provide public health infrastructure in slums and inscribe the name of their party on the facility provided. If the programme or manifesto of the party does not suggest that it stands for the interests of the poor (or if its main political and financial support does not come from the working class), one may regard such populist acts with some cynicism. Nevertheless, many public health improvements have been made because of processes that were not intended primarily to benefit the poorest strata in a society.

It is important to stress that the reduction in many diseases has involved improvements in public sanitation (cleaner air, water, and food), a rise in personal nutritional status, and an increase in the individual's knowledge of disease transmission. A good example of all this is tuberculosis. The incidence of this disease and mortality from it has fallen continuously in Britain since the latter part of the last century, although no medicine to cure it existed and no injection for prophylaxis was available until after the Second World War (see Figure 6.3). The reduction must have come about because of the more wide-ranging developments just listed (though scholars still debate which was the most important of them). Tuberculosis is still a major killer in Asia and Africa: we are particularly aware of it in urban areas but this may be because that is where records are best kept and where patients congregate in the hope of hospital treatment. A cure is now available but to control the disease it is first necessary to identify all tuberculosis cases. This is not easy as the symptoms are less visible than those of smallpox and many sufferers perceive a social stigma that inhibits them from seeking a cure. Once the disease is diagnosed, it is crucial that the whole course of treatment is followed carefully. Otherwise the bacteria in the body adapt to the low or infrequent dosage with which they are bombarded and the patient may pass on drug-resistant strains of the disease to others. The other technological weapon is the BCG vaccination. Unfortunately health programmes have not attempted to inoculate the whole population (which is really what is needed as the bacteria can survive in the body for years, so that treatment of localities of high incidence is insufficient to eradicate the disease), nor is the BCG vaccine 100 per cent effective. The contrast with smallpox vaccination is evident. In the light of these problems, and consid-

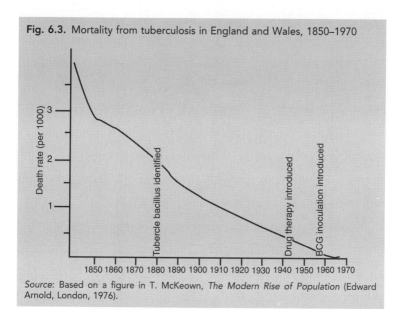

Fig. 6.3. Mortality from tuberculosis in England and Wales, 1850–1970

Source: Based on a figure in T. McKeown, *The Modern Rise of Population* (Edward Arnold, London, 1976).

ering the experience of Britain mentioned above, public health analysts have argued that tuberculosis has to be tackled on many fronts at once. Improvements in nutrition, air quality, and availability of space (avoidance of overcrowding) have to be made simultaneously. This amounts to a programme of complete social reform, indeed of economic development itself. As we have said, total social environmental reform is costly and lags behind, while resources are pumped into industry and agriculture, not to mention armaments.

In some ways the diarrhoeal diseases are even more difficult to control. They consist of a host of bacteria and viruses such that the different curative drugs are more effective against some than others. Identification is difficult, the symptoms being similar in most cases. No vaccine is available for most types of diarrhoeal disease. At present, there is no certainty of control without the guarantee of clean water and food. This, in turn, presupposes adequate drainage and sanitation. With appropriate development strategies, control is no doubt possible: infant and child mortality in Britain was as high at the end of the last century as it is in some of the poorest countries of Asia and Africa today (see Figure 6.4). The diarrhoeal diseases were then the major cause of death in young children. At the turn of the century infant mortality from diarrhoea used to peak in the hottest months of a hot summer: one of the causes is believed to be the contamination and deterioration of cow's milk used for infant feeding (especially before refrigeration became

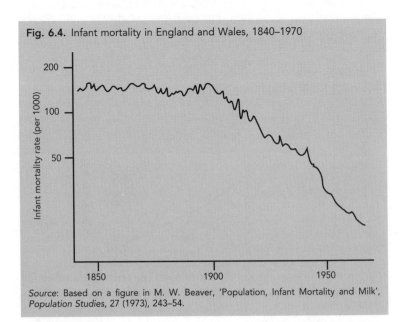

Fig. 6.4. Infant mortality in England and Wales, 1840–1970

Source: Based on a figure in M. W. Beaver, 'Population, Infant Mortality and Milk', *Population Studies*, 27 (1973), 243–54.

widespread). As the environment became more sanitary and milk was kept free from dust and dirt, the problem diminished.

Air pollution is believed to contribute to the severity of many diseases that affect the lungs and chest, such as bronchitis, tuberculosis, and lung cancer. Yet, all over the world this has been one of the last of the environmental problems to be addressed. In Britain, it was not until the 1950s that any serious controls were imposed on factory and domestic emissions of smoke. Until then, major winter 'fogs' in large cities led directly to a massive increase in heart and chest disease mortality. Even today in parts of England the quality of the atmosphere in areas of heavy industry (on Teeside for instance) leaves much to be desired. In the United States, pollution from automobiles in some cities sometimes combines with the weather to produce conditions that are dangerous enough for the local authority to advise people not to leave their homes. Similarly in China, although serious efforts have been made to clean water supplies and infant mortality has declined partly as a result, air pollution remains the last major environmental hazard. Why has it been the last problem to be tackled?

Atmospheric pollution is a clear case of an externality. We referred to an example earlier of its incidence between producer and producer. The serious health implications derive from its incidence between producer and consumer (as when industrial smoke falls on residential areas) or between consumer and consumer while using an industrial product, such as automobiles or domestic coal. Unlike water, the question of public resources for infrastructure does not arise. The State cannot cleanse the air for public consumption. It can legislate. In so doing, as we have pointed out, it directly confronts the interests of industrial producers. The latter tend to be more powerful politically than the resentful taxpayer (of whatever social class). Thus, car manufacturers have fought to prevent legislation on safe emissions, industrial companies to escape responsibility for massive and lethal air pollution such as occurred in India at Bhopal, and cigarette manufacturers to maintain the unrestricted right to advertise their products. The socialist countries too, in their drive for heavy industrialization—the corner-stone of their economic ideology—consistently neglected the safety of factory emissions. Of course, consumer behaviour bears part of the responsibility also: to some extent people choose to smoke cigarettes and to burn domestic fuels like soft coal. Some products do more harm than others, but people are acting under considerable constraints. For instance, the range of tobacco products or fuels available at prices that the poor can afford is limited. Some of the safer products, such as processed fuels giving low carbon emission, are very costly. Overall, producer-consumer externalities (such as factory smoke in the air or chemicals in the river) have been far more difficult to address politically than consumer to consumer externalities (such as domestic sewage in the water).

The political lobby for air pollution control is growing. The middle-class consumer is becoming more involved in self-protective action, although the poor suffer most from air pollution—partly because their dwellings tend to be sited in low-cost areas downwind of factories or next to main roads. There is increasing awareness that nobody can escape from the implications of a heavily polluted atmosphere in the end, as the state of some American and European cities now shows.

In the eighteenth century in the West, as in much of the world today, disease was regarded as 'outside' the social system. It was a God-given problem and neither preventive nor curative action could prevent its direst effects. To use the economist's term, most disease was regarded as exogenous. Gradually that view has become eroded. More diseases have become understood in terms of their social context; preventive solutions have therefore been addressed, though they have often turned out to be expensive, thereby delaying their adoption. Nowadays many analysts view all diseases as endogenous to the social system. Disease incidence is now seen as inextricably bound up in social and economic factors. Two case studies will help to illustrate this point. One is of leprosy. The other is of AIDS.

Case studies of two dreaded diseases

Leprosy has long been thought of as the dreaded disease. Its worst clinical manifestations—infected and often mutilated limbs and deformed faces—have inevitably resulted in this fear. The difficulty in identifying its cause and the chain of transmission not surprisingly led to leprosy being regarded as the archetypal exogenous disease—a punishment perhaps from God. The germ responsible for the disease was discovered in the late nineteenth century. By the 1940s a cure was developed in the form of a drug that had to be administered over a very considerable time, years rather than months. These were crucial steps on the road to making the disease understood as endogenous (at least to our biological universe). Further work on the transmission of the disease has helped towards our understanding of it as endogenous to the social system also. The main route of transmission is probably like that of tuberculosis, through the exhalation and inhalation of the bacillus. Therefore, overcrowded living conditions make its spread more likely. Furthermore, it seems that ill-nourished people are more likely to develop the disease. In a sense therefore, leprosy has been brought in out of the realm of the supernatural and the unknown. That does not, of itself, make eradication easy. New and powerful drugs have now been discovered that reduce the time taken for treatment to a maximum of three years and in most cases to only eighteen months. Unfortunately, the importance of adhering precisely to the course of drugs and the difficulty of identifying new sufferers from the disease, who show none of the advanced symptoms but who may be afraid to identify themselves, makes eradication through the 'campaign approach' very difficult.[5] BCG vaccination probably bestows some immunity according to recent research.

The historical experience of Western Europe shows that leprosy can be eradicated without any of these modern curative or prophylactic technologies. Slowly but surely the disease disappeared. Almost certainly this was due to improved nutrition, better living conditions, and better personal hygiene. As with tuberculosis, improved incomes and housing, less overcrowding, and more widespread knowledge of the nature of the disease could render it extinct. However, these are all social factors inherent in the development process. They depend on economic growth, on the reduction of poverty, on the creation of social infrastructure, and on the sharing of knowledge throughout a society. The more leprosy is studied the more it is seen to share the social characteristics of other less dreaded diseases. In fact it need not be dreaded at all.

Similar considerations apply to AIDS, whose progress has only been monitored comparatively recently. A certain amount of energy and talent has been wasted on trying to discover from where the disease came. This discussion was tantamount to attributing an exogenous cause. If one did trace the origin of AIDS to a particular locality, would that help us to understand its current progress and incidence throughout the world or to break the chain of transmission, any more than attributing the origin of leprosy to a punishment from God? The first studies of AIDS in Africa focused on transmission through sexual intercourse. However, contaminated blood circulates in society in other ways. Public (and private) curative health systems have been implicated in passing diseases on through poor institutional hygiene—unsterilized needles, for example. Intravenous drug users also spread the disease. Only when all these routes for the spread of infection have been investigated thoroughly can we claim to regard AIDS as truly endogenous to our social system. This may be politically difficult, for it calls into question the safety and efficiency of government health departments and private clinics.

Furthermore, the study of AIDS in isolation from the study of sexually transmitted diseases and reproductive health in general is pointless. The social conditions that have produced high levels of sexually transmitted diseases in particular regions throughout the twentieth century are much the same as those that favour the spread of AIDS—for instance the separation of spouses through migration for work, destitution, and severely limited earning opportunities for women. With the more recent development of international travel for commerce and tourism, a further economic route of transmission has been opened up that explains the simultaneous spread of the AIDS epidemic in all continents of the world. As with other disasters, like famine, governments have been slow to acknowledge the existence of the disease within their borders. They fear loss of face and, of perhaps more importance, loss of trade. Nevertheless, despite initial denials, more enlightened governments have admitted to the problem and begun preventive programmes (both Thailand and India delayed recognition, and then reacted constructively in this way). Until a cure for AIDS is found, it will be rightly feared far more than leprosy but its spread is entirely endogenous to the social and economic system.

To monitor the progress made in health improvement around the world,

---

BOX 6.1. STANDARDIZATION TO ELIMINATE AGE COMPOSITION EFFECTS

Why are the birth rate and death rate 'crude'? The reason is that the death rate is made up of two components:

- the age-specific mortality rates;
- the proportion of the population in each age group.

Similarly the birth rate reflects both the age-specific fertility rates and the proportions of the population in each age group.

We illustrate this with reference to the crude death rate using the age-specific mortality rates (ASMR) from Box 2.2 (but call Taiwan 'Country A' to develop a general argument). The crude death rate is a kind of average of these rates but is not their arithmetic mean. That would be calculated by summing the rates and dividing by the number of age groups, which would imply that each age group made an equally important contribution to the total population. In fact some age groups have more people in them than others. In Taiwan the younger age groups have more people in them than the older age groups. So, we need what is called a *weighted average*.

Suppose we took a simple average. Summing the rates and dividing the total by ten (in the case of Country A) is equivalent to multiplying each age-specific mortality rate by 10 per cent. Therefore, to take into account the fact that each age group does not have exactly 10 per cent of the population in it, one multiplies each rate by the actual proportion of the population in the specific age group, as follows:

Table A: Country A

Age group	Population ('000s)	Proportional distribution of population	ASMR	ASMR weighted by age distribution
<1	255	0.041	0.0341	0.00140
1–4	766	0.123	0.0077	0.00095
5–14	1,806	0.291	0.0011	0.00032
15–24	849	0.137	0.0022	0.00030
25–34	868	0.140	0.0029	0.00041
35–44	737	0.119	0.0049	0.00058
45–54	507	0.082	0.0101	0.00083
55–64	273	0.044	0.0254	0.00112
65–74	103	0.016	0.0618	0.00099
≥75	45	0.007	0.1579	0.00111
Total	6,209			0.00801

BOX 6.1. continued

In Box 2.2 total deaths came to 49,940. Box 3.1 showed how to calculate the crude death rate (CDR):

CDR = $49,940 \div 6,209,000 = 0.00804$ or 8.0 per thousand.

This is the same as the weighted average of the age-specific mortality rates with the proportion in the age groups as weights (i.e., 0.00801; there is a small difference due to rounding).

This should make it clear that in fact the crude death rate has two components: mortality rates by age and age composition. If either of these changes, the crude death rate will change. For example, if the number of people in the age group 65–74 increases tenfold and the corresponding deaths tenfold also, one gets the following:

Table B: Country B

Age group	Population ('000s)	ASMR	Deaths
<1	255	0.0341	8,695
1–4	766	0.0077	5,822
5–14	1,806	0.0011	1,986
15–24	849	0.0021	1,783
25–34	868	0.0029	2,517
35–44	737	0.0049	3,611
45–54	507	0.0101	5,121
55–64	273	0.0254	6,934
65–74	1,030	0.0618	63,650
≥75	45	0.1579	7,106
Total	7,136		107,225

Thus, in Country B:

CDR = $107,225 \div 7,136,000 = 0.001503$ or 15.0 per thousand.

This is nearly double the crude death rate calculated previously. Yet, the only change we made was to increase the size of the elderly population. The mortality risks remained the same. Clearly a rate that is so sensitive to age composition is rightly called 'crude'. Comparisons of the death rate in two countries with different age compositions (like the two examples shown here), reveal nothing about life chances or health conditions in the two countries. In fact, many of the more developed countries have higher crude death rates than many less developed countries for this reason.

One way to adjust for this is to multiply the age-specific mortality rates for the two countries being compared by the proportions of the population in each age group in one country. This is known as *age standardization*. Proceed as follows:

> **BOX 6.1.** continued
>
> - Obtain the age-specific mortality rates for Country A.
> - Multiply each of these by the population in the age group in Country B.
> - Add up these deaths and divide by the total population in Country B.
> - The result, fifteen per thousand, is the death rate for Country A (Taiwan) standardized on the age distribution of Country B.
> - As Country B has been used as the standard, no adjustment is needed for Country B.
> - The crude death rate for Country B (fifteen per thousand) can now be compared directly with the standardized death rate for Country A.
>
> Any difference between them is now purely due to differences in their mortality by age. Here there is no difference. This is what you should have expected for the only difference between the two countries lies in their age composition, not in their mortality rates by age (or mortality risks per person). The same standardization can be done for the crude birth rate.

it has become customary to use measures of mortality. We have already referred to the use of the infant mortality rate in this way. A measure often used to summarize the mortality experience at all ages is the crude death rate. This is the sum of all deaths during a year divided by the total population at the midpoint of that year The problem with this measure is that it is influenced by the age structure. A population with a large number of elderly people will have a high death rate even if the mortality risk of each elderly person (the age-specific mortality rate) is relatively low (as in Western Europe today). The higher the proportion of old people in the total population, the higher the crude death rate even if age-specific mortality remains the same. Consequently, the crude death rate in Britain is higher than that in China and the death rate will inevitably rise again in China even if age-specific mortality continues to fall at every age. One way round this problem is to *standardize* the death rate to neutralize the effect of the age composition: Box 6.1 explains what the problem is and one way to solve it. However, a better measure of health (or at least lack of death) is life expectancy, or life expectation at birth. This measures the number of years a person is expected to live on average, or the average age at death. We leave the calculation of this measure until we have discussed life tables (Boxes 9.3 and 9.4).

Notes

1. The army and the civilian administration were usually housed on the outskirts of the towns (in locations still often referred to as 'cantonments'). This kept them away from the worst risks of disease through poor sanitation and air pollution. Until the middle of the nineteenth century, however, sanitation in the barracks themselves was rather poor. Moreover, such locations were no protection against malarious mosquitoes (that is, those that have bitten an infected human being).

2. In India the death rate began to decline hesitantly during the first decades of the twentieth century. Much of that decline can be attributed to the demise of plague, but it is less clear how far public health measures were responsible for that demise. Usually, we think of the demographic transition as starting properly in the 1940s.

3. There is some dispute as to how much of that decline can be attributed to the malaria control campaign. A conservative estimate produced by an epidemiologist, Ron Gray, is that 25 per cent of Sri Lanka's post-Second World War mortality decline was due to it (see Figure 6.1).

4. Technically this is known as a negative externality. If on the other hand the externality causes some indirect benefit (free of charge), then this is known as a positive externality.

5. Physical mutilation only occurs in untreated cases. The early stages of the disease manifest themselves in anaesthesia (lack of sensation) on surface areas of the limbs—the afflicted areas being identified by a pale patch of skin. This is when the disease is infectious and needs treatment to prevent its spread. The further development of the anaesthesia leads to limb damage and other complications, by which time, ironically, the patient is no longer a public health hazard but is suffering the maximum harm to him or herself alone. So, one has the difficult task of eradicating the disease when it is of the least personal trouble to the individual.

Part IV

Political Economy and Birth Control

7 | Fertility Decline in the Course of Development

The nineteenth-century European fertility decline

Earlier chapters have looked at the changes in fertility that occur in cyclical fashion in response to short-run changes in economic prosperity, harvest failures, and so on. Longer-term changes both up and down, or long swings as we have called them, have also featured in the discussion. The causes seem to have been diverse, ranging from changes in migratory behaviour to the influence of religious ideologies introduced from outside.

We have not yet discussed the question that many people believe to be the most important of all. Why does fertility decline dramatically, and apparently without reversal, in the course of the demographic transition? (See Figure 7.1.) What is the relationship between this process and that of economic development or industrialization? To put it more concretely, why did fertility start to decline throughout Western Europe in the nineteenth century at about the time of the spread of the Industrial Revolution? Are we witnessing the same process as the countries of the developing world begin the process of industrialization today?

We introduce this question with a brief review of what happened in nineteenth-century England. This was the century when industrialization really got under way, starting with the development of the capitalist mode of production and its attendant technological revolution in textile manufacturing (which dates from the late eighteenth century) and continuing with the iron and steel revolution of the mid-nineteenth century. Most significantly from a demographer's point of view, these technical and economic changes were accompanied by a substantial shift of population from rural to urban residence. In 1800, only 25 per cent of the population lived in towns and cities, by 1860 it was 62 per cent, and by 1900 it was 78 per cent. From the 1870s, fertility began to fall. It continued to do so unchecked until by the 1920s it reached the low level that continues to obtain (with fluctuations) today.

No simple explanation exists of why the industrial and demographic revolutions occurred in sequence in this way. Yet approximately the same experience occurred all over developing Europe. Some scholars have suggested that rising incomes and the increased availability of manufactured goods on

Fig. 7.1. The demographic transition

(a) *In Asia and Africa at about 1980*

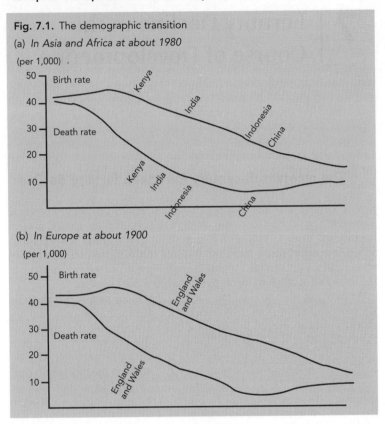

(b) *In Europe at about 1900*

the market resulted in a substitution effect in household behaviour. In other words, people began to spend their incomes on household items rather than on bringing up large numbers of children. If this is so, distinguishing different social and economic classes in the analysis is important. It is debated whether the working class benefited from industrialization until the twentieth century. It is also observed by demographers that the working classes were the last to reduce their fertility, again not doing so until the early twentieth century.

The effect on fertility of industrial or factory employment is also ambiguous. In some heavy industrial areas of Europe, marital fertility rose at first only to decline later. Perhaps one should look specifically at employment of women, which was less in heavy industry than in light industry. It seems that the age of marriage was higher among women living in textile towns than elsewhere. So counter-effects seem to have worked simultaneously during industrialization to raise and to lower fertility, depending on the type of industry.

Employment of children was important in the early days of the Industrial Revolution (as they were the cheapest source of labour). While Factory Acts began to limit children's employment from the early years of the nineteenth century, only in 1901 was a really comprehensive Act passed. Children ceased to be a source of income for poor families. Elementary school attendance had been enforced since 1880. By then it was also becoming clear that the demand for skilled labour was growing faster than the demand for the unskilled, thus raising the appeal of secondary education. All these developments made the reproduction of the labour force more costly, and children (as they became of higher quality) more expensive to rear.

Unlike the case of the mortality transition, the State was not involved explicitly in the historical fertility transition. It certainly did not promote fertility decline. This is evident from an extraordinary event that occurred in England. The date of the precipitous fall in fertility in England is somewhere in the mid-1870s. In 1876, two social reformers, Charles Bradlaugh and Annie Besant began to distribute a pamphlet in England written by an American and called *The Fruits of Philosophy*. Its title disguises the fact that this was a sort of birth control manual.

There was an outcry by the social establishment against this act. The *Daily Telegraph* accused the distributors of sabotage similar to those who poisoned the drinking water! A leader writer wrote:

to publish for indiscriminate sale in the open streets a work which while professing to deal with questions of population and national prosperity, in reality suggests vice of a character so abandoned, revolting, and unnatural, that to see its precepts accepted as 'philosophical fruit' would be to witness the first beginnings of the downfall of this nation . . .

These sound like the prejudices of Thomas Malthus. Interestingly, it appears that the Malthusian argument was still close to the surface. Poverty was still thought to be related to too rapid population growth. Consider the words of another newspaper at the time, the *Bradford Observer*:

No one can deny that the population question is one of extreme difficulty, of urgent importance in India, where we are staying [i.e. preventing] the 'natural checks' of famine, plague, and war, and introducing nothing in their place; of urgent importance too at home where the population tends to increase faster than the means of subsistence. But . . .[1]

There is no evidence that the State was interested in trying to control population growth, or at least not through family planning. In contrast, the distributors of the book were taken to court. This publicity had one unintended effect. The sales of the book skyrocketed. By the late 1870s, far more people must have known about birth control techniques than if the government had started a programme itself. Furthermore, social behaviour in the context of economic change disregarded the outdated admonitions of newspaper leader writers. Fertility fell dramatically.

Twentieth-century fertility transitions

What is different about the fertility experience of the twentieth century is the role played by the State. As we saw in Chapter 6, the State became involved in mortality control in Asia and Africa, often with the encouragement of Western and international organizations, for a variety of reasons. In many ways these are related to the development of national and international capitalism. While birth rates remained high, one effect of rapidly falling death rates was rapidly increasing population growth rates.

Chapter 3 briefly discussed ways in which increased rates of population growth may adversely affect economic growth. The faster demographic growth, the more children there are in the population relative to adults. Put simply, this is because while fertility remains high more people are being fed into the base of the population pyramid than are taken out through mortality higher up: the base begins to bulge (see Box 7.1 and Figure 7.2). This means that the dependency ratio (defined as the ratio of the population below the official age of waged work (say 15) and above the normal age of retirement (say 65) to the population of working age (15–64)) goes up. Those not at work need schooling, health care, clothing, and feeding. These are

---

BOX 7.1. HOW POPULATION GROWTH AFFECTS AGE COMPOSITION

A little calculus can show that if the growth rate of the population is higher (through natural increase), the population will be younger. The higher the growth rate, the higher the percentage of population under any given age. Although we suggested an appealing way of understanding this in the text, actually it follows from the interaction of both fertility and mortality and is not due to fertility alone. If a population is growing fast in the stable state, then each age group must have been smaller twenty years ago. Those aged 20–4 years are the survivors from a smaller birth cohort than the 0–5 year old population. The ratio of the younger to the older age group will be quite high, say 2:1. In contrast, if the population is stationary in the stable state, then each age group must have been the same size twenty years ago. Therefore the current 20–4 year old population come from a birth cohort that was the same size as the birth cohort from which the current 0–4 year old population comes. So the ratio of the younger to the older age group will be close too 1:1 (only a little above due to some of the earlier birth cohort having died before reaching 20–4).

This process is illustrated in Figure 7.3. It compares a hypothetical population that is growing hardly at all because of its very severe mortality with another hypothetical population that is growing very fast because it has much lower mortality but the same level and pattern of fertility. In both cases the simulated populations are in the stable state and are projected forward fifteen years. The youthfulness of the population in the second panel is due solely to its lower mortality and the resulting rapid growth rate. By contrast, Figure 7.2 can be interpreted as illustrating the effect of fast growth due to a high total fertility rate.

Fig. 7.2. Effect on the age structure of decreasing fertility when age-specific mortality is held constant

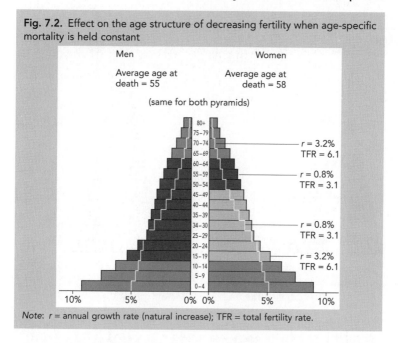

Men

Average age at death = 55

Women

Average age at death = 58

(same for both pyramids)

r = 3.2%
TFR = 6.1

r = 0.8%
TFR = 3.1

r = 0.8%
TFR = 3.1

r = 3.2%
TFR = 6.1

Note: r = annual growth rate (natural increase); TFR = total fertility rate.

costly expenditures for society, some of which are borne directly by the State. It is believed that these expenditures eat into the surplus available for investment in agricultural infrastructure and industrial machinery and therefore hold back the pace of economic development itself. More recently, rapid population growth has been held responsible for migration from rural to urban areas that has led to congestion and insanitary living conditions. As ecological issues begin to attract our attention, population growth is accused of laying waste to the forests (as discussed in Chapter 4). In fact, all these supposed disadvantages of population growth are very controversial and we will not discuss them further here. What matters is whether the owners of capital and middle-class citizens in general either genuinely believe that population growth is a crucial problem or want to use population as a scapegoat in the face of other difficulties that they cannot solve. For centuries the State, if it had been concerned at all with demographic matters, had been concerned to *increase* the rate of population growth. In the 1950s for the first time, it became seriously involved in trying to *decrease* the rate of growth in many countries in Asia and to a lesser extent Africa. Far from expressing abhorrence at the 'fruits of philosophy', it began to distribute them eagerly by promoting birth control techniques.

Family planning programmes have not always been primarily responsible for the dramatic fertility decline that many Asian countries have experienced already and some African countries are embarking upon. Sometimes,

Fig. 7.3. Effect of rapid growth on the age structure when age-specific fertility is held constant

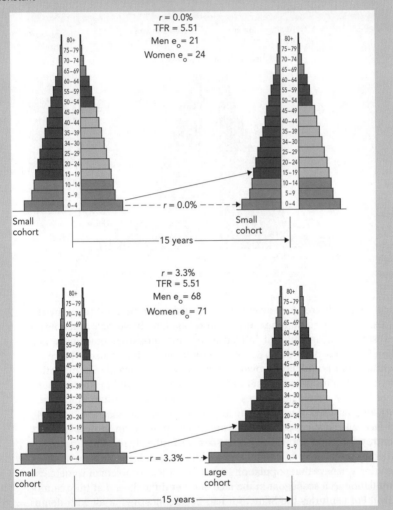

Note: Comparison of the upper two pyramids with the lower two pyramids shows that more rapid natural increase leads to a younger population even when it results from lower mortality (r = growth rate, TFR = total fertility rate, e_0 = average age at death).

the birth rate had begun to decline before the major launching of family planning by the State. In Taiwan, for example, households began to acquire modern consumer goods like radios before the birth control programme really got under way. It was found subsequently that the households who were adopting lower fertility norms were those in possession of these modern goods. It seems likely that there would have been a fertility reduction without the State-sponsored programme. There has also been a great deal of discussion of the birth control programme in Thailand, especially as this was heavily sponsored by Western governments and included the introduction of a new birth control technique, the injectable (known as Depo-Provera). This was a controversial contraceptive because it had not undergone adequate trials in the West when it was introduced in Thailand and was suspected of being implicated in the development of breast cancer. Again, students of Thai demography have pointed out that fertility began to fall before the introduction of this much acclaimed and much criticized programme and continued to decline at much the same rate afterwards.

Despite popular belief, birth control is not the only important mechanism in fertility reduction. Sri Lanka is held up as an example of a poor Asian country where fertility has declined substantially. An analysis of the proximate determinants responsible for this (these were introduced in Chapter 3), shows that a rising age at marriage has been largely responsible for this decline. The same can be said of Malaysia in the 1960s. These changes in marriage patterns have little to do with the activity of the State, although the State has been involved in birth control in both these countries.

One contrasting example to those just described is Indonesia. Until 1970 the total fertility rate was steady at the relatively high rate of 5.6 (nearly six live births per woman). In 1970 a family planning programme was introduced in Java. Over the five years 1970 to 1975 fertility fell to 5.1, and from 1976 to 1979 to 4.7. The fall was mainly due to contraception, rather than delayed marriage. It would appear that the programme was responsible. However, the decline also coincides with Suharto's economic development programme and his encouragement of consumerism. So immediately the picture becomes less clear. Controlling for one event while changing another is not possible in history (although statistical methods exist for simulating such controls in the analysis of historical data).

There have now been many studies, using large samples of the populations concerned, that have sought to tease out the main social and economic factors responsible for the fertility decline that has occurred in virtually every country of Asia (and some countries in Africa).[2] It is not an easy job to do this statistically and one cannot be over-confident in the results. However, in most such studies the education of women is apparently an important factor. That is to say, households that have lower fertility, or have experienced greater use of family planning, tend to have more highly educated mothers in them than the rest.

For women to continue their education beyond primary school, though not necessarily further than that, seems important in fertility determination. But why is it important? One has to establish that this is a truly independent effect and does not simply signify that households with better educated women tend to have higher household incomes and more modern expenditure patterns or better educated men, both of which might be the real reason for the fertility decline. Some studies have controlled statistically for these alternative explanations. For instance, even in Pakistan, where at the national level not much change in fertility has been observed, sample surveys have shown that households with better educated women have lower fertility, whatever the level of education of the men in the household.

It is often argued that education improves a woman's status in the sense that it gives her more confidence and ultimately power in the household, not just greater respect. This would be important if women are being forced to bear large families by their menfolk, who might feel that they gain status from having many children, especially sons. What is slightly puzzling about this argument is that it cannot be applied to the experience we described in the previous section. After all, women in the nineteenth century in England did not even have the vote, so it is unclear that education, to the extent that they received any, improved their status. Similarly, in Saudi Arabia today many women are highly educated but women are not allowed to drive a vehicle. Their education does not expose them to society, new ideas, or travel. Nevertheless, to assume that women everywhere tend to prefer not to have many births in close succession is reasonable. Short birth intervals are good neither for mothers nor for their children. It is also reasonable to assume that many women would prefer not to go on bearing children into their late forties. Women who lack autonomy may face social or family pressure to bear many children, and especially sons, that forces both these patterns of childbearing on them.

Similar arguments have developed around the question of women's work and fertility. We shall return to this later but comment at this stage that the impact of paid work depends on what sort of work is being undertaken and the reason that a woman enters the labour market in the first place. Work can bring independence and status or it can be thoroughly degrading and undertaken only under the compulsion of the utmost poverty. It is as difficult to unravel the relationship of female employment to fertility decline in present-day Asia as it was in nineteenth-century England. A woman's participation in the work-force may result in delayed marriage. So also may the prolongation of her education. The purpose may be to enhance the income and prestige of the household and so make a daughter a more attractive marriage partner.

This discussion has illustrated how social change may affect marriage, the ultimate family size, and even the spacing of births. Age-specific fertility data collected after the start of a fertility transition show that different patterns of fertility decline exist (Figure 7.4). For example, delayed ages at first

Fig. 7.4. Effects on fertility schedule of delayed marriage, spacing of births, and termination of childbearing

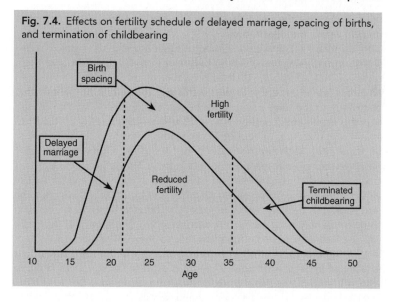

marriage result in a rightward shift in the rising portion of the age-specific fertility schedule. Greater spacing of births (i.e., longer intervals between births) lowers the overall level of the schedule. Decisions to limit surviving family size and to stop childbearing in one's thirties result in a slice being taken out of the declining portion of the age-specific fertility schedule. Taking all these three effects together, lower fertility ultimately results in a more pointed schedule, with a peak that is lower than before.

Many determinants of fertility decline are not easily measurable. The circumstances of different social groups or classes at different stages in a nation's economic development may differ in ways that promote and retard fertility simultaneously. This has led many scholars to feel that, besides statistical analysis of large population samples, one needs small-scale intensive anthropological-style investigations really to understand the processes at work in fertility decline. Field studies in Indonesia and India (in Kerala) have detected two contrary processes operating simultaneously—both lowering fertility. Those sectors of society that have benefited from the new industrial revolutions in Asia have seen advantages from fertility decline in terms of more household resources for education, the possession of consumer durables, and upward social mobility. This picture may have applied to the middle class in nineteenth-century England also and the better-off farming communities of nineteenth-century Japan. On the other hand, the poor and the landless see diminishing advantages of having many children as the prospects of employing them on their land or in the overcrowded cities become grimmer than they were thirty years ago. So fertility falls also among the poor, though not to benefit from prosperity but to prevent a slide into destitution.

In a similar vein, Seccombe has argued that households engaged in cottage industry, using family labour only, can intensify their labour use in a recession and so maintain their household incomes. Such households need abundant labour to be able to react in this way. In contrast, households that contribute to the wage labour force of capitalist industry have no control over the employment of their labour. Therefore, high fertility is no advantage. These two types of household can readily coexist side by side, at least for some time, with contrasting patterns of fertility. Other scholars have observed the opposite reactions at work in India. Households who feel their trade to be a diminishing one that has lost out to capitalist enterprise, like village shoemaking, prefer smaller families and expect their children to be occupationally mobile, that is, to get out of their family trade. In contrast, some households engaged in the service sector, like domestic sweepers, who are located near to metropolitan centres observe that the rapid expansion of the urban middle classes creates a shortage of domestic labour that is reflected in rising wage rates. They are encouraged to rear many children who will stay in the same trade (though migration may be necessary). Detailed case studies yield a complex and varying picture of fertility trends and their determinants but eventually we may begin to discover patterns of behaviour and responses to economic change that extend across cultures and continents and over time.

It used to be fashionable to list the reasons why fertility was expected to remain high in the developing world. The value of children as a source of security (as well as of labour) was one of the main reasons stressed. Yet, as we have seen, fertility fell in the West long before the State developed systems of social security to replace the family. Similarly, the persistence of high infant mortality was often cited. Yet, infant mortality had fallen to 100 per thousand or below in many Asian countries by the start of the 1960s. In England fertility began its rapid decline while infant mortality was still around 150 per thousand. Those who judged that fertility would not decline in the major countries of Asia have been proved wrong. Indonesia, India, and China (to name the three largest) have all begun their fertility transitions (see Figure 7.1). Research has increasingly focused on why fertility began to decline amid so much poverty, rather than on why it has not yet begun.

Declining fertility is not necessarily a reason for rejoicing. Some sectors of society may be reducing their fertility because of their poverty, not in spite of it, and certainly not because it is going away. However, much of the alarm that used to be expressed over population increase was unnecessary. State involvement in popularizing or making more available modern contraceptives has undoubtedly helped households to act on their need to limit their families more efficiently. History demonstrates that people know how to manage their human and non-human household resources. Economic and social changes affect households' fertility behaviour. To some extent this occurs whatever government may wish or will.

Notes

1. It is curious that the problem of population growth in India should be alluded to about seventy years before the beginning of the demographic transition there. Perhaps the British wanted to think they had been more successful at reducing the death rate than they were.

2. In Chapter 3 we described the prejudice that assumed that historical Asia was different from Europe in respect of fertility regulation. Similarly, despite the example of fertility decline in East Asia, as late as the 1970s some demographers believed that South Asia would not follow suit. Cultural norms and economic backwardness were cited as the reason. In fact, economic change was taking place and ideas were changing too; during the 1970s part of South Asia began to enter the fertility transition. Similarly, until quite recently some demographers hesitated to predict fertility decline in Africa, again citing poverty and culture. They were also wrong. Fertility has begun to decline, notably in Kenya, which was formerly a very high fertility country, but also in several other African countries.

8 | Case Studies of Fertility Transition in Asia

Fertility transition in China

One of the more remarkable stories of fertility decline in a developing country can be told of mainland China. It is remarkable in that one might not have expected a sustained decline in fertility to take place in a poor agricultural country. It is also important in that the global impact of the decline is substantial because of the enormous size of China's population—one-fifth of the world's total.

In China, the State has been deeply involved in health and welfare since the Communists took over government in 1949 under Mao Zedong. We have already referred to examples of disease control. The Chinese State has been characterized by huge swings in its approach to strategy and ideology. At times the economy seemed to be out of control: the famine described in Chapter 5 fell into one of these. In the 1950s, the peasantry were organized into communes with the State providing a floor beneath which the food consumption of each family should not fall; families were also supposedly guaranteed basic health and education needs. Unfortunately, the communes could not guard against a crisis in macro-political management—hence the famine. Nevertheless, infant and child mortality fell to quite low levels in many parts of China by the 1980s—with infant mortality rates of around fifty per thousand. This suggests that government policies had been rather effective.

Ideology first approved strongly of population growth and growth in the labour force as the source of wealth. Most of the early infrastructure built by the communist regime, consisting of massive dams and other public works, was constructed almost entirely by hand (as it had been in the past—see Chapter 3). 'Our population is our strength' was the slogan of the day.

The first efforts to control population growth were made in the 1960s. These were soon abandoned, not so much through any reversal in policy but because of the lack of direction experienced during the 'cultural revolution', a period of political and ideological turmoil. None the less, in the cities at least, where living space was getting very constrained because little urban construction had taken place since 1949, people were less impressed by the initiatives of the State. They were faced with an economic reality that made

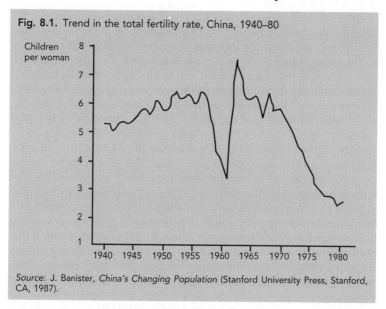

Fig. 8.1. Trend in the total fertility rate, China, 1940–80

Source: J. Banister, *China's Changing Population* (Stanford University Press, Stanford, CA, 1987).

family growth undesirable and they responded accordingly. In some cities, like Shanghai, fertility fell regardless of the State's intentions.

In the country as a whole, however, the total fertility rate was still about 5.8 (in 1970), which is typical of pre-transition fertility levels in Asia. It was really only in the 1970s that the birth control programme began. The slogan of the day was 'later, longer, fewer'. This was meant to encourage a later start to childbearing, longer intervals between births, and fewer children on completion of family building (refer again to Figure 7.4). It is important to appreciate that the rural fertility transition dates back to this period (see Figure 8.1). In China, any mention of birth control is often associated with the 'one-child programme' of the late 1970s: in fact, much had happened before then.

The one-child programme

The most ambitious birth control programme ever launched by the State in any country was initiated in China in 1979. The target was for most couples to pledge themselves to having only one child.

Why was the Chinese State so concerned to limit its population growth (after earlier periods of welcoming population growth, or at least treating the issue with ambivalence)? One can read what the Chinese authorities apparently wished to tell the world at the time in an English language study by two prominent demographers (Liu Zheng and Song Jian). 'Although initially the impact of a fast growth of population on the economy is not immediately apparent, the steady increase in the size of the population brings a series of problems in its wake, particularly in terms of grain and market supplies, housing, education, and employment.' Thus, the problems of population growth were apparently seen in the same light as in the capitalist economies: the huge dependency burden was making its impact felt, for example on the cost of schooling: 'the strain caused by such a large enrolment on educational funds, supply of teachers, basic construction investment, the printing of teaching materials etc. is enormous.' More importantly the same study goes on to argue. 'The most serious pressure placed on the national economy due to the excessive growth of population is felt in the provision of employment.' This statement represents either an extraordinary ideological U-turn or an appreciation of a dramatic change in the Chinese economy. Labour, once the source of wealth, was now facing diminishing rather than increasing returns. It may have been judged that the need was no longer for massive infrastructural works opening up new lands for cultivation, but for the more intensive farming of existing lands, requiring small-scale rather than large-scale irrigation. The large works had been completed and capital had been created in the form of dams and hydroelectric systems. Now the concentration should be on their effective use.[1] In fact earlier Marxists had argued that, if population ever became a problem, a socialist society could best deal with it. The Chinese State was demonstrating whether this was true.

Ironically, however, the means adopted in the programme initiated in 1979 included economic incentives for people to pledge themselves to have no more than one child. In other words, the State was using the principles of the market to implement its policies (whereas earlier it had adopted a more socialist approach concentrating on ideological exhortation). Couples were induced to sign a document making this pledge. In return they received a certificate. The monetary incentive (which was delivered in 'work points', or claims over commodities and services, in the rural areas) was described as a subsidy. It was intended to help ensure even greater chances of good health for the single child, and allay any fears people might have of losing a child through disease—particularly through nutrition-related disease arising out of poverty. The money offered, five yuan a month, amounted to about a tenth of the average wage in State industry at the time. It was no doubt a higher proportion of the income of most agricultural workers. This was to be paid continually to each eligible couple for fourteen years!

A cash reward was also paid on the spot for sterilization: fifty yuan for those with one child and thirty yuan for those who already had two. Non-monetary rewards for signing the one-child pledge included priority access to urban housing space for those working in the cities. This was a strong incentive as a severe housing shortage had resulted from the concentration on rural development over much of the time since the 1949 revolution.

On the other side of the coin, disincentives were set up to having more than two children. These became harsher over time and in some parts of the country were applied even to those who refused to stop at one. For example, after a re-enforcement of the policy in 1983, some provinces reduced the incomes or bonuses of workers who refused to sign the pledge.

Incentives were also introduced to marry later: longer paid vacations after a wedding were granted to those who did so. The legal age for marriage was 18 years for women and 20 years for men but the State favoured what it described as the 'optimal age'. This was 22 and 30 years for women and men respectively. The existence side-by-side of an optimal and a legal age caused some confusion later. When the legal age of marriage was raised people confused it with optimal age and responded by getting married earlier, which was not the intention. The complexity of control regulations is typical of the Chinese family planning programme and its evolution. There were, for example, several exceptions to the 'one child' rule. These proliferated as time went on. From the start, while ethnic minorities were encouraged to sign the one-child pledge, they were none the less relieved of the sanctions applied to those who went beyond two children. Birth control is a sensitive issue and the Chinese Government was concerned to cultivate the minorities politically to protect the frontier regions where they lived.

All these regulations were backed up with an intensified mother and child care programme. Besides material incentives, the exhortatory features of the communist State were mobilized in a propaganda campaign. From time immemorial, States have sought to advertise themselves or their wishes through placing messages on simple articles of everyday use. For example, the Chinese, who are among the largest users of tobacco in the world, have used matchboxes to induce people to sign the one-child pledge. Bizarrely, some posters and even matchboxes had slogans on them in the English language: perhaps they were meant to impress visiting foreigners (who might bring financial aid) as much as the local people.

The practice and problems of the programme

To make the intensification of the family planning programme from 1979 onwards a success, huge pressure was put on officials to fulfil birth targets for the locality within their control. This led to a rather bizarre process of planning at the local level who was allowed to give birth in any given year. So as not to overstep their targets, local officials put enormous pressure on women who had an unplanned birth to undergo an abortion. Some of these abortions were carried out late in the pregnancy and the programme began to fall into disrepute. Overseas observers hesitated between commending the Chinese for their serious attempt to control population growth and condemning them for doing it so forcibly. Western scholars displayed a remarkable degree of double-think, a criticism they themselves had made of the communist regimes. As we shall see, this policy of forced abortions resulting from target setting and communal rewards is similar to the system of 'motivator fees' and forced sterilizations adopted at times in India and elsewhere. The democratic capitalist State is capable of just as heavy a hand.

One potential problem was whether the State could deliver the rewards or not. If the adoption of the one-child norm had become really widespread, the financial implications for the State would have been substantial. Furthermore, given the wild swings in Chinese ideology and consequent strategy that had characterized the past, could one believe that the financial subsidy would be continued for the promised fourteen years? The State had a credibility problem. The peasant was cautious. Effectively, this meant that the future value of the subsidy was heavily discounted in people's minds.[2]

The most extraordinary problem the programme may have faced stemmed from the simultaneous introduction of radical economic reforms. The one-child programme coincided with an economic liberalization programme that brought the market into the economy. In particular, for the first time since 1949 Chinese agricultural workers were allowed to farm private plots and make money from so doing, as well as working communally. Much communal land was divided to enable farmers to have responsibility for their own land (the scheme was known as the 'responsibility system'). This put labour back into the control of the household, just as it had been on peasant farms. More hands would allow farming families to make more money. Hence the reforms provided an incentive to have more children or at least more than one. Some scholars, however, have argued that the effect of these economic reforms should not be exaggerated. By now in China, as elsewhere in Asia, more hands were less useful than better educated children. Therefore, downwards economic pressures on fertility desires were beginning to develop anyway among the Chinese peasantry. This coincided happily with the State's family planning intentions. Economic reforms would have had little impact on the trend.

It can be argued more strongly that a further effect of the economic reforms, after some time at least, was to enable some peasants to get sufficiently rich not to bother about the incentives. They could easily afford to pay the fines. What was needed was a means-tested system of fines and incentives, related to incomes. This would have been too complicated even for the Chinese to administer.

In practice, some provinces of the country, for example Guangdong, did not implement the one-child programme rigorously at all. With the breakdown of the commune system and the increased responsibility of the peasant households for their own affairs, the very mechanism of political control was weakened! Nevertheless, the degree of success achieved (which we will review shortly) may be due to the relatively high degree of social security still provided by the communes despite their diminished role.[3] In this, the Chinese State may be contrasted with capitalist States such as India, where the security of the poor peasant and landless labourer is far less assured and children have provided the only guarantee of income or health care to be relied upon. While being far from perfect, the Chinese Government probably provided a better deal. The lower mortality rates which everyone accepts have been achieved in China may be cited in evidence.

Let us turn to look at the results of the programme. In summary, the target of persuading the vast majority of the population to sign the one-child pledge was achieved only in certain provinces of the country. As far as fertility rates are concerned, which are the hard evidence of the success of a programme, the decline was well under way before 1979, as we have noted already (see Figure 8.1). It continued thereafter, following almost the same trend as before. In 1970 the total fertility rate was 5.8 children; in 1977 it was 2.8, and by the 1980s it was close to the replacement level of 2.1. By the mid-1980s, the birth rate was below twenty per thousand, and the growth rate close to 1 per cent a year. For such a level to have been reached in a population of a billion people is a remarkable achievement. Most critics would agree that this has been a desirable reduction given the reduced availability of land and the low level of capital accumulation achieved so far. It is extremely unlikely that continued growth in the labour force would have raised incomes per head, as labour shortage was very much a thing of the past. Fertility would probably have declined spontaneously, but much more slowly than it did with the help of the programme, which sought to establish new norms—albeit forcibly at times. Equally, it is very likely that the same fertility levels could have been achieved, though perhaps a little later, by continuing the programme of the early 1970s without the Draconian measures of the end of that decade.

Economic change and opportunity still dominate fertility decisions in many households. Therefore spatial differentials persist in China as in other societies. One finds lower fertility in better-off provinces and, as we have remarked, in urban areas where there is the greatest squeeze on living space. Economic conditions still seem to prevail in fertility determination but clearly the State can accelerate change.

The coercive aspects of the one-child programme generated much resentment. To prevent a collapse in the programme, the State began to introduce exceptions to the one-child rule besides those already granted the ethnic minority populations. For example, in the 1980s one was permitted to have a second child without loss of privileges or fines in certain areas, such as mountainous regions. Here population densities were far below average anyway. Arguably larger labour forces would be useful in undertaking programmes of reforestation. However, the expressed rationale behind the relaxation was a pragmatic one designed to make the programme work: 'better to prevent a massive leak by opening up a few small ones', as the planners put it. Such demographic fine-tuning is probably unique in world history.

Perhaps the greatest irony in the programme is one that only students of demography can appreciate thoroughly. The one-child programme was unnecessary! A population of 1.2 billion was often quoted by the Chinese government as the ultimate target. Demographers have calculated that such a target could have been reached with two children per couple if they started on their childbearing much later and spaced the births with a four-year interval between them. This is because the natural growth rate of a population can be reduced either by reducing the net rate of reproduction (as the Chinese sought to do) or by increasing the mean length of the female generation—that is, the number of years it takes for a cohort of women to reproduce themselves. The alternative policy would also have been difficult to enforce as it implies that women starting their family are in their thirties. Arguably this would have been more acceptable than allowing families only of one child.[4] It would have avoided the intermediate and unpopular stage of a net reproduction rate less than one, for clearly the one-child target was a temporary one. A population that failed to replace itself forever (by allowing each woman to generate only one-half the total children needed for her own reproduction) would eventually die out.

As it is, the draconian programme has left the population with some enduring problems. People who are now young are going to grow old with only one child to look after them. The State will face the consequences of one working member (or producer) in the economy having to support two elderly people (or consumers) needing services like medical care as well as food. One hopes that the resilience and ingenuity of the Chinese Government enable it to solve this new population problem when it develops.

Fertility transition in the Indian subcontinent

In the Indian subcontinent, the public health programmes already mentioned (above all the successful reduction in malaria and the near-eradication of smallpox) had lowered the death rate substantially by the end of the 1950s. Economic planners had been formulating plans based on a population growth of between 1 and 1.5 per cent a year, which they assumed would continue into the foreseeable future. If the birth rate was around forty per thousand, this implied that the death rate would be around twenty-five per thousand or above. There were no reliable data for the whole country to support or dispute this estimate. It meant that if the economy grew at 5 per cent a year, incomes could grow at approximately 3.5 per cent a year and would double in about twenty years (see Table 8.1).

The first reliable demographic data on which to base an estimate came with the taking of the 1961 Census. The result was a shock for the Planning Commission. Between 1951 and 1961 the population had grown at an annual average rate of just less than 2 per cent a year. Clearly fertility had been underestimated in the guesswork just described. Probably more impor-

Table 8.1. Growth in population, income, and investment as envisaged in the Second Five-Year Plan of India

	First Plan actual (1951–6)	Fifth Plan projected (1971–6)
National income (Rs millions)	10,800	27,270
Investment rate (%)	7.3	17.0
Population (millions)	384	500
Incremental capital–output ratio	1.8:1	3.7:1
Per capita income (Rs)	281	546

Source: India, Planning Commission, Second Five-Year Plan (New Delhi, 1956).

tantly the death rate had been overestimated. The health programmes and economic development of the 1950s had brought mortality down sharply, probably to close to twenty per thousand. All this information came in the wake of serious food shortages arising in the late 1950s. The response of the Government of India was to spend ten times as much on family planning as it had done before.

It was in the mid-1960s that the State began to take family planning really seriously. During the 1960s the economy began to falter, with serious balance of payments problems arising by the middle of the decade. Furthermore, food shortages again required international aid to prevent starvation. It was understood by now that the international capitalist community regarded population control as necessary for the successful pursuit of economic growth and abolition of poverty. In contrast, the international communist community still regarded population growth as desirable (or at least irrelevant to the question of economic development). India was in a crucial strategic position and exploited the fact by obtaining aid from both the communist USSR and the capitalist USA. Only the USA, however, could be relied on to deliver food. Its strong anti-natalist position was probably important in forcing the Government of India to take population control seriously. Public expenditure on family planning was stepped up from one-third of 1 per cent to more than 1 per cent of public expenditure, thus becoming a substantial proportion of the health budget. With international assistance the family planning administration began to deliver the intra-uterine device (IUD), carrying out insertions through rural clinics. Although there was no coercion, the programme was ill-managed, with inadequate training and poor follow-up. The complications that are bound to occur with this method of birth control (interference with the menstrual cycle) were not appropriately explained or rectified. Many women were soon unwilling to continue with its use, with the result that can be seen in Figure 8.2.

The State can be criticized for clumsy programmes and for failing to blame itself when they went wrong. Instead of rectifying the programme, the Government assumed that the problem lay with the women themselves.

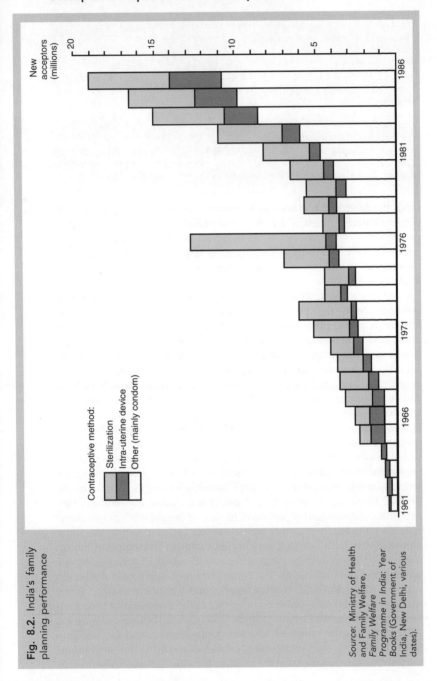

Fig. 8.2. India's family planning performance

Contraceptive method:

Sterilization

Intra-uterine device

Other (mainly condom)

New acceptors (millions)

20

15

10

5

1961 1966 1971 1976 1981 1986

Source: Ministry of Health and Family Welfare, *Family Welfare Programme in India: Year Books* (Government of India, New Delhi, various dates).

It started a new programme, this time putting the responsibility on men. India's condom campaign was one of the more imaginative of its kind in the developing world. The device was widely distributed at subsidized prices, using consumer goods companies (concerned with the sale of household items like tea and soap) for distribution and the village shop as the retail outlet. As in China, propaganda for the programme used posters and advertisements on articles of everyday use, for example coins.

Turning to Pakistan, it may come as some surprise to learn that the State sponsored its own family planning programme in the mid-1960s. With Islam as the established religion, the atmosphere would not seem propitious for the adoption of birth regulation. However, although Islam encourages procreation and prescribes early and universal marriage, it does not clearly prohibit contraception (or even abortion). Different doctrinal authorities come to different conclusions on this matter. In Pakistan, as in India, the IUD was the favoured contraceptive device, again putting the responsibility on women. Use of contraception remained uncommon, however. A survey in 1968 showed that only 6 per cent of women in the reproductive years were using any form of birth control. Although a new programme was started in Pakistan in the 1970s, implementation again fell well behind the expressed intentions. There were still few clinics in the countryside through which family planning could be promoted. Distributing contraceptives through channels other than the health services would have been unacceptable. Moreover, many people believed that Islam prescribes procreation even though it does not. Any economic disadvantage of large families had not made itself sufficiently apparent to break through this series of barriers.

We referred earlier to the way in which the population 'problem' is sometimes made the scapegoat for other ills facing a society. In the early 1970s the Congress party of India won an election after an electoral campaign in which it had promised to 'abolish poverty'. As the decade wore on it became ever more apparent that such a promise was not likely to be fulfilled. Despite economic growth rates that remained on average above the rate of population growth (though not by far), the fruits of that economic growth were not being distributed in a way that would reduce the proportion of the population below the poverty line. Landlessness was increasing and major industrial enterprises were beginning to substitute capital for labour. Government employment-generation programmes were too small to offset these tendencies (except in emergencies, like famines or elections). Aware of its loss of credibility, the Government turned increasingly to highlighting its family planning programme and to putting the blame on population growth. In the early 1970s, the method increasingly preferred by the State was male sterilization. From the point of view of the State, this has the virtue of ending rather than delaying childbearing. One hundred rupees, which amounted to three to four weeks' wages at the time, were offered as 'compensation' for the operation. Sterilization camps with a carnival-like atmosphere were organized. Not surprisingly, it was disproportionately the poorest families that agreed to undergo the operation in order to collect the financial compensation. Subsequent studies have shown that many regretted their action.

In 1975 the Government declared a State of Emergency and instituted a programme of reform with family planning high on the agenda. Supported by the propaganda line that population was a pre-eminent problem, heavy-handed tactics (as later in China) were resorted to. Substantial 'motivator fees' were offered to anyone who could find people willing to participate in the birth control programme. Government servants were promoted for actively supporting this campaign. In some northern states of India the activity went too far. Sterilization was forced upon people who were either unwilling or ineligible (for instance couples who were beyond the age of childbearing anyway). It is little exaggeration to say that when democratic elections were eventually held, the Congress party lost its majority in those areas where its programme of family planning (among other excesses) had been most ruthlessly indulged in.

Caldwell, a demographer who has spent much time in villages in the south of India, argues that the Indian family planning programme had 'not created a demand for birth control . . . but it had accelerated change' that was taking place in any case. Clearly such acceleration may be in the public interest. For instance, if the State provides education at communal expense for young children, then individual couples are relieved of this part of the financial burden of large families. They may be inclined to have more children as a result, bearing in mind their earning potential as they grow up. If they had to pay for their children's schooling themselves, they would have had fewer.[5]

A democratic society should be worried if individuals are being made to suffer unduly for the common good. Very strong motivation or outright compulsion are serious infringements of personal liberty. By the 1980s the opinion of the international capitalist community was turning against the promotion of population control at any cost. The anti-abortion lobby was gathering strength by then in the United States. There were also increasing reservations about the coercive nature of some programmes. Therefore, political support for family planning began to diminish. Some economists, like Julian Simon, argued that population growth could still be beneficial, as in the past, or at least neutral in its effect on economic development. The actual empirical evidence remained, and still remains, ambiguous.

In this international context, it is not surprising that the family planning programme started in Bangladesh in the mid-1960s and strengthened in the mid-1980s came in for considerable international criticism. Despite being a Muslim country, Bangladesh engaged in a programme that became every bit as aggressive as that in India during the State of Emergency. Incentives included six weeks' wages for women, towards whom the programme was primarily aimed, plus the gift of a sari for anyone agreeing to undergo sterilization. As in India, there were motivator fees also. Schemes such as these are always open to abuse. During the 1984 floods, there were reports of officials acting beyond their brief and withholding government relief food aid from women who refused to allow themselves to be sterilized. Such abuses encouraged some foreign donors to withdraw support from the Bangladesh population control programme.

The underlying strength of social interest in birth control can be seen from the fact that, even after periods of excess such as the Indian Emergency, the number of acceptors of family planning methods continued to increase (see Figure 8.2). In India, by the mid-1980s a quarter of couples were 'protected', that is to say were using some reliable approach to birth prevention. Can one detect any effect on fertility?

The birth rate is known more accurately in India nowadays than it was in the 1950s. A closely supervised system of registration in a sample of the population exists and the national figure is estimated (within quite small margins of error) from that. There is no doubt that, by 1990, the birth rate had come down to between thirty and thirty-five per thousand. This represents slow but distinct progress from the 1960s, when the birth rate must have been over forty per thousand. Studies of the 1970s showed that the total fertility rate fell from around six to around five live births during that decade. These studies also confirm that birth control within marriage was the leading explanation.

In Bangladesh a decline in fertility has only been detected recently. Sample surveys suggest that total fertility was around five in the early 1990s, whereas it was closer to seven well into the 1970s. The level of contraceptive use reported is also high. Some would explain this by an improvement in women's status as they seek freedom from male domination. Some think that changes in ways of thinking (perhaps stimulated by aspirations for modern goods of which people have become increasingly aware) has been dominant. Others would explain the change in terms of increasing landlessness and land fragmentation that have rendered additional labour of very little value to families. It is likely that these motivations have a differential impact on different classes. They may all be operating simultaneously in the country as a whole.

One has to be careful when interpreting statistics based on a single year's data. It is possible for fertility to dip and then recover. We have seen how this may happen in famine. Being able to look at fertility according to the age of the women is particularly useful. If the older women in a survey have reduced their fertility, this probably means they are stopping childbearing earlier. However, if the youngest age group reduces its fertility, this may be a temporary decision. Perhaps women delay starting childbearing because of a national crisis or a sudden increase in work opportunities for women. Five years later these women may catch up by having more children than usual for their age group to compensate for their earlier low fertility. Clearly behaviour of this kind does not lead to a permanent reduction in the total fertility rate, year by year (or what is known as the *period* total fertility). By

Table 8.2. Cohort and period fertility rates in Bangladesh

Age	1954–8	1959–63	1964–8	1969–73	1974–8	1979–83	1984–8	Decline 1974–8 to 1984–8 (%)
10–14	0.0276	0.0191	0.0218	0.0199	0.0152	0.0150	0.0126	17
15–19	0.2518	0.2576	0.2435	0.2497	0.2323	0.2084	0.1822	22
20–24		0.3479	0.3439	0.3386	0.3272	0.3078	0.2599	21
25–29			0.3310	0.3116	0.3033	0.2969	0.2254	26
30–34				0.2728	0.2605	0.2324	0.1692	35
35–39					0.1810	0.1557	0.1141	37
40–44						0.0763	0.0555	
45–49							0.0176	
TFR (period)							5.18	
TFR (cohort aged 45–49)[a]							7.39	

[a] Calculated for ages 15–49, from 1954–8 to 1984–8.

Source: M. D. Huq and J. C. Cleland, *Bangladesh Fertility Survey, 1989* (National Institute for Population Research and Training, Dhaka, 1990).

the end of their lives, these women could end up having the same number of children as women who were born before and after them. The only difference is that they have spaced their children differently, starting slowly then catching up. Their total fertility accumulated through their life (or what is known as *cohort* total fertility) would not have dipped at all. For some purposes, studying cohort behaviour is useful. Table 8.2 shows the experience of women in Bangladesh, bringing out the distinction between cohort and period fertility rates. If fertility was not changing at all, the cohort and period rates would be the same.

Little fertility decline had occurred in Pakistan by 1990. Nevertheless, high fertility does not prevail across all socio-economic strata in the population. Fertility in households of the highest status, whose men and women are in professional occupations, is a little lower than average. This is most marked if the women in the household are better educated. As we discussed in Chapter 7, education may affect many things. Perhaps what is important is that it gives women the self-confidence to exercise some power in household decision-making and to discuss issues thought inappropriate for family discussion in other households, namely how many children would best suit the household's circumstances and aspirations and how much childbearing and rearing it is reasonable for the women to undertake.

Although economic growth has not been rapid in Pakistan, it has been sufficient to make many households considerably better off than ever before. People possess consumer durables they never used to have. Many of the work-force have worked at some time or other in the affluent Gulf states. This has put even rural families in touch with modern lifestyles. Aspirations may conflict with large numbers of children consuming household resources. It would not be surprising if a pent-up desire for fertility reduction exists, that a more determined State-sponsored programme could help to release. Nevertheless, by 1990, the use of contraception was hardly above 10 per cent.

Several scholars claim to have detected an increase in self-assertion among women in Pakistan and Bangladesh in recent years. This may have been promoted by greater participation in the work-force outside the family or the family farm. While women's work in urban factories is often of low status, for instance in the stitching trade in the cities of Bangladesh, it does serve to take women out of the closeted environment of a traditional Islamic upbringing.

Attitudes to childbearing have begun to change in India, especially in the more prosperous households that gained from the growth in agricultural productivity associated with the Green Revolution. In the Indian Punjab farmers tell a different tale about children nowadays from the one they told twenty years ago. We quote (from the study by Nag and Kak) the words of a blacksmith in 1970 and then in 1982, when the same man was contacted again. In 1970 he said: 'I have no money and the Co-operative Society only loans to farmers. If I have sons they will work outside, labour like animals, but save. A rich man invests in his machines. We must invest in our children. It's that simple.' In 1982 his view was that 'There is plenty of work for me to do. New technology has not made me useless. Of course I have to work very hard in my old age. My sons don't help me. These days very few do. It is better to have a small family.' Furthermore, it seems that the new technology and increased commercialization have encouraged the view that some education beyond primary level is worth while. Educated sons and daughters can get worthwhile jobs in towns and cities or even overseas. Farmers in the Punjab use migrant labour from Bihar to do the manual work required. Young children are no longer required to work in the fields. Chemical spraying is a man's job, whereas weeding by hand was once a child's. Young men, more aware of the better things in life, no longer want the drudgery of working in the fields. Besides, technical competence in agriculture increasingly presupposes literacy, if only to read instruction manuals and package labels.

All this amounts to observing that different types of economic change are taking place in particular social strata and locations in the Indian subcontinent. Many of these seem to have had an impact on the readiness to accept the message of State pronouncements on family planning. This is not to deny that progress is slow in South Asia, and very slow in comparison with what has been happening in China. One reason may be that life is still very precarious for the many households that have remained untouched by migration, women's work, new agricultural technology, and so on. As in the past, children provide the best security and feel duty-bound to provide it on the spot if their parents fall sick and are unable to work. These services are not provided by the State, nor by any local institution. Note the observation of the blacksmith just quoted that even the local co-operative would not lend to a landless family. Thus, again, one needs to make class distinctions in the analysis. One also has to distinguish different areas within the nation, which may reflect cultural factors. In some states of India female literacy is much lower than in others and, arguably, patriarchal values are stronger, making the lives of women precarious and oppressed. Similarly, landless labourers have obtained more bargaining power in some states than elsewhere and have achieved a degree of self-reliance. Some parts of the country remain essentially feudal in their mode of agriculture, with no assured recognition of the rights of sharecroppers. Security is therefore something that can vary within a country. In China, the State communist system still provides some of those basic requirements that elsewhere children supply for their families (though life for some minority ethnic groups is distinctly less secure).

Notes

1. Some would argue that the large-scale approach was never appropriate in the first place. The capital quickly created often became useless through inappropriate design. Moreover, some long-term ecological damage may have occurred as a result.
2. Economists will recognize that this means the present value of the award (or stream of subsidies) was much smaller than it would have been if people had believed that they would continue to get the subsidy for the full promised term.
3. Although we argued earlier that lack of security seems not to have deterred European families from fertility reduction a century earlier, security is a more important consideration among poor rural farmers in a developing country like China or India than among an urban middle class and relatively prosperous industrial working class such as characterized Britain, for example, at the turn of the century.
4. This may be seen from the following. Take a cohort of women and assume that they double their number through reproduction by the time their daughters have survived to become mothers (allowing for mortality). Thus, we have a *net rate of reproduction* (NRR) of 2 (see Box 2.3). This is exactly the same as saying that the population of women will grow through natural increase so as to double in the space of a generation. In algebraic notation, this can be written as $100e^{rT}$, where r is the natural increase rate and T the mean length of the female generation (see Box 1.1). The two quantities are the same and this remains true whether the number of women doubles in a generation, remains the same, or changes by some other amount. Thus:

$$\text{NRR} = e^{rT}.$$

Hence:

$$r = \frac{\log_e \text{NRR}}{T}.$$

Therefore, as we assert in the text, the growth rate r can be reduced (and a target population size reached more slowly) either by reducing the NRR or by increasing T.

5. Economists will recognize here a distinction between private and public costs and benefits. One might ask why the State should become involved in family planning at all. Why not leave people to make their own decisions? And why not leave private enterprise to market birth control methods? The problem is that, if the State has already subsidized schooling for children (and even in some places school meals also), then it has adopted in effect a pro-natalist policy. It may seek to neutralize this therefore by subsidizing birth control methods at the same time. Of course, as we have pointed out, the State became involved for many other reasons as well.

Part V

The Demographic Impact of Industrialization

9 | Urbanization and Migration

Introduction

Urbanization is a process of great demographic significance. It transfers populations to a very different social, economic, and physical environment. It also transfers people into a very different demographic environment, one that is itself often changing rapidly with further social and economic consequences.

The national age structure is a composite of the many different age structures that characterize the different communities that make up the national population. If we think of those communities in spatial terms, we can see that the nation consists of villages, towns, and cities each with their own age and sex distribution. The contrast between the age-sex distribution in one local community and another may be extreme. One may consist mainly of old people, another of young people, and a yet another mainly of men of working age. In particular, the rural age distribution and the urban age distribution are often very different. Even within the urban population marked contrasts exist between towns. We explore these in the discussion that follows.

What are the implications of local demographic differences? We have already discussed how important demographic dependency is in determining the economic consequences of demographic growth. Too many young people could raise the costs of development by requiring heavy educational expenditures. Similarly, too many old people could raise the costs of welfare expenditures. These dependency relationships are a direct result of the age distribution and local governments have to face their consequences. Furthermore, demographic growth at the local level consists both of natural increase (the difference between births and deaths) and net migration (movements of people into an area minus movements of people away from it). In combination, these two forces may produce rapid local growth or no growth at all. The perceived economic and social consequences of the rapid growth of towns are often deplored. Critics refer to unemployment, congestion, and slums. Equally, the economic rationale behind the growth of towns and cities is not always fully appreciated. Some scholars believe this force to be the engine of development.

We discuss both the good and the bad aspects of urbanization and the policy issues implied. First, we concentrate on why urban populations have grown so rapidly in Asia and parts of Africa since the 1940s. Since many of these countries embarked on major programmes of industrialization over this period, we focus on the relationship between industrialization and urbanization or, to put this in other words, the economic rationale of industrial towns.

The rationale of the industrial town

Producers

The economist Adam Smith is well known for describing the advantages to be obtained from specialization in the process of manufacture. His observations were made at a pin-making factory but we use the example of garment manufacture, as the textile industry has been so important in the industrialization of many developing countries today. It is a slow process for one man or woman to make a whole garment, from the spinning of the cotton thread to make the cloth, to the final stitching together of the woven pieces. A much speedier operation can take place if one worker, or group of workers, does all the spinning required, another the weaving, another the dyeing, and another the stitching. The repetition of tasks, while boring, means they can be done more quickly. The result is a rise in labour productivity, that is, output per person per hour. This argument, while technically valid, presupposes that someone can reorganize labour in this way. It also presupposes that the desire to raise productivity exists. In short, such manufacturing makes sense in the context of the rise of capitalism and the emergence of entrepreneurs who wish to maximize profits and who therefore seek to raise productivity. The first workshops of the Industrial Revolution were of the kind just described. The initial demographic implication of this is that industry, instead of being carried out in numerous cottages scattered around the rural villages, became more concentrated in specific localities.

The next step in the process of industrialization is for some of these tasks, which are simply the repeated movement of human limbs, to be speeded up even further by applying power-driven machinery. Again, the more machines of a similar kind that can be fitted in one factory, the better. Hence spinning mills and weaving mills are set up separately. It saves space to have several storeys of machines in one building, rather than several single-storey sheds. Economies of scale are immediately apparent. Although machines might seem to replace labourers, the net effect of scale economies (implying much greater production and labour) and mechanization (which reduces the demand for labour) is that the work-force at a factory site becomes larger not smaller. The scale effect dominates the mechanization effect. (Again we assume that someone provides the investment finance, which presupposes the rise of a capitalist class.) The growth of industrial capital in industry proceeds apace and with it, though not necessarily at the same speed, the growth of the working class.

The demographic impact of the process does not stop here, however. Suppose an industrial enterprise, a machinery-manufacturing unit for example, employs 5,000 workers on one site. That work-force will need to spend most of its wages on food and other necessities (especially in a poor country with low wages). Many of these goods and services will be provided most cheaply if they are made or processed on the spot. This implies what we might term a local multiplier effect. If a factory is set up in a village, the men's wages represent effective demand that will increase employment of other local people. Some may migrate in to obtain employment in this way. The local employment multiplier depends on the general level of mechanization in the country and the transport infrastructure, among other things. Let us suppose, however, that it takes two more workers to provide the service and consumption needs of the original worker in the machinery-construction plant. The work-force therefore becomes the 5,000 original workers plus 10,000 multiplier workers, or 15,000 in total.

When eventually the total work-force becomes settled, it will presumably set up households in the expanding town. If the average household size is five people, that is, the main wage worker, his or her spouse, and three children, the total population comes to 75,000. However, if some households contain two wage workers, we may have overestimated. Assuming that this is true of one in five households, then a better estimate of the total population might be 60,000.

It is now apparent how important a single industrial investment may be in changing the demographic distribution in a country. In our example, recruiting 5,000 workers to start a new enterprise leads to the development of a town of 60,000 people in as long as it takes the investment to come on stream—perhaps three years. This is an urban growth rate of 83 per cent a year.

The 1950s and 1960s were characterized by industrial investments of this kind, whether to substitute for imports or to boost exports. It is partly as the result of this economic drive for industrialization that the world's population is set to become 50 per cent urban by the year 2000. India's population was only about 10 per cent urban before Independence. By 1981 it had become 25 per cent urban. Similarly, China progressed from being 10 per cent to 25 per cent urban over roughly the same period.

The economic advantage of scale that we have described is technically known as an 'internal economy', meaning that it is enjoyed by one specific industry. In addition, economists describe what they call 'external economies of scale', or sometimes 'economies of agglomeration'. If several different industries locate in the same place, their unit costs will be reduced. There are several reasons for this.

First, if several industries share infrastructure like paved roads, then costs per industrial unit (or per unit of output) fall. A new engineering plant may require the construction of railways and roads that it cannot use fully. This makes the fixed day-to-day maintenance costs (and repayment of interest on capital borrowed) very high. Thus, the returns to the capital invested in this infrastructure would be small. However, if another major factory can be persuaded to locate in the same area, for example a fertilizer plant, then the costs can be shared.

Secondly, if the output of one factory is the input to another it often makes sense for the two plants to locate close together to reduce transportation costs. Spinning and weaving mills may develop nearby for this reason.

The third reason for agglomeration relates to the labour market. Marx drew attention to the value of having a pool, or reserve army, of labour from which capitalists could draw their labour as and when they needed it. This tends to keep wages down. If employers have to recruit fresh workers from the rural areas whenever an economic boom occurs, they would be involved in an expensive operation or might have to raise wages to attract employees. If many factories locate in one place, a large number of workers are thrown on to the labour market simultaneously whenever the business cycle turns down. Nevertheless, at any time, some firms will be going bankrupt while others are starting up and some firms will be substituting capital for labour while other expand their use of both. Thus, there are always some unemployed workers available to join a new firm at a low wage.

The urban labour force and the pool of unemployed are supplied from several sources. Their relationship is only partly determined by the rise and fall of industry or the growth of mechanization. Natural increase in the urban area is one source of workers. We return to this in detail later. In many cities in Asia today the death rate is quite low on average and the birth rate, although it has fallen, is still between ten and twenty per thousand higher than the death rate. Such rates yield natural increase of up to 2 per cent a year (with a birth rate of thirty per thousand and a death rate of ten per thousand, for example). In Europe before this century, death rates were so high that natural increase could hardly provide sufficient labour to supply the urban labour market. Indeed, in some cities the death rate was higher than the birth rate. Migration was the major component in growth. Without it the urban population would simply have drained away. In much of Asia and Africa today this is not generally the case. Migration may be responsible for half or less of urban growth. In India, for instance, natural increase has fuelled half the country's urban growth and migration the remaining half.

As manufacturing becomes more sophisticated and machinery requires greater skills for its operation, entrepreneurs look for technical skills in the work-force that they recruit. If they place their factory where no other industry exists, they have to recruit and train their workers themselves. If they locate where industry has long been established, they are more likely to find skilled workers available. With time, special training schools may be established by the bigger firms or groups of firms. New factories entering the town can avail themselves of these workers at little or no extra expense to themselves. The advantages of a large and diversified labour market (with workers trained in various skills) are very substantial.

Owners and managers of industry also like to congregate together for less tangible reasons. Social reasons are important but so is the more practical need to communicate quickly and easily with each other. This is desired so as to co-ordinate investment and output decisions. With good telecommunications networks, the need for physical proximity is reduced. Nevertheless, it remains very important in those developing countries where making a telephone call to a neighbouring city is costly and time-consuming. Business managers face difficulties in obtaining spare parts for their machinery if their supplier is located in a distant town. It is not unknown to find junior managers on long-distance train journeys carrying spare parts in bulging brief cases!

There are, however, costs involved in locating one industry close to another one to gain these advantages. This policy may take a factory further away from the source of some of its raw materials. An industry like the iron and steel industry, for example, that is located close to the supply of its bulky inputs, like iron ore or coal, will not attract other industries whose bulky inputs, crude oil for example, can only be obtained elsewhere. Some towns fail to become agglomerations of the type we are describing above for just that reason. In an extreme case, they may remain like 'monocultures'— growers or producers of one product only. We say more about such towns later.

All these economies of agglomeration lower the unit costs to an individual industry. In Figure 9.1 the cost curve curves downwards because of the internal economies of scale to which we referred in the description of a textile factory. It shifts down when external economies occur as other industries locate in the town.

A consumer goods industry also gains economic advantages from having consumers of its products located in towns or cities, rather than scattered over the countryside. A large and growing market was identified as one driving force of the Industrial Revolution in Europe. As Marx commented, 'the rising demand for clothing materials, *consequent on the growth of population* [my emphasis], the demand for luxuries favoured generally by the extension of commerce, gave weaving a quantitative and qualitative stimulus'. Not only was delivering goods to an agglomerated population easier, it was also easier to stimulate demand by advertising. Moreover, the demonstration effect of richer people on poorer people was stronger the closer their proximity in large numbers. In short, capitalism loves cities.

Fig. 9.1. Industrial cost curves subject to economies of scale

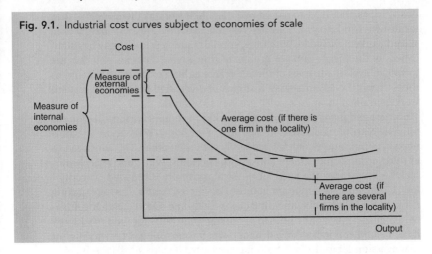

Consumers

People, whether considered as consumers or as labourers, require infrastructure such as roads and water supply once they congregate together to serve industry. It is possible to think of the city as an industry in itself, producing safe water, good drainage, clean air, and other amenities. The cost of so doing depends on the number of people involved. Building water works and so on to cater for small towns is costly. Thus, the cost per head of urban services falls as the population agglomeration increases (Figure 9.2). In this respect, as with industrial production, a larger city is better than a smaller one.

Eventually, however, costs per head begin to rise. At what size of population agglomeration this happens depends on many things. The geography of the locality will determine costs of infrastructural extension. It may become necessary to carry water from a much more distant source. Building may begin to encroach on rich agricultural land. Air pollution may become more costly to control once a particular population density is reached. For these and other reasons the cost curve may begin to turn upward (Figure 9.2). There is a widespread tendency to believe that cities are becoming too big when these or other factors raise the costs of urban management. This is a mistake that fails to identify the cause of the problem.

Air pollution, water scarcities, blocked drains, and untreated sewage are all familiar experiences in the cities of Asia and Africa and widely deplored by the rich and poor alike who live in them. The immediate problem that underlies them is inadequate management by those who run the city. If the city can be regarded as an enterprise, then the managers should produce products and services that are in demand and, of course, charge the cost of

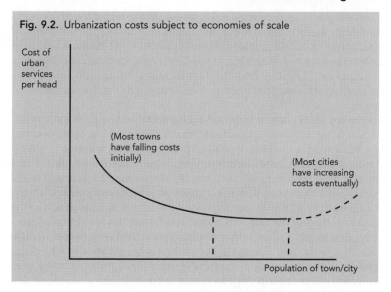

Fig. 9.2. Urbanization costs subject to economies of scale

Cost of
urban
services
per head

(Most towns
have falling costs
initially)

(Most cities
have increasing
costs eventually)

Population of town/city

so doing.[1] The users (sometimes called polluters if they are using clean water or air into which to discharge their wastes) should pay. To be fair, the rich should pay more than the poor but this is not of direct relevance to the current discussion.

The indirect effect of charging for the urban services may be a demographic one. If an industrial factory has to pay for the water it uses, then its unit costs will rise and it will pass on as many of these as it can in higher prices to the consumer. This may mean that the amount it can sell is limited so that it closes a factory. The demand for labour falls and the pool of unemployed rises. This should discourage migration for jobs and reduce direct recruitment from the rural areas. Similarly, if urban labourers have to pay for the cost of drinking water when previously they obtained it free, then they will seek a rise in wages to compensate. If this is achieved, the costs of industrialization increase again and labour demand decreases. Alternatively, those who are not employed in the wage labour sector or are unable to obtain an increase in wages, will suffer from their increased expenditure requirements and will cut back on other consumption. As we noted in Chapter 2, this may mean cutting back on food. Whether or not the people already in the town have the option of returning to rural areas or migrating to a new town where charges are less, further migration from outside will be discouraged. Indirectly, therefore, the rising cost of urban living has had demographic consequences. These have come about through the price or taxation system, not through direct migration controls.

As we discuss later, many migrants do not have the option of returning to their villages. In such circumstances, for the State to regard the city as a kind of refugee camp is fair. If the State is unable to improve the conditions of agriculture, it should provide incomes or work for the destitute who have arrived in the cities. It also has to pay for services for them. The necessary finances must be raised from the more fortunate through differential rates of taxation or through price discrimination (charging the rich more than the poor).

The key point is that it is the activity itself, like polluting the water or air, which is the problem that needs addressing. If the polluter is made to pay for the activity, economic or political pressure to limit it develops. Simply trying to limit the size of a city by controlling migration has no effect. Fewer people may come in to the city annually but they continue to add to the pollution until the city develops a major environmental problem. In any case, much of aggregate urban growth comes from natural growth of the residents themselves, not from migration (though this is not true of every city). One should also remember that factories in rural areas have done huge amounts of damage through pollution. Moreover, villagers in one village pollute the water that flows down to another. Epidemics of cholera have spread in recent times in this way. It is not urbanization or urban growth *per se* that is to blame for the misuse of public resources.

Rural-to-urban migration

The neo-classical approach

Towns and cities grow as a result of both natural increase and the inflow of migrants exceeding the outflow. Too much attention has been paid to migration and not sufficient to understanding the demographics of the natural increase component. However, it is time for us to turn to the debate on rural-to-urban migration. Many people believe that this migration is 'excessive', but such terminology merits some reservations. We have already pointed out that the 'excessive' use of urban resources is not directly the result of demographic factors.

The neo-classical school of economists is characterized by a belief in the predominance of human choice. They would analyse flows of migration in terms of the outcome of thousands of individual decisions to migrate and are less concerned by the processes that lead to these decisions, or by whether the decisions are taken under duress. The principal exponent of the neo-classical approach to migration has been Michael Todaro. He studied population movements in Kenya. Most migrants were heading for the city of Nairobi, which seemed odd to some observers as Nairobi had a serious unemployment problem. Few industrial or government service sector jobs were being created year by year and the waiting list for such employment was steadily rising. Why then did people continue to come into the city rather than continue to farm the land? Were their actions irrational?

Todaro revealed the logic in this behaviour. People correctly perceive that a huge gap exists between their average annual earnings as farmers (say $100) and what they would be paid in government service (say $300). They also perceive correctly that their chances of getting a job as a civil servant are slim. This can be expressed as a probability of success, say 30 per cent. Thus, the prospective migrant might reckon his chances of getting a clerical job in government service as roughly one in three. A 30 per cent chance of an income of $300 represents an 'expected' income of $0.3 \times \$300 = \$100$. As the prospective migrant's income from farming is $100 there may not be much point in changing jobs. If the government suddenly expands one of its departments, increasing the demand for clerical staff, then the chances of getting such a job might go up to one in two. This implies an expected income of $0.5 \times \$300 = \$150$. Clearly this is better than being a farmer and farmers would migrate to the city. If an individual turns out to be unlucky and does not get a job he will probably remain in the city for another chance. Only after waiting in vain for a year or two would he return to his village. During the waiting period he would effectively be added to the unemployed. Thus, there will always be more people in the city than government or industrial jobs but this does not mean that migrants are being irrational. Todaro went on to make this model rather more realistic. He appreciated that migrants waiting for jobs do not necessarily remain totally unemployed. They usually find some work that gives them a little money to survive on while waiting around in the city. Figure 9.3 shows how the model developed to allow for this and other considerations.

Although it did not say so explicitly, this theory seemed to imply that all potential migrants were very much alike. They all faced roughly the same probabilities of getting government or industrial jobs. This meant that one could foresee what would happen in response to the creation of a specific number of new jobs: more migrants would come in and unemployment would go up by a predictable amount. This was thought to have important policy implications for both Kenya in particular and developing countries in general. One of these is that preventing the growth of income differentials between rural and urban areas is desirable. In the short run this was thought to imply curbing urban trade union wage demands. In the long run, it requires investment in rural areas to raise productivity and incomes there.

The reader will notice that this is a rather different interpretation from that offered by Marxist analysis, to which we referred earlier. The previous discussion assumed that industrialists and capitalist governments favour the creation of a pool of labour that was either unemployed or engaged in poorly remunerated activities, as this serves to keep wages down and to inhibit the formation of trade unions (which find it much easier to operate in large organized enterprises). To Marx it would not have made sense to think of governments seeking ways to eliminate unemployment. The prob-

Fig. 9.3. The Todaro migration model in outline

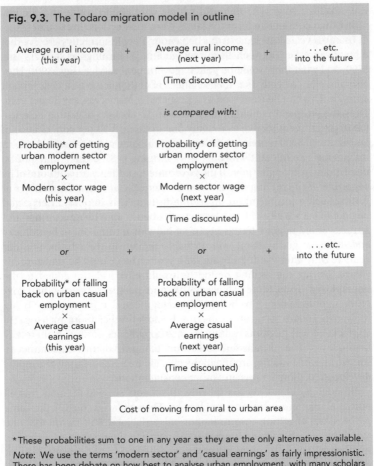

| Average rural income (this year) | + | Average rural income (next year) | | + | . . . etc. into the future |
| | | (Time discounted) | | | |

is compared with:

| Probability* of getting urban modern sector employment × Modern sector wage (this year) | | Probability* of getting urban modern sector employment × Modern sector wage (next year) |
| | | (Time discounted) |

| *or* | + | *or* | + | . . . etc. into the future |

| Probability* of falling back on urban casual employment × Average casual earnings (this year) | | Probability* of falling back on urban casual employment × Average casual earnings (next year) |
| | | (Time discounted) |

−

| Cost of moving from rural to urban area |

*These probabilities sum to one in any year as they are the only alternatives available.

Note: We use the terms 'modern sector' and 'casual earnings' as fairly impressionistic. There has been debate on how best to analyse urban employment, with many scholars using the terms 'formal' and 'informal' instead. Time discounting means that estimates that lie further into the future are given diminishing importance in the calculation.

lem that Todaro sought to explain would not be regarded as a problem at all, at least not for the capitalist State.

Researchers in both Africa and Asia have objected to Todaro's way of looking at things. They point out that in practice the chances of getting a job differed substantially from person to person for reasons that were social rather than random. People with 'the right connections' have a much better chance of getting a government job than those without. People from a particular caste or tribe might enjoy a high probability of a job in government or industry; those from another caste or tribe might have virtually no chance of one. Although some advantage is obtained from having a good education, rigidities of a social and cultural nature remain that favour some social groups over others. In India, for example, industrial employers used to go around the villages recruiting labour. Migrants who left for the city knew they had a job awaiting them: the probability of getting a job was therefore close to one. At the same time, landless labourers finding themselves with less and less work (perhaps because of mechanization or through the bringing in of labour from outside the village) would look toward the city as a provider of sustenance, even if they had to labour as porters or street sweepers all their lives. Being of low caste they might believe correctly that their chance of getting a good job in a big industry was close to zero. Nevertheless, their expected income from small jobs in the city was better than half-starving as an underemployed agricultural labourer. In Kenya itself, where Todaro was working, the Luo and the Kikuyu did not face the same chances of obtaining employment in government service, precisely because one tribe had better 'connections' than the other.

There continues to be a great deal of research into how much social mobility there is in the cities of the developing world. Most studies suggest that people do not move on from casual work in trades and services to employment in government or industry within a couple of years of arrival in the city, as Todaro seemed to suggest.

The simple neo-classical model was not intended to incorporate non-economic factors that also determine whether migration takes place or not. As we go on to discuss, demographers are interested in the implications of migration for subsequent urban growth. This depends largely on the sex composition of migration streams. In practice, many women migrate to urban areas along with their husbands. Some migrate to join husbands already established in the city. Others may be brought into the city to marry young men already there (whether themselves migrants or not). Much female migration is related to marriage and has a mixture of social and economic determinants.

Women who migrate as part of a family unit may end up entering the labour market after they reach the city. What made it economically feasible to migrate, however, may have been the provision of family accommodation by the employer to their husbands. Industries that are eager to keep their work-forces, perhaps because they have invested heavily in their training, are more likely to provide such accommodation (subsidized at the employer's expense). In such circumstances, therefore, to assume that the female migrants had moved in response to employment opportunities would be wrong.

The freedom of women to migrate is conditioned strongly by social acceptability. Generally it has been unacceptable in Hindu and Muslim cultures for young women to migrate alone in search of employment. The decision to migrate does not rest with the woman as family elders can prohibit (in this case) their daughters from moving. In other societies migration of single women is acceptable. In Japan, for example, women made up nearly 80 per cent of the labour force in the textile industry in the early twentieth century. Most of these women were unmarried migrants who lived in dormitories in the cities. In Southern Africa nowadays, women migrate to the urban centres to work as domestic labour for middle-class families. When their husbands migrated to work in the South African mines, they stayed behind to provide the agricultural labour. With more migration to Black African cities and less to the mines, the pattern and extent of female migration has changed. Just as the family may prohibit some of its members from migrating, it may also put considerable pressure on some of its members to migrate against their will. The family head may force women to go out and supplement the household income: it may not be their own choice. Similarly, the eldest son may be told to seek work in the city to finance specific requirements of the household, especially the education of the younger children.

The very idea of a 'choice' to migrate becomes questionable when a whole family unit is in economic distress. The extreme of famine, discussed in Chapter 5, is a case in point. Yet famine apart, day by day some households find themselves increasingly in debt. Having sold all they have, they are left with no option but to migrate (assuming the local landowner does not wish to retain their services through some kind of bonded labour). In such circumstances, urban incomes and the chances of urban jobs scarcely enter the equation. Migration is a matter of survival and destitution in the countryside is no more favourable (usually less) than destitution in the city. Studies in northern India have shown that those villages that have the greatest rate of out-migration are those where the inequality of land distribution is also greatest.

From these few examples it can be seen that several different types of migration exist, with differing demographic characteristics. Some migrant flows consist of young men alone. Others comprise young men and young women—perhaps with the latter following the former only after a time lag. In yet others, couples migrate with their young children. Finally, in cases of distress, whole households may move, including the aged—though the latter may fail to survive the journey.

The measurement of migration is important, so as to identify the main source of urban growth and enable us to discover where migrants come from. Unfortunately, information on migration is not easy to obtain. Ideally, one wants to count people who are on the move. Designing a survey that would achieve this is almost impossible. Few countries maintain a registration system of migrants within their national borders and those that do so have great difficulty in ensuring that it is a complete record. In countries where migration to cities is supposedly restricted, a substantial amount of illegal migration takes place. Thus, probably the only reliable record on migration is obtained from those decennial censuses that include a question on the recent movement of people into the present locality. As the census usually collects information on the age and sex of everyone, including recent migrants, it is possible to compare the demographic characteristics of migration streams to different localities (or those from different localities). If a record can be compiled from the census data of people who moved into a city within the last year, an approximate measure of current migration can be obtained and expressed as a rate by dividing by the population total obtained at the census. This is called the *gross in-migration rate*

BOX 9.1. MEASURES OF MIGRATION

Let us start with the following definitions:

P = the population of the region experiencing migration. (Strictly this should be counted mid-year, though for some purposes it may be necessary, or even desirable, to count or estimate the population at the start of the year.)

M = number of migrants into the region in one year.

E = number of migrants out of the region in one year.

O = population with the characteristic of having been born outside the region.

Then:

the in-migration rate is: M/P,

the out-migration rate is: E/P,

the net migration rate is: $(M-E)/P$, and

the proportion ever-migrated is: O/P.

If the region is a national entity, the terms immigration (for M) and emigration (for E) are customary.

From a strictly demographic point of view the growth of a region is defined as:

$$R = B - D + (M - E),$$

where B = births and D = deaths. This assumes that the boundaries of the region have not altered. In fact, the growth of a town between two censuses is often:

$$R = B - D + (M - E) + T,$$

where T is the population transferred to the town by enlarging its official boundary to incorporate neighbouring populations. This may be simply a nuisance (if boundaries are enlarged arbitrarily). Alternatively, it may indicate genuine growth in the population of the town during the decade, with migrants settling just outside the existing boundary. The geographer, economist, and demographer have to exercise judgement together in describing the components of urban growth in such cases.

(see Box 9.1 for details). It is at best a crude measure, not only because people may forget precisely when they made the move or simply may not wish to reveal their migrant status, but also because of a methodological problem. People who set off to come to the city within the year, but who died *en route*—not an unusual occurrence in time of drought or famine— are not included in the count of migrants because they never arrived in the city to be counted.

A structural approach

The models we have just described refer to a very limited period. They do not place migration in the context of long-term economic change and development. This section attempts to do this.

The main differences between feudal and capitalist agricultural systems are outlined in Chapter 1. Labour is not very mobile in feudal systems. It tends to be tied to the land on which it works. For example, sharecropping allows tenant farmers to claim a share of the food they grow but requires them to remain on the land to undertake work demanded by the landlord. Necessities like clothing and cooking utensils are obtained locally from cottage industries. Very little cash enters the economic system or is obtained as a return for labour. Most remuneration is in kind. All this restricts mobility. It is true that some pre-capitalist modes of production, such as pastoralism, do entail physical movement, but not to towns or cities.

It is only when capitalist relations of production become established that labour is both free and required to move. Labour is needed on large farms only seasonally and is paid for specific jobs like harvesting. For the rest of the time workers are free to migrate. Farm workers are paid largely in cash: so they have the means to migrate and establish themselves in an urban economic environment. It is not only large farms that need wage labour. Plantations and mines are generally run on capitalistic lines. The major movements of male labour in Southern Africa have been in response to the demand for labour in the mining industry.[2]

The development of manufacturing industry along capitalistic lines has been chiefly responsible for rural-to-urban labour migration. Economic historians like Arthur Lewis, writing about West Africa, regard this process as the major determinant of a shift in the structure of the labour force, from being predominantly in the primary sector (e.g., agriculture) to being predominantly in the secondary and tertiary sectors (i.e., manufacturing and services). When he was writing, West African farms tended to be small-scale and owner operated (a characteristic that remains to some extent true). Rural capitalism had not developed very far, though the crop produced was often a commercial one such as cocoa. Family labour was free to move, however, and some young men were encouraged to do so. With increased investment in industry, the marginal product of labour increases (i.e., the

Fig. 9.4. The dual-economy model of migration

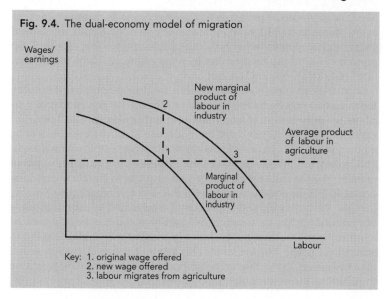

Key: 1. original wage offered
2. new wage offered
3. labour migrates from agriculture

curve shifts outwards—see Figure 9.4). This enables industrialists to offer higher wages than the average product of labour in agriculture. This in turn attracts labour off the land.

Classical economists like Arthur Lewis thought that this process would continue until all 'surplus labour' was removed from agriculture. In other words, all labourers whose marginal product was less than what they consumed (assumed to be equal to the average product) would leave farming. After that, the analysis becomes more complicated as average product, and hence average income, begins to rise in agriculture as well as in industry. Marxist economists, on the other hand, have not regarded surplus labour in agriculture as a static quantity waiting to be drained away into industry. They see the creation of unemployed labour in rural areas as a direct result of the process of capitalist farming. As farmers accumulate land, they drive off the tenanted labour, turning it into wage labour employed only where and when the need arises. Surplus labour is a relative concept in that it only exists because of this process. Moreover, no reason exists why it should disappear as capitalist farming becomes more widespread. Whether one follows the approach of Lewis or Marx, the outcome is similar. Labour, and therefore population, transfers from rural to urban locations as part of a process of capitalist development. This is necessary to the system. It is not the outcome of incidental choices about where to live.

This is a simplified exposition of various schools of thought. We have said nothing about where the food comes from to feed the labourers who have left the land. Clearly, unless a surplus of food (or something to exchange for imported food) can be produced this process cannot be pursued. To some extent, the surplus that can be made available from agriculture will depend on the rate of population growth in agriculture also. This aspect of the process has been explored further by other economists who have elaborated such 'dual economy' models.

An interesting attempt was made to link the demographic transition with the migration process by the geographer Zelinsky. He argued that surplus labour in agriculture arose largely because of the fall in the death rate. The large rise in natural increase that resulted meant that, whatever the existing mode of production, large amounts of labour became surplus in rural areas. This led to a drift toward the towns. He claims that in practice the onset of mortality decline and acceleration in rural-to-urban migration were coincidental. In fact the empirical evidence is less easy to establish than Zelinsky thought. We have argued that periods of acceleration in natural increase occurred long before the demographic transition, but that they did not lead to urbanization. Only careful analysis of particular cases could establish to what extent labour became surplus because of eviction of tenants, rather than because of an increase in the proportion of the population to survive from birth to the working ages.

Migration in southern Africa

International migration within southern Africa has colonial origins. The mining companies of South Africa, engaged in the exploitation of gold and diamonds, needed huge amounts of labour. Whether or not sufficient cheap labour could have been found within South Africa itself, migrant labour from other countries was always favoured. Temporary international migrants have the advantage of docility resulting from their relative insecurity in a foreign land. They are often prepared to put in large amounts of work for a relatively low income. Their wages represent a considerable improvement over what they could hope to earn in subsistence agriculture and enable the migrants to meet expenditures relating to marriage or education that they could otherwise not cover. The demographic character of such migrations is male and young. Women stay in the home country, working on the land and for the household, along with their children and aged dependants.

Although this pattern of international migration lasted for half a century, by the 1980s some changes could be observed. For political reasons, the Republic of South Africa was increasingly recruiting labour from its own rural black population. This partly displaced the international migrants just described. At the same time, the demand for labour had risen in the countries that used to supply the international labour. In particular, after independence, Botswana and Zimbabwe began to develop urban centres requiring labour and to attract migrants to these instead. Here the migrants comprise both men and women, though the movements still have a temporary (or 'circular') character. Migration to the South African towns had also become increasingly female. The predominant occupation of women is as unskilled workers in the service sector, especially as domestic servants for the growing middle class. In this respect there are similarities with the more developed urban regions of Latin America.

The economic implications of international migration are important. When large numbers of men work abroad, useful earnings may flow into their home economy. Equally, however, a serious strain is put on agricultural production. In particular, specific types of labour become short and those left behind cannot immediately become adequate substitutes. For example, men are needed to plough the fields and women do not usually herd cattle in southern Africa. We will come across a similar situation in Chapter 10 when we discuss migrations from east to west Asia. To help fill the labour gap, children are removed from school. This has damaging effects on the long-run development of the economy. As we have noted, however, there are specific reasons why cash from such migration is useful. Nowadays, a cash income may be necessary to ensure that there is continuing agricultural activity on the land over which a household lays claim: otherwise its right to that land may not be secured.

Circular migration in southern Africa also has indirect implications for both fertility and mortality. The poor conditions of employment in the mines used to lead to appallingly high levels of mortality and widowhood in the countries of the migrants' origin. In the past this was probably sufficient to lower fertility below what would have occurred had the migrants stayed at home. Improving health conditions in the mines, as company owners felt the need to invest more in the quality of their labour, have reduced the excess mortality of miners. However, the fact of separation itself has a similar, if more temporary, effect of reducing fertility. It has been estimated that some six months may be added to birth intervals by a typical history of spousal separation. Such separations are also implicated in marital breakdowns—in themselves a tragedy and one that again causes a reduction in fertility. Furthermore, migration and its attendant absences from home have been associated throughout the century with an elevated incidence of sexually transmitted diseases. After the advent of penicillin and other drugs in the 1940s, these diseases were less often fatal, but their effect on sterility, and so fertility, is evident in relatively low fertility levels in the past. These rose in the 1960s and beyond. More recently, sexually transmitted diseases have come to include AIDS, which again has no cure at the moment. This is raising mortality again. As we argued at the start of the chapter, migration exposes migrants to new environments and may itself produce new demographic regimes.

The demography and evolution of industrial towns

Clearly, the demography of individual towns and cities has several components but reflecting on this statement for a moment might be useful. First, what are the components of the crude growth rate of a town? They are the crude birth rate, the crude death rate, the gross in-migration rate and the gross out-migration rate (see Figure 9.5). What then are the components that make up the crude birth rate, this being in many ways the most complex of the four factors in urban growth? They are the population married by age, marital fertility, and the age composition of the urban population. Unlike rural localities, towns are usually subject to substantial net in-

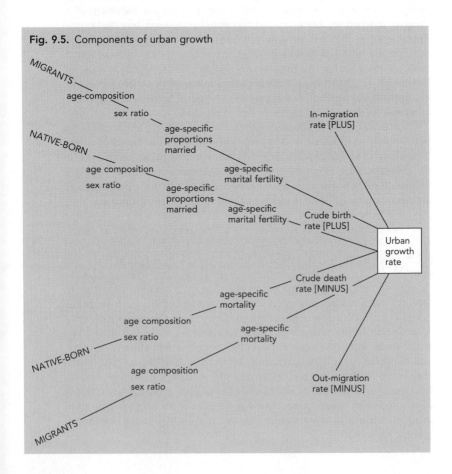

Fig. 9.5. Components of urban growth

migration. The different patterns of migration that we have already discussed are themselves important determinants of the three components of the crude birth rate. Thus, the pattern of growth in towns differs from most national populations and many rural populations.

The age and sex distribution of in-migrants can affect the propensity to marry. If migration differs between the sexes, fewer marriages will take place within the urban population. Migration by young people may slow the rate of marriage formation in a country as a whole. Secondly, marital fertility is likely to be lower if individuals of either sex migrate rather than couples. This is true even if married individuals migrate, because the separation of spouses can significantly lower fertility. A. F. Weber, a statistician who wrote with insight on the demographic characteristics of urban areas in America and Europe at the end of the nineteenth century, was not impressed by the prospect of unbalanced sex ratios in towns: 'Wherever there exists a considerable preponderance of one sex over the other, in point of numbers, there is less prospect of a well-ordered social life.' The third way in which migration may affect the birth rates in cities is through its influence on the age composition. If migrants tend to be young adults, the age composition is tilted in favour of high birth rates because there are a lot of births when there are many potential mothers in a population even if each woman has only two children. Areas that are subject to heavy in-migration of women aged 15 to 49 years therefore have a higher birth rate than populations with a more regular age distribution (i.e., closer to stability). It follows from this that we cannot compare two localities by comparing their crude birth rates. If the data are available, we need to compare the total fertility rates (see Box 2.3). Alternatively, we need to find some way of standardizing for the effect of the age composition (see Box 6.1). Again Weber has an intriguing sociological comment, followed by a sober demographic observation:

As a result of the presence of a relatively large number of persons in the active period of life in urban populations, one would expect city life to be easier and more animated, the productive classes being large and having a smaller burden to bear in support of the unproductive classes. One would also expect to find more energy and enterprise in cities, more radicalism, less conservatism, more vice, crime and impulsiveness generally. Birth rates should be high in cities and death rates low, on account of age grouping [i.e. age composition].

It should be apparent by now that cities can develop very different demographic characteristics depending on the predominant nature of their migration streams. We have described how the demography of these streams is conditioned by social and cultural factors. It is also possible to link the demographic characteristics of towns to their economic characteristics or functions. This is particularly easy to illustrate empirically if a town has a predominant economic function or industrial character, rather than a mixture of many. While most towns have a mixture of functions, a few regularly occurring types exist. Popular terminology suggests this: towns are known as 'textile towns' or 'steel towns', 'mining towns' or 'market towns'. In addition, 'holiday resorts' and 'retirement towns' are familiar in the more developed countries.

Let us refer to a few industrial types of towns. Early modern industrialization developing on capitalist lines usually involves light industrial manufacture, like food processing or textile spinning and weaving. In many societies, textile manufactures employ women as well as men. Thus, the textile industry produces manufacturing towns having a predominance of young people but with no predominance of one sex over the other. If the town continues to grow through steady additions to its stock of factories, the age structure will look not unlike that of the rural hinterland, except that it will lack old people for some time.

Many countries in Asia, however, embarked on a different industrialization strategy, especially soon after they gained independence from the colonial powers. The aim was partly to ensure self-sufficiency by the local production of the inputs required for growth of the factory sector and its attendant infrastructure. This involved the setting up of heavy industry such as iron and steel manufacturing. These industries are subject to huge economies of scale. The more steel produced in a single plant, the cheaper it is to produce it per tonne.[3] When such plants are first set up, large numbers of young adult migrants are recruited to run them. Usually they are predominantly male. After some time families are formed, either through the men bringing in women to marry, who subsequently bear children, or through their bringing in, from their place of origin, their wives and children already born to them. The age and sex structure of the town usually changes dramatically in a short time therefore—more dramatically than in light industrial towns.

Mining towns, on the other hand, may never achieve a balanced sex ratio if they are regarded as dormitories. In such cases the migrants tend to return home at regular intervals and may never settle permanently in the town. They will be replaced by young men of a new generation. The age structure of such towns always remains dominated by young men.

The age and sex structure of a town reveals something about its social character and even something of its industrial character. It is an important component in our understanding of what the town is like. The demographic structure may also tell us something of the history of the town. The best way to visualize these contrasting demographic scenarios is to look at the population pyramids for localities. They often differ quite dramatically one from another. The national age distribution is an average of these (a weighted average). We show a few representative types of urban age distribution from Indian data in Figure 9.6. Box 9.2 explains how to prepare such pyramids correctly if the data have been tabulated by age groups of varying length, which is a common occurrence in the preparation of tables in order to save space.

Fig. 9.6. Contrasting urban age distributions in India

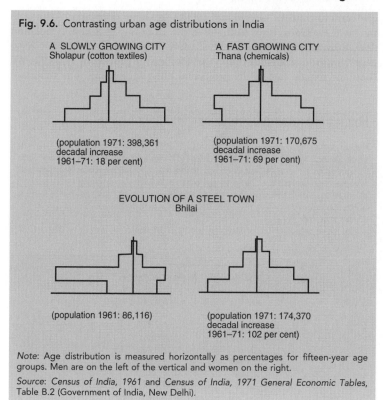

A SLOWLY GROWING CITY
Sholapur (cotton textiles)

(population 1971: 398,361
decadal increase
1961–71: 18 per cent)

A FAST GROWING CITY
Thana (chemicals)

(population 1971: 170,675
decadal increase
1961–71: 69 per cent)

EVOLUTION OF A STEEL TOWN
Bhilai

(population 1961: 86,116)

(population 1971: 174,370
decadal increase
1961–71: 102 per cent)

Note: Age distribution is measured horizontally as percentages for fifteen-year age groups. Men are on the left of the vertical and women on the right.

Source: Census of India, 1961 and *Census of India, 1971 General Economic Tables,* Table B.2 (Government of India, New Delhi).

The first thing to observe about the urban age distributions shown in Figure 9.6 is that they lack symmetry. The second thing that is clear is that they can change greatly over time. Both these observations are evidence that urban populations are a long way from being stable in the demographic sense. The reader will recall that a stable population is one that is subject to unchanging mortality and fertility and is unaffected by migration. Under these conditions the growth rate remains constant. So does the age structure of the population. The population pyramid that results has a symmetry and regularity that differs from what we usually observe for towns and cities. The most common characteristic of a city's age pyramid is a tendency to bulge on the male side at the young adult ages. The direct cause of this is in-migration and this is the major reason that such populations are not stable.

Populations tend to re-establish stability even if they have been subject to some destabilizing shock, such as an inflow of migrants, in the past. Intuitively this is not difficult to imagine. Migrants eventually form families and give birth to children, get old and die like any other population. With time the town re-creates itself naturally in the same way as a rural population does. Proving this mathematically is more difficult and we shall not do so here. However, as an illustration we simulate the process in Table 9.1. We show the female side of the projection only. At the start, one thousand

BOX 9.2. POPULATION PYRAMIDS

A population 'pyramid' is really a form of histogram. While the latter present ages (or age groups) along the horizontal axis and numbers or proportions (frequencies or relative frequencies) up the vertical axis, population pyramids reverse this convention. The only problem that arises in drawing these graphs is what to do if the age interval changes from, say, five years to ten. A particular instance of this problem occurs in all population pyramids at the top of the age range.

Consider the data in Table A for a city of 75,000.

Table A

Age group	Male population
0–4	6,784
5–9	5,986
10–14	4,788
15–19	4,088
20–24	3,990
25–34	6,386
35–44	4,388
45–54	2,792
55+	798
Total	40,000

One calculates the proportional distribution by dividing the male population in each age group by the total population of both sexes. For example, for the 0–4 age group:

$$6,784 \div 75,000 = 0.090.$$

This gives us a complete proportional distribution. However, when drawing a histogram one should take a standard interval and keep to it. Select the smallest interval for which data are available. Here, this interval is five years and we adjust the population numbers (and their proportions) for which we have data on ten-year intervals. For the 25–34 year age group:

$$6,386 \div 75,000 = 0.085,$$

and the adjustment is:

$$0.085 \div 2 = 0.042.$$

Generally, if the standard interval is i and a particular interval is n, adjust the population in an age group (or its proportion) P as follows:

$$P \div n/i.$$

BOX 9.2. continued

When the data are tabulated with an open-ended interval such as 55+ years, it has to be closed arbitrarily, say at age 75. This makes the last interval twenty years, which is four times the standard width. So, divide the last number, 798 (or its proportion), by four. Deciding the age at which to close a pyramid involves judgement: if one chooses too high an age (e.g., 100 years), it produces an elongated space-wasting pyramid; if one chooses too low an age (e.g., 60 years), it will produce a curious 'hat' on the top of the pyramid (which is worse, since it is unlikely that everyone died by the age of 60).

Table B

Age group	Proportion in age group	Adjusted proportion in the age group
0–4	0.0904	same
5–9	0.0798	same
10–14	0.0638	same
15–19	0.0545	same
20–24	0.0532	same
25–34	0.0851	0.0425
35–44	0.0585	0.0292
45–54	0.0372	0.0186
55+	0.0106	0.0026 (closed at 75)
Total	0.5331	

The male population is slightly over half the total and the male half of the standardized pyramid looks like this:

Figure A.

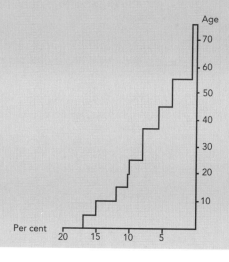

Table 9.1. Simulation of convergence of a migrant population on a stable age distribution

Age	0	10	20	30	40	50	60	70	80	90	100
0–4	0	341	224	156	244	219	198	221	216	209	216
5–9	0	177	269	137	176	210	171	181	191	181	183
10–14	0	0	281	184	129	201	180	163	182	178	172
15–19	1,000	0	162	245	125	160	192	156	165	175	165
20–24	0	0	0	253	166	116	181	162	146	164	160
25–29	0	879	0	142	216	112	141	169	137	145	153
30–34	0	0	0	0	218	143	100	156	140	126	141
35–39	0	0	744	0	120	182	93	119	143	116	123
40–44	0	0	0	0	0	181	119	83	130	116	105
45–49	0	0	0	609	0	99	150	76	98	117	95
50–54	0	0	0	0	0	0	144	95	66	103	93
55–59	0	0	0	0	459	0	74	113	57	74	88
60–64	0	0	0	0	0	0	0	99	65	45	71
65–69	0	0	0	0	0	270	0	44	66	34	43
70–74	0	0	0	0	0	0	0	0	47	31	21
75–79	0	0	0	0	0	0	92	0	15	23	11
80+	0	0	0	0	0	0	0	10	1	10	9

women migrate and form a new town. Ten years later they have married and borne children, as well as ageing in the process. Twenty years later the children have grown up and some of them have started bearing children. So the demographic process goes on. Without any further change (age-specific fertility and mortality being held constant and no more migration occurring), this population begins to undergo the demographic evolution that establishes the stable population. One hundred years after the initial migration, the age distribution has become reasonably constant, year after year.

To carry out this simulation, we have to convert age-specific mortality rates calculated from data obtained from a vital (birth and death) registration system into *survival ratios*. Box 9.3 shows how this is done and hence how a *life table* is constructed. This is a concept that lies at the heart of demographic analysis. Life tables are an essential input into population projections as shown in Chapter 10. The simulation in Table 9.1 made a point but in practice towns do not become so isolated after the initial migration inflow as the example presented there. They continue to attract further migrants, though the scale of subsequent migrations may be small in comparison with those in the first few years if, as in our simulation, the industry was established initially on a greenfield site. Thus, urban populations continue to be unstable in the demographic sense.

The age structure of an urban area has social and economic implications no less important than those national age structures. The case of the heavy industrial town raises questions about future employment potential. If families are formed in such new towns, the lower end of the age pyramid fills rapidly, as sons and daughters are born to the original migrants. Some fifteen years after the initial migrants arrive, a second generation needs employment. The problem with heavy industry from this point of view is that a steady increase in new investment and jobs does not usually occur. Major new investments are made all in one go. There follows a time lag before any increase in capacity is laid down. The investment cycle does not coincide neatly with the human reproductive cycle: or it is pure chance if it does. In theory, the second generation 'problem' can be solved by the sons and daughters of the migrants migrating out to another urban area. In practice, people are not as mobile as this.

The fortunes of particular towns rise and fall along with their industries. An industry may lose its competitive advantage. For instance, if labour costs rise, exports of textiles will fall as countries with cheaper labour take over the market. Alternatively, a raw material, like offshore fish stocks or a seam of iron ore, is exhausted. Either a new location is opened up to replace the old one or the country may lose the industry altogether, as imports become cheaper than domestic production. Such change and flexibility may be to the national advantage but their local impact can be painful. The rest of the local population often depends on the core industrial work-force demanding services and consumer goods. Thus, the failure of an industry is magnified through a negative multiplier (as we noted in the context of famine in

BOX 9.3. LIFE TABLES

A life table shows the proportion of the population that can be expected to survive from one age to the next, or more usually from one age group to the next (this is the abridged life table). Obviously this information is invaluable for making population projections from one year to the next (or for five years ahead). It has other uses also, but most of these fall outside the scope of this book.

The raw data for construction of a life table consist of registered mortality rates according to age and sex of the deceased. It is mentioned in the main body of the text that these data can be incomplete and inaccurate and that models are often constructed for use in projections. For the moment, however, assume that the data are available.

Look at the diagram presented as Figure A.

Figure A.

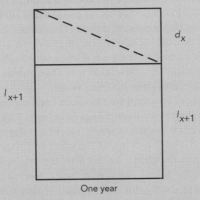

One year

The number alive at the beginning of the year is l_x and the number alive at the end of it is l_{x+1}. The number that die is d_x. The subscripts are added to indicate the age to which the measures refer. For example, l_2 is the number alive on their second birthday and d_2 refers to deaths between the second birthday and the third birthday. Assume that deaths are distributed evenly throughout the year, so that the number surviving declines arithmetically (a straight line with a constant negative slope as drawn above). The proportion of those alive at the start of the year who die during it (termed q_x) is calculated as follows:

$$q_x = \frac{d_x}{l_x}.$$

Looking at Figure A, we can see that the age-specific mortality rate i.e. the number of deaths during that year divided by the population estimated at the mid-point, in each case referring to age x, is:

$$m_x = \frac{d_x}{l_x - 0.5d_x}.$$

BOX 9.3. continued

Substituting this expression for m_x:

$$\frac{m_x}{1+0.5m_x} = \frac{\dfrac{d_x}{l_x - 0.5d_x}}{1 + 0.5\dfrac{d_x}{l_x - 0.5d_x}}.$$

The right-hand side simplifies to:

$$\frac{d_x}{l_x} = q_x.$$

Thus, proportions dying can be calculated from the mortality rates:

$$q_x = \frac{m_x}{1 + 0.5m_x}$$

where m_x is the age-specific mortality rate at age x.

Raw registration data and a census count can supply all the information that is needed. Having calculated q_x, the proportion surviving over the year from the start, p_x, is:

$$P_x = 1 - q_x.$$

Until now it has been assumed that the period in question is one year but in abridged life tables it is usually five years. Demographers represent this with a second subscript before the p or q, for example $_5p_{10}$ is the probability of surviving from one's tenth birthday to one's fifteenth birthday. It has also been assumed that deaths are distributed evenly throughout the period in question. This is empirically valid except for the early years of life, where constructing the life table from data for single years of age is important.

Now we can build up a life table. One usually starts for convenience with a round number of births, say 100,000, and obtains the proportions surviving and the number alive at each exact age following birth (l_x). Note that by exact age we mean the number who reach their 'xth' birthday. Hence l_5 represents the number who live to their fifth birthday. Abridged life tables usually include the values of l_x at five-year intervals, but they also include l_1 since mortality in the first year of life is relatively high and the infant mortality rate is identical to q_0 (see Box 2.2). For some purposes l_2 is also used.

The life table might start as follows:

$$
\begin{aligned}
l_0 &= & 100{,}000, \\
l_1 &= l_0 \times p_0 &= 88{,}169, \\
l_5 &= l_1 \times {_4}p_1 &= 81{,}848, \\
l_{10} &= l_5 \times {_5}p_5 &= 80{,}100, \\
l_{15} &= l_{10} \times {_5}p_{10} &= 78{,}771, \text{ and so on.}
\end{aligned}
$$

Projections require data in five-year age groups as this is the way that the census usually reports the population to be projected forward. The l_x's are converted to an approximation of the number of people from our original 100,000 who are alive between the ages x and $x + n$ as follows. Take, for

BOX 9.3. continued

example, the number alive between exact age 5 and exact age 10. This is approximately equal to:

$$\frac{l_5 + l_{10}}{2} \times 5.$$

In the example considered here this comes to:

$$\frac{81,848 + 80,100}{2} \times 5 = 404,870.$$

The same procedure can be adopted for each age group. For example the number alive between exact ages 10 and 15 years is calculated as:

$$\frac{80,100 + 78,771}{2} \times 5 = 397,178.$$

Another way of looking at these numbers is to think of them as person-years lived by the original 100,000 between these birthdays (which are five years apart). It is less than 500,000 because of mortality, which has reduced the original 100,000 to about 80,000 by their tenth birthday and to even less by their fifteenth.

These persons alive are symbolized as $_nL_x$. The subscripts refer to years lived after exact age x for a duration of n years. In our example:

$$_5L_5 = 404,870 \text{ and}$$
$$_5L_{10} = 397,178.$$

The same procedure can be repeated down the life table.

Two qualifications are necessary:

- Simple averaging like this is inadequate at the start of the life table since the steep decline from very high levels of mortality in infancy is not even approximately linear. A weighted average is used instead for the numbers alive both at 0–1 years and at 1–4 years. One suggested weighting scheme (due to Reed and Merrell) is:

$$_1L_0 = 0.276l_0 + 0.724l_1, \text{ and}$$
$$_4L_1 = 0.034l_0 + 1.184l_1 + 2.782l_5.$$

- At the end of the life table, finish off as follows:

$$_\infty L_x = l_x / _\infty m_x,$$

where x is the oldest age, and $_\infty m_x$ represents the mortality rate for the oldest age group, for example 75 years and above. If necessary, this final death rate can be estimated as follows. If the oldest person dies at age w, assuming a linear decline in the cohort's size (in this case from l_x to 0 between x and w), person-years lived between x and w are $0.5l_x(w - x)$. Therefore:

$$_wm_x = \frac{l_x}{\dfrac{l_x(w-x)}{2}} = \frac{2}{w-x}.$$

BOX 9.3. continued

The last life table function the construction of which we discuss here is the survival ratio. It is used in projections. The ratio measures the proportion of the population in one age group, say x to $x + n$ years, that are alive n years later in age group $x + n$ to $x + 2n$. The survival ratio column in the life table is obtained by dividing each $_nL_x$ value by the previous $_nL_x$ value as follows:

$$_nL_{x+n} / {_nL_x}.$$

Thus, in our example, the proportion surviving from the age group 5–9 to become 10–14 years is:

$$\frac{_5L_{10}}{_5L_5} = \frac{397,178}{404,870} = 0.9810.$$

This survival ratio can now be used to project the population aged 5–9 years five years into the future. The procedure is explained in Box 10.1, which presents an example of an abridged life table that includes all the important life table functions.

Chapter 5). If the population ages and is not replaced by new migrants but loses its young people through out-migration, the dependency ratio goes up. The old people may rely on remittances into the town from sons and daughters working elsewhere. This can be a precarious position in a poor country. Furthermore, if the town's services were financed from local taxes, then the tax base is eroded through the departure of business and the exodus of the productive work-force. It is little exaggeration to say that closing down an industry can mean closing down a town.

Policies exist to address this predicament. Even capitalist States, anxious to avoid the economic and social costs of chronic unemployment, have tried to attract new investment into such localities by subsidizing their capital costs. In some countries, like Japan, whole work-forces have been offered to expanding industries to avoid redundancies. For political and economic reasons, some governments have nationalized declining industries to keep them alive through heavy subsidies. All such measures have a cost but alleviate some pain. The question in each case is what is the optimal solution.

This section concentrates on the urban age structure and its determination through migration and births. Still, just as towns differ in their birth rates, so they differ too in their death rates. Again these have two components: age structure and age-specific mortality. In historical Europe the latter used to be higher in urban than in rural localities. That is no longer the case in the developing world. One reason for this is the rise of modern curative medicine. This is provided by individual doctors, clinics, pharmacies, and hospitals. All of these are easier to reach in urban than in rural areas. Moreover, their services are widely known among urban populations, including the poor. Seeing doctors' surgeries in slum areas is no longer unusual. Another reason for lower urban mortality is access to food. In countries where malnutrition is still a cause of death, urban localities offer better access to food scraps or charitable handouts than villages. Furthermore, environmental conditions are often no better in villages than in towns. Water is as likely to be contaminated by bacteria and viruses carrying cholera and other diarrhoeal diseases, breeding grounds for malarious mosquitoes abound, and tetanus is often present in the soil. On the other hand, air pollution will usually be less severe in the countryside, although air quality within badly ventilated dwellings may be poor.

Mortality differs from town to town depending on, among other things, the class composition of different localities. Metropolitan cities with a large professional and managerial class often have light mortality. New towns, planned from scratch to accommodate the workers in a newly established heavy industry also often have low mortality, even though the population is predominantly working class. The highest mortality probably occurs in older (and sometimes smaller) towns, with less productive industries, a population experiencing stagnant or declining income, and decrepit social infrastructure. In addition, market towns may lack the economic advantages of industrialization but suffer all the disadvantages of congestion. It should be apparent that one needs to compare similar income strata in order to interpret the effect of different environmental conditions on the health of the people. The lowest income groups in cities sometimes endure appallingly high mortality, comparable with that of similar economic groups in the countryside. More often their mortality rates are lighter—at least where data allow one to make such comparisons (see Table 9.2).

Mortality differentials within cities are striking. The upper-middle class usually has survival prospects similar to those in the developed world. Hence infant mortality rates often differ between the poorest 10 per cent and the richest 10 per cent by a ratio of around ten to one. Even within the

Table 9.2. Infant mortality rates in India for rural and urban areas according to father's occupation

Father's occupation	Infant mortality rate (per 1,000)
Rural	
Cultivator	125
Agricultural labourer	137
Urban	
Manual worker	113
Non-manual worker	27

Source: Census of India, 1981.

working classes, major differences are apparent: the author found that infant mortality doubled from around forty to around eighty per thousand between planned industrial housing areas in an Indian steel town and makeshift slum localities. Such spatial differentials reflect both social and environmental influences on health.

Unfortunately, comparing data on mortality city by city is difficult. Aside from problems of differential accuracy, age composition differs dramatically from town to town. Towns that are growing rapidly and have a young age composition inevitably have a low crude death rate. Towns that have been in existence for a long time have a high crude death rate owing to their older age composition. The only solution to this measurement problem is to obtain, or estimate, age-specific mortality figures. Then one can either standardize the crude death rates (as in Box 6.1) or calculate the most useful summary measure of mortality, *life expectation at birth* or *life expectancy*. This calculation involves converting age-specific mortality rates into survival ratios (as explained Box 9.3) and then calculating the appropriate average (Box 9.4). Life expectancy measures the average age at death of a group of individuals born at the same time who experience specified age-specific rates. Because it examines the experience of a single cohort, the statistic is unaffected by the age composition of the population. Where data allow, life expectancy is the measure used most commonly to indicate the health of a nation and to illustrate intra-national differentials.

Case study of Jakarta

To illustrate what may be learned about a city's history from its age structure, we look at the population pyramid for Jakarta in 1961 (Figure 9.7). What strikes the eye? The bulge in the age groups 20–4 years and 25–34 years reveals that this is a city that has been experiencing the in-migration of young adults with men slightly predominating over women. The distinct hollow in the 10–14 year age group is less easy to explain. Careful inspection of the age pyramid for all of Indonesia in 1990 (Figure 10.1) shows that a similar deficiency exists there for the age group 40–44 years. This suggests that some event depleted the number of children born or surviving from a period ten to fourteen years before the 1961 census.

Indonesia's history in the mid-twentieth century was punctuated by a series of largely man-made disasters. The depression of the 1930s ruined the colony's economy, which was dependent on exports to the developed world. In the early 1940s the Japanese occupied the islands. In the late 1940s, the country fought for its independence. The latter struggle not only cost lives, but undoubtedly suppressed births. This is the missing cohort that fails to show up more than twenty years later in the national and the capital's age distribution.

BOX 9.4. LIFE EXPECTANCY

In the life table the column headed $_nL_x$ represents all the years of life that the original birth cohort of 100,000 (l_0) live during each period of n (usually five) years. (Often this is referred to in speech as 'the big L_x column'.) The sum of this column is therefore the total years of life these 100,000 people enjoy. For example, one person may live two years and die in childhood, another may reach age 50 and then die, while a third, more fortunate individual enjoys one hundred years of life before dying. The sum of these years of life divided by the number of persons (100,000) is the average number of years lived or the average age at death.

To rephrase this statistic in terms of probabilities, it can be thought of as the expected age at death faced by any individual starting off life in this population or, as it is more frequently put, the *expectation of life* at birth. This is therefore calculated as follows:

$$e_0 = \frac{\sum_{x=0}^{\infty} L_x}{l_0}.$$

Although life expectancy at birth is a statistic that is familiar to most people, life expectation can in fact be calculated for any age: for example, life expectancy at age 5 indicates the average number of years of life left to those who have reached age 5, and life expectancy at age 80 is the number of years an 80-year old person lives on average at that level of mortality. It does not of course represent the average age at death of people surviving to a particular birthday—for this one must add on the years that they have already lived.

More generally, life expectancy e_x is calculated follows:

$$e_x = \frac{\sum_{y=x}^{\infty} L_y}{l_x}.$$

(Recall that the l_x column stands for the number surviving to exact age x.)

In most life tables, life expectancy increases for several years after birth, before it begins to shorten with increasing age. This is to be expected. Mortality is much severer in the early years of life than it is in late childhood and early adulthood (recall the shape of the age-specific mortality schedule). Once someone has survived their first few years, they enjoy a reasonable prospect of living to old age even in a developing country with high overall mortality risks.

The use of life expectation at birth as a summary measure of survival (or its inverse, mortality) is favoured because, unlike the crude death rate, it is not affected by age structure. Its drawbacks are:

- It cannot be calculated accurately without good data on ages at death (so that one can construct a life table).
- It is strongly influenced by infant and child mortality, and therefore for some purposes may give a misleading impression. This can be put right, however, if e_5 is used as an additional summary measure.
- It suffers from the same problem as the total fertility rate: they are both calculated from current cross-sectional data, but they sound like measures that can be used to project into the future. In fact, circumstances may change altering the mortality risks of those currently being born (e.g., a new breakthrough in the treatment of cancer or increasing risks from a new disease like AIDS).

Fig. 9.7. Population pyramid for Jakarta, 1961

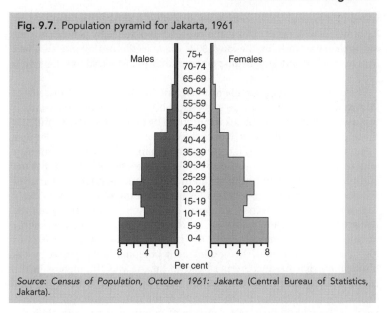

Source: Census of Population, October 1961: Jakarta (Central Bureau of Statistics, Jakarta).

Jakarta's population has grown rapidly. In 1961, it was 2.9 million, having grown over the previous decade at an annual average rate of 5.6 per cent a year. During the next decade, the city's growth abated a little. The population reached 4.5 million in 1971 (a growth rate of 4.6 per cent annually). During the 1960s the rate of natural increase for the country was 2.1 per cent a year. If Jakarta had approximately the same rate of natural increase as the rest of the country, then a little over half its growth came from net inmigration.

Jakarta suffers from the problems that afflict most metropolitan cities in Asia and Africa, and many smaller towns. Provision of public infrastructure has lagged behind need. In 1970, 80 per cent of the population lived in non-permanent shelter and 90 per cent were without a private water connection. It is easy to feel some disgust at this state of affairs without fully realizing what it implies. These are, after all, the conditions in which most of the rural population of Indonesia live. They are indicative of the poverty of most people in the country and the low productivity of the work-force in comparison with more developed countries. It is the fact that such conditions repeat themselves in a capital city, where much wealth is also concentrated, that makes them more noticeable. One cannot argue convincingly that the city's population was unable to pay for its requirements, since central government collects substantial tax revenues from its inhabitants. To some extent it is this that makes it impossible for the city itself to raise revenue from its own population. Instead, it relies on the return of some central government funds to pay for the infrastructure needed to control flood waters, for example, and so improve sewerage. A second problem that Jakarta shares with other cities is the congestion of space by people carrying out their daily work. By the late-1960s roads in the central city area had become packed with small transport operators and with traders selling their produce from the footpath.

The response to these problems that came in 1970 from the Governor of Jakarta was typical of responses to these problems elsewhere in the world. It was assumed that the problems were caused by population growth and that this was due to in-migration. Hence the city was declared 'closed'. Further migration was restricted by a registration system, under which permission had to be obtained to visit to the city and the return fare deposited with the authorities. After six months the migrant had to provide evidence that he or she had obtained a job, otherwise they had to return to the countryside.

This was an unsatisfactory response. Lack of jobs was probably not the real problem, as Todaro had shown. Moreover, if there was an excess supply of labour, natural increase within the city was as responsible for this as migration from outside. The employment potential is illustrated by the observation that the income per head in Jakarta was the highest in the country. Such a position usually creates many service and trade-sector jobs for the poor in response to the demand of the not-so-poor. On the other hand, if the real problem was shortage of public infrastructure, then the potential demand of the city should have been tapped by local taxation and the necessary investment undertaken.

Nevertheless, we inhabit the world of the second best when it comes to policy. There was probably some virtue in trying to ensure that each new migrant could earn a living. In practice the system of regulation failed to work, however. As one commentator put it: 'Despite registers, control cards, cash deposits and transmigration, the Indonesian capital . . . leaks internal migrants like a sieve.' Another policy adopted was to exclude traders and pedi-cycles from certain zones of the city. This may have worked better. It has also been tried in other cities of Asia. On the whole, it would be better to provide some legal sites and charge high rents for them, than simply to zone whole areas. Whichever policy is adopted, it is likely to be ignored if bribery of officials is rife. As Jakarta has become richer, moreover, the city has ground to a halt again—this time because of the large number of private motor vehicles on the roads.

During the 1970s a serious attempt was made to improve the sanitary infrastructure in the areas of Jakarta that consisted of unserviced non-permanent shelter (known locally as *kampongs*). Upgrading settlements such as these is much cheaper than bulldozing them and building again from scratch to unrealistically high standards. The result is a relatively healthy environment to live in at a price that the poor can afford (though in Jakarta, as elsewhere, international finance has been sought to assist the redevelopment programme). The cost of upgrading the *kampong* population worked out at $28 per head. This was a manageable cost in relation to the average income of $313 in Jakarta in 1970. Between 1969 and 1974 about a quarter of the *kampong* population were upgraded in this way.

By 1981 the population of the city had reached about seven million and by 1991 about ten million. Thus, growth had slowed again to around 4 per cent a year during these two decades. It might be thought at first that this is evidence that the anti-migration policies have had some success. However, the 1990 population pyramid for the whole country (Figure 10.1) shows that there may have been another reason for the decrease. The four youngest age groups are about the same size. This is usually evidence of fertility decline. As the family planning programmes of the 1970s probably had most impact in the major cities, a reduced birth rate will have contributed to the slowing of urban growth.

Notes

1. There is a long and technical discussion among economists as to how exactly to set the charges. The basic problem is that, if average costs per unit of service are falling, it is necessary to charge a price that will cover average costs, not just marginal costs.
2. The focus of this chapter is on rural-to-urban migration but different countries define urban areas differently. In some cases mining localities with their attendant colonies of workers are regarded as urban, in others they are defined as rural.
3. The reason for this is partly one of geometry. Vessels such as blast furnaces in which the iron is purified at high temperature require relining with heat-resistant brick at regular intervals. The smaller the ratio of the surface area to the volume of the vessel the lower the proportion of the vessel's time spent out of work and, as a result, the more profitable the enterprise becomes. The larger a container's volume, the lower the ratio of its surface area to volume becomes.

10 | Population, Employment, and Education

Introduction

Look at the population age pyramids for the countries lying in the south and east of Asia (Figure 10.1). One thing is immediately apparent: the great diversity of these age structures. This reflects the fact that they are caught at a single point of time in a process of change. Some countries, like Bangladesh and the Philippines, still have the characteristic distribution of a population growing at more than 2 per cent a year. The pyramid has a broad base that gradually diminishes towards the higher age groups. Other countries, like Japan and Hong Kong, are well on the way to an age structure like that of many Western populations. The distribution is rather uniform from bottom to top and the population growth rate has fallen to less than 1 per cent a year. Thailand and many of the East Asian populations exhibit undercutting at the base, implying that smaller cohorts of young people are now being born than in earlier years.

A growing number of countries in South and East Asia are industrializing rapidly. Japan is already fully industrialized; Korea and Taiwan are well on the way. Even India and Pakistan, while still predominantly agricultural, have sustained substantial industrial growth, especially since the start of the 1980s. Until now this book has concentrated on the issues facing agricultural economies that have only partly industrialized. We conclude the book by looking at the role that population plays in the 'newly industrializing countries', that is, those where industrialization is now the dominant characteristic of the economy in terms of both output and employment. In particular, we examine the effect of changes in the population's age structure on prospects for industrialization. What implications does this have for industrial employment? How are these mediated by the education policies of the States concerned? What are the implications for trade and international migration in the region?

Chapters 3 and 7 referred to the relationship between demographic and economic growth depicted in the literature on Harrod's single-sector growth model. One of the main issues discussed was whether the productivity of investment might fall if too many resources had to be devoted to social investments, many of which, like housing and education, need to be par-

Fig. 10.1.(a) Contrasting age structures in the countries of Asia

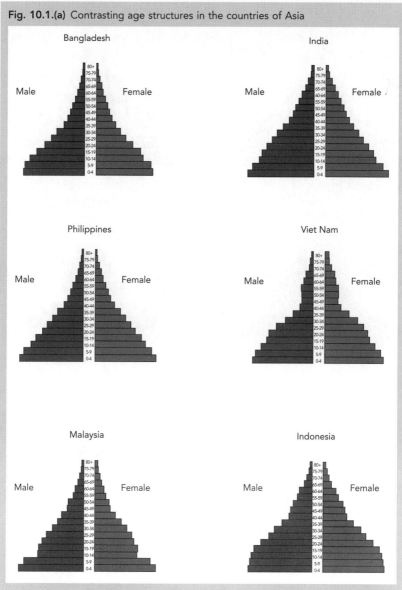

Source: United Nations, Department for Economic and Social Information and Policy Analysis, *World Population Prospects: the 1994 Revision* (United Nations, New York, NY, 1995).

Fig. 10.1.(b)

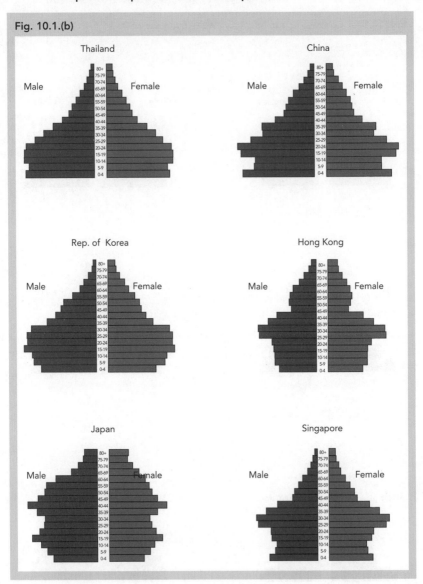

ticularly high in populations with young age distributions. Any such fall in the productivity of investment would slow the rate of economic growth. It was not until recently that demographers and economists became concerned that the same problems would arise if the population was growing too slowly. The eventual demographic implication of this is an old age

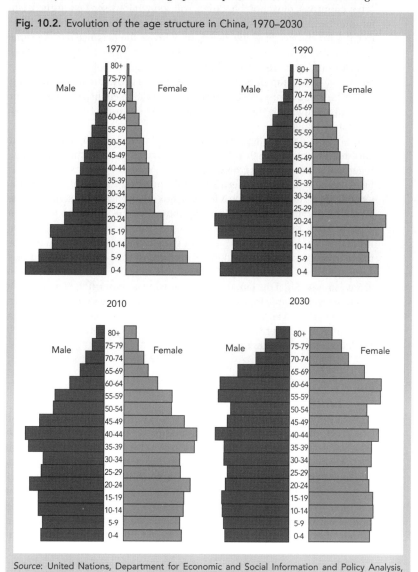

Fig. 10.2. Evolution of the age structure in China, 1970–2030

Source: United Nations, Department for Economic and Social Information and Policy Analysis, *World Population Prospects: the 1994 Revision* (United Nations, New York, NY, 1995).

distribution. Ageing of the population makes demands on resources for health and old age care that never pay off economically in a more productive work-force. This is an issue that many countries in Europe are facing. It will soon also be one for much of South-East and East Asia. Because of its early fertility decline, ageing is most advanced in Japan (see Figure 10.1) but other countries, most notably China, will soon follow (see Figure 10.2). Not far into the next century, the need to make the social investments required to cater for the needs of the elderly may lower the productivity of overall investment and hence slow their rate of economic growth. Arguably those countries in Figure 10.1 with bulges in the middle of their age pyramid are enjoying a demographic advantage. They have a high ratio of economically active to non-active people. Therefore, most of their investment can be devoted to enhancing the productivity of the work-force. This, however, is a temporary situation.

Apart from dependency, the other focus of models that relate economic and demographic growth is on a rather obvious issue. If the population, regarded as consumers, grows rapidly, the increase in consumption per head will be slower than otherwise.[1] While the extension of this argument to an analysis of the labour force is less obvious, it is basically the same. Labour has to be provided with tools and equipment. If the growth in the labour force is faster, the growth in equipment per labourer will be slower. To put it another way, with faster population growth, more equipment has to be made available simply to equip new entrants to the labour force and prevent equipment per head from decreasing. New equipment and tools count as investment. So, if the labour force is growing, a proportion of investment has to be used simply to maintain the existing level of capital per labourer. Simulations by Coale and Hoover in the 1950s showed that, for India, about two-thirds of the country's investment was used up simply to keep up with the labour force growth, that is to stand still.[2]

Employment

The single-sector growth model had little to say about employment. As it assumed that no scope exists for substitution between labour and capital, the rate of employment growth was governed by the rate of capital growth (for any specified level of capital productivity). If this is less than the rate of population growth then, in the stable population at least, the number of unemployed persons increases permanently. If, on the other hand, the rate of capital growth began to exceed the rate of population growth, a labour shortage would develop. This would be unsustainable without labour immigration.

Single-sector growth models are not particularly useful in interpreting the dynamic changes that occur with development. This requires disequilibrium rather than equilibrium analysis. In practice, considerable substitution of capital for labour has occurred. Movement of labour from one sector of the economy to another, for example from agriculture to industry, has been largely determined by the amount of substitution of capital for labour in each sector. Increasing capital intensity in the industrial sector might slow the speed of transfer of labour between the two sectors. This would mean that, although the rate of industrial growth might be quite fast (as in India or Pakistan), the proportion of labour still left in agriculture would not diminish significantly (as it has failed to do in India over most of this century). This is not really the place to discuss whether this is good or bad. We could note, however, that it often means that the benefits of industrialization are distributed to only part of the labour force. Even if most of a country's national income derives from industry, some scholars regard it as odd to describe it as industrialized while most of the labour force remains in agriculture.[3] The contrast between the different regions of Asia regarding the transference of labour between these sectors is brought out in Table 10.1. Some East Asian countries went initially for a strategy of labour-intensive industrialization, mainly based on the textile industry. This enabled them to move the labour force more rapidly between the sectors.

Where does population growth enter this scenario? If rate of natural increase is high, the growth of labour supply will be similarly fast. This makes it more difficult to transfer labour sufficiently fast to reduce the proportion of labour in agriculture. If no natural increase occurred, all growth in the industrial labour force would reduce the labour force in agriculture. If the

Table 10.1. Share of labour force in agriculture in selected Asian countries (%)

Region and country	1970	1985
East Asia		
South Korea	50	25
Taiwan	35	17
South-East Asia		
Indonesia	62	55
Malaysia	48	36
Philippines	54	49
Thailand	72	69
South Asia		
Bangladesh	74	64
India	74	69
Pakistan	57	53
Sri Lanka	51	44

Source: International Labour Office, *Yearbook of Labour Statistics* (Geneva).

rural population has a positive rate of natural increase, this is not necessarily so.[4] However, while population growth slows the pace of transfer of labour out of agriculture and into industry, its part in this should not be exaggerated. Industrial sectors often grow by more than 5 per cent a year. Some Asian countries have achieved sustained rates of more than 10 per cent. As rapid population growth only reaches 3 per cent a year or so, it is not an important brake on the process of transfer in such economies. Thus, we stress that capital-labour substitution is vital to the explanation of employment absorption or lack of it. A 10 per cent growth in industrial output does not necessarily mean a 10 per cent growth in labour demanded by industry.

So far the implications of population growth for employment have been discussed on the assumption that the participation rate remains the same: that is to say, that no change occurs in the proportion of able-bodied people who are working outside the household in each age group. This assumption, however, while reasonably valid for males between the ages of 15 and 65, is quite invalid when we consider the female work-force. In practice, there are contrasts between countries and changes over time in the female participation rate. In Latin America, and to a lesser extent Asia, more women have entered the industrial labour force since the mid-1970s. There are several reasons for this. One is that in a period of recession firms tend to reduce their permanent labour forces and reduce their costs by employing casual or part-time labour. Women are more likely to work on these terms, largely because in many households they are forced to work to supplement the reduced wages and employment of the male members that occur during a recession.

Recession apart, firms across the world have been seeking out cheap labour to lower the costs of manufacturing. One can see this taking place in individual economies where firms conduct an increasing amount of their production through subcontracting to small firms or to family-run workshops. In the latter, at least, women are often the major labour source. They work between domestic jobs and often their remuneration is based on the amount of work they do (the number of items, or parts of items, manufactured) rather than the hours worked. In practice, this often works out to be the equivalent of a low hourly wage.

This process is well illustrated by the practice of international firms. Increasingly these have come to regard the whole global economy as their factory. They divide the manufacturing process, undertaking aspects of it in different countries to avail themselves of the cheapest costs. Processes that are labour intensive are allocated to countries where the appropriately qualified labour is available in greatest quantities (in relation to the demand for it). In these, labour will usually turn out to be the cheapest. They will also be among the poorer countries of course, as their relative lack of capital (among other things) lies behind their poverty and accounts for their relative abundance of labour in relation to capital. Many countries have set up export processing zones to push forward this process. Such zones often discourage the formation of trade unions, which may have some effect on wages in the manufacturing sectors of developing countries. Within each country, these firms seek out the cheapest possible labour—and women are a typical source. In the early 1980s, in South Korea 30 per cent of textile workers were female; in Hong Kong 40 per cent of apparel and footwear producers were female; and in Singapore nearly 50 per cent of electronics workers were female.

On the brighter side, women in Asia are gradually improving their educational attainment and their status in society. Even in those countries of South Asia where women have long been effectively prevented from active participation in the labour market except in the lowest-status jobs, changes for the better are beginning to take place. Increasingly women are acquiring the qualifications for a professional career. However, the contribution made to the increasing labour-force-participation rate for women by this process is inevitably very small so far.

The fact that the proportion of women in the manufacturing work-force was higher in East than in South Asia both in 1960 and twenty years later in 1980 reflects the points made in the last two paragraphs. In South Asia less than a quarter of the manufacturing work-force is female, in East Asia more than one-third. Economic as well as cultural differences explain this. Export-oriented industrial policies, which tend to raise the employment of women, were adopted only recently in South Asia, but are well established in most of East and South-East Asia.

The changing demography of the countries of East Asia has begun to have a remarkable impact on the economies and labour markets of the region. As a result of high birth rates and rapidly declining death rates in the 1930s, 1940s, and 1950s, the supply of labour continued to grow rapidly in these economies until the 1960s. However, substantial fertility decline began to take place as early as the late 1940s in Japan and by the late 1950s and early 1960s in other countries of East Asia. This meant that the new entrants to the labour force ceased to grow in number in the mid-1960s in Japan and the mid-1970s in Taiwan, South Korea, Hong Kong, and Singapore (see Figure 10.1). This demographic factor may have put some upward pressure on wages. Of course this does not follow automatically. Underemployed labour may be held back in agriculture or there may be a reserve of urban-based labour available for hire—migrants waiting for better jobs or labour displaced from work by capital substitution, for example. Both forms of surplus will keep wages down even if the growth of labour through natural increase slows. In the rapidly growing economies of East Asia, however, much of the labour surplus had been squeezed out of the economy by the 1970s. Women represented the last source of cheap labour available to industry.

Figure 10.3 illustrates this process in Singapore. The increase in female participation in the labour market had clearly begun by the 1970s. Note that this was before the male cohorts entering the labour force began to decline,

Fig. 10.3. Changes in labour-force participation in Singapore, 1966–88

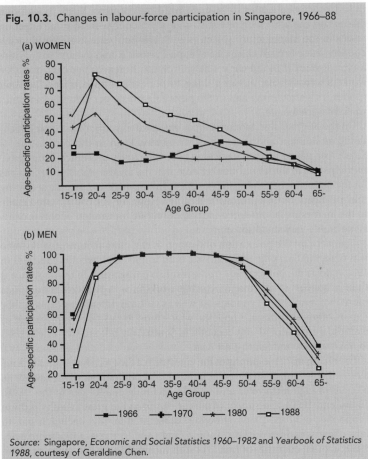

(a) WOMEN

(b) MEN

■—1966 ◆—1970 —★—1980 —□—1988

Source: Singapore, *Economic and Social Statistics 1960–1982* and *Yearbook of Statistics 1988*, courtesy of Geraldine Chen.

demonstrating that demographic factors are not the only cause of these changes. By the 1980s, the increase in female participation seems to have slowed. Controls have been adopted in Singapore to try to hold in check the likely rise in wages that will follow from the decline in the supply of men and of women. Taiwan and South Korea will soon be in a similar situation. Thailand is not far behind.

There is an interesting demographic dilemma here. One reaction to an emerging labour shortage is to encourage women to have children and ensure an increasing supply of future labour. This discourages any immediate increase in women's participation in the labour force. Indeed participation might decline as a result. The other strategy to address these demographic and economic changes would be to accept that this relative labour shortage is an inevitable and perhaps desirable feature of the process of economic development and to allow wages to rise. This means that the country becomes less competitive in international markets in the processing or production of labour-intensive goods. Firms will begin to look elsewhere for their cheap labour. This is exactly what has happened in Asia. Bangladesh, whose labour is still plentiful and cheap, is undertaking an increasing share of textile production. As with the East Asian economies, women have become a major source of labour (despite traditional restrictions on women working outside the household).

As labour becomes more costly, it only remains internationally competitive if it is also more productive. This may mean that the country has to specialize in more capital-intensive forms of production. It may also require a labour force that is better educated and trained. These are complicated issues in the theory of international trade that we cannot elaborate here. What is clear is that, for the argument to go any further, one has to take into account the level of education and other skills that the population has and the development of these human assets over time. We now turn to this.

Education

In the original single-sector economic growth model, educational expenditure was treated by some economists as an investment that was too slow-yielding to be comparable with that in capital equipment. As children take ten or fifteen years before they contribute their accumulated education and skills to the production effort, using resources for education was thought to lower the productivity of investment (at the margin). That was one reason why a fast-growing population was a brake on economic growth. The age structure that resulted was young and this increased the demand for educational expenditures.

To some extent these ideas have become outdated. In practice, the amount that a country spends on education has not borne much relation to the age structure of the population. Some States have simply crammed more children into existing schools. In economic theory also, new ideas have gained acceptance. The additional contribution made to society in general, and to material production in particular, by additional years of education is believed by some scholars to be difficult to measure and is likely to be underestimated in any quantitative analysis. Whatever the theoretical case, in practice considerable resources have been devoted to education in various South and East Asian countries. The experience of educational attainment also differs dramatically between the different countries in the region.

Education statistics should be looked at separately by age group and by educational level: primary, secondary, tertiary for example. In practice, there is no uniformity in the way that levels are distinguished in different countries. Table 10.2 shows ratios of enrolment to population in the age group 6–11 years. Enrolment simply tells us how many pupils entered school at that level at the start of the year. It does not say whether they continued in regular attendance throughout the year. Dropping out is a serious problem in many countries. The age at which the pupil signed on is not recorded. It is likely that some pupils enrolling in primary schools are older than 11 years. Either they are returning to retake a year or they are enrolling for the first time, having failed to do so when they were in the usual age range. These factors mean that the enrolment ratio can exceed 100. This would occur, for example, if all eligible 6 to 11-year-old children and some of those aged 12 to 15 years enrolled at the primary level. Apart from these interpretational problems, problems exist with the accuracy of the numbers themselves. As with vital statistics data, the collection of educational data often relies on local officials and even local schoolteachers themselves. Apart from the nuisance of maintaining the records, such staff may inflate the figures to show how successful their school or district is at getting local children into school and keeping them there.

Table 10.2. Proportion of children aged 6 to 11 years enrolled in primary school in selected countries of Asia (%)[a]

Region and country	1970	1990
East Asia		
Japan	99	101
Hong Kong	117	106
South Korea	103	108
China	89	135
South-East Asia		
Singapore	105	110
Thailand	83	85
Philippines	108	111
Indonesia	80	117
Malaysia	87	93
South Asia		
India	73	97
Bangladesh	54	73
Pakistan	40	37
Sri Lanka	99	107

[a] Figures for the nearest available year to the column heading.

Source: World Bank, World Development Report 1992 (Oxford University Press, New York, NY, 1992).

For the purposes of illustration we will trust the accuracy of the data. Table 10.2 reveals the contrast between, for example, Pakistan, where in 1983 even the male enrolment ratio was only 63 per cent, and Indonesia, with an enrolment ratio of 117 per cent. Dropout ratios are also revealing, although the data available are out of date. For example, when India's enrolment ratio was between 80 per cent and 100 per cent for males and between 40 per cent and 70 per cent for females, which seem quite respectable levels, the dropout ratio was as high as 60 per cent. In the East Asian countries in Table 10.2, the dropout ratio was less than 10 per cent at the same date. So the proportion of children actually attending school at any time was much higher than in South Asia. South-East Asian countries lay somewhere between these two extremes. Turning to secondary education enrolment, Table 10.3 shows how rapidly East Asian countries have expanded their attempts to get children to continue their education. Enrolment ratios have gone up by around 40 per cent over the quarter century. This illustrates the point that the labour force in these countries is becoming rapidly more qualified (at least in the sense of having achieved higher schooling levels).

The effect of these different rates of schooling on the labour force can be judged from data for the early 1980s. In East Asia about 30 per cent of the labour force is trained to secondary school levels. In South Asia the propor-

Table 10.3. Proportion of children aged 12 to 17 years enrolled in secondary school in selected countries of Asia (%)[a]

Region and country	1970	1990
East Asia		
Japan	86	96
Hong Kong	36	[b]
South Korea	42	87
China	24	48
South-East Asia		
Singapore	46	69
Thailand	17	32
Indonesia	16	45
Philippines	46	73
Malaysia	34	56
South Asia		
India	26	44
Pakistan	13	22
Sri Lanka	47	74
Bangladesh	[b]	17

[a] Figures are for nearest available year to column heading.
[b] Not available.

Source: World Bank, World Development Report 1993 (Oxford University Press, New York, NY, 1993).

tion is below 15 per cent. It can be argued, though not proven, that the wide spread of primary education in Korea and Taiwan encouraged the rapid movement of the population out of agriculture into industry. Simple mechanization in both sectors of the economy became universal more easily as the population could at least read and write. South-East Asian countries lagged behind in this respect, though they went forward with secondary and tertiary education. South Asian countries expanded their supply of tertiary educated labour well ahead of what the economy could absorb. This was counter-productive to some extent as some of these graduates migrated overseas. Expansion of the tertiary sector occurred despite these countries' poor coverage at the primary level and high illiteracy rate.

Now that the East Asian economies face a new era of competition for cheap labour and wish to upgrade the skills in their labour force, they have to encourage the spread of secondary and particularly tertiary education. Japan completed the transition to a highly educated work-force well ahead of the other East Asian states. By 1960, 90 per cent of its labour force had at least secondary education.

The young demographic structure of a population can be paradoxically both helpful and unhelpful in the achievement of a universally well-educated or well-trained labour force. As we have noted, the yearly increase in the size of the cohort of children entering school puts an increasing strain on resources. About 40 per cent of a population whose growth is 2 per cent a year will be less than 15 years of age. A stationary population has only half that proportion. In that respect Japan and Singapore have a distinct advantage over India and the Philippines. However, the other consideration is that it may be only the young who can be trained in the latest skills and technology. Retraining older cohorts is more difficult. It takes longer and is therefore more costly. Thus, populations that have an older labour force that is renewed at a slower rate by smaller cohorts of school leavers are less well refreshed by new ideas, skills, and technologies. This is a problem that Japan is now facing. It is shared by the industrialized countries of the West. Furthermore, if wages are paid on an incremental scale that relates to the age of the worker, older work-forces become progressively more costly to maintain as they age. In fact, these issues are probably more complicated and controversial than we have suggested here. The important point that the discussion again illustrates is the principle that no demographic structure is ideal. Slow demographic growth causes problems just as fast growth does.

International competition and international migration

The newly industrializing countries are becoming increasingly anxious to develop their human resources. The comparative advantage that they once had was based on abundant cheap labour and is being gradually worn away. They see that the way to maintain international competitiveness is to develop a skilled labour force that can use more sophisticated technology. A better-educated population is probably necessary for this. These countries are pursuing the course of dynamic comparative advantage, as economists term it. They are looking ahead to where their international competitiveness will lie in the future and preparing for it now. Meanwhile, countries that are further behind in the development process can benefit from their abundant resources of less-educated labour by taking over the economic niche that the newly industrializing countries filled in the past. While they too have to look to the future, their immediate problem is the large and growing cohorts of young men and women seeking jobs. In China, these cohorts started to shrink in the 1980s (see Figure 10.1). In India, they will cease to grow in the 1990s. While fertility decline is now well established in both countries it takes fifteen to twenty years before this begins to affect the labour force.

In those countries that still need employment growth, there are many industries that can continue to grow while maintaining a high labour-to-capital ratio. Some people have argued that this is best done through small-scale and decentralized industries, for example, processing agricultural products for food and clothing. However, neither small-scale nor decentralized development necessarily saves on capital. Unless a network of roads and railways has been established through the country, the delivery of supplies to, and the collection of finished goods from, many producers distributed widely is costly. Large amounts of capital in the form of transport facilities and equipment are required. Stocks of unfinished goods spend a lot of time waiting to be moved or in transit. All this amounts to the underuse of capital, which is equivalent to a low employment-to-capital ratio. Centralized factories do not have this problem. They can employ labour for two or three shifts to keep production continuous and ensure the full use of fixed capital equipment. On the other hand, the managers of such factories tend to displace their labour forces by investing in more capital-intensive equipment to avoid problems of labour management and the threat of rising wages. One can envisage some optimal combination of factory industry and small-scale workshops located in fairly centralized localities, if not necessarily the largest cities. However, the economics of the problem is still a matter of controversy, largely because the data are not available to support one argument as against another. This then is the challenge of the 1990s and beyond, especially in those countries of South and South-East Asia where the labour force will continue to grow for some time yet.

We have looked towards the future by consulting population pyramids and making rough predictions from them. One would like to be more precise than this and to make concrete short-term predictions with hard data. How could we provide such figures? Until now we have tended to assume that those who are already born will survive to join the labour force. Strictly speaking, however, only part of the birth cohort will survive. We can calculate what that proportion will be if we have estimates of the probability of dying at each year of age appropriate to the population in question. Sometimes we can use the most recent data on mortality from vital registration to construct these probabilities and from them the survival ratios we require (as in Box 9.3).

In many countries, however, vital registration is not sufficiently accurate for us to use the data from this source directly. It is one skill of the professional demographer to be able to reconstruct more accurate mortality data from surveys. This skill is beyond the purview of this book. Demographers have also observed that death probabilities follow distinctive patterns by age that change in a fairly predictable way as the overall level of mortality varies (i.e., as life expectancy goes up or down). From this knowledge they have constructed model tables of survival probabilities.[5] These can also be used in projections, so long as one knows the overall level of mortality in the population in question. This can be estimated from surveys or from census data, using techniques based on intercensal survival. Again this is the province of the professional demographer. Whatever the source of one's survival ratios, their use is straightforward. It is illustrated in Box 10.1, where we project the male labour force in Singapore five years ahead. (We make one important assumption in this projection: that there will be no significant international migration.)

There is one important economic and demographic option open to the newly industrializing countries that we have only alluded to in passing. This is the international migration of labour. The countries of East Asia that are now facing labour shortages could ease their difficulty by allowing the immigration of labour from elsewhere in the region. Those countries having difficulty in absorbing the labour they themselves have could supply that labour to the countries in need. In practice, this exchange is not so easy to organize. Racial and nationalist concerns make some countries hesitate to allow foreigners to work on their soil, though in the end economic compulsion usually wins the day.

Most international labour migration has been in the direction of the oil-rich countries of West Asia. Here the labour shortage was not caused by a demographic decline. In fact, natural increase rates in most West Asian countries are among the fastest in Asia, at around 3 per cent a year. With the phenomenal increase in capital from the sale of oil at enhanced prices since the 1970s, a huge increase in labour was needed to realize this in infrastructure on which to base future industrialization. Additionally, labour was needed to operate an expanding services sector (even if industrial manufactured goods were imported rather than made indigenously). The labour came readily from Pakistan, India, Bangladesh, and Sri Lanka. One-third of the increase in Pakistan's labour force went to West Asia between 1978 and

1983. From the 1980s substantial flows of labour began to come from South-East Asia, especially Thailand and the Philippines and later Indonesia.

The effects of this strategy have not always been as acceptable as it might appear from our analysis so far. The demand is mainly for construction labour. As a result these skills became scarce in some of the countries from which the migrants came. This problem occurred in South Korea, which contributed some labour despite incipient shortages in its own economy. However, some countries have responded favourably by regarding their skilled labour as an exportable asset, from which they can recoup their investment in human capital. Migrants send back and eventually bring back

---

BOX 10.1. POPULATION PROJECTIONS

One can estimate the total future population by extrapolating the growth rate. We do not discuss such projections here but assume that interest exists in the future age structure of the population and the growth of the population of labour-force age. To carry out a *component projection* of the population by age, one needs the information on mortality contained in an appropriate life table. If the population of children is also of interest, one must project how many births will occur in future. This requires assumptions about age-specific fertility.

The most difficult aspect of population forecasting is to decide what will happen to vital rates in the years ahead. Future mortality and fertility can be estimated using very complex methods or very simple assumptions. Either way, the principle is to extrapolate past levels and trends. The difficulties involved are compounded by the imperfect demographic data available for many countries, with the result that it is unclear what levels of fertility and mortality are currently. Even if registered mortality and fertility are not completely accurate, however, a life table may have been constructed or a model life table found that is consistent with age structures and growth rates over the previous decade. Similarly, a survey may have provided recent information on fertility.

Here we focus on the projection method itself. We illustrate it with data on men in Singapore and start with a model fertility schedule thought appropriate for Singapore in the early 1990s (Table A), a model life table with a life expectancy believed to be similarly appropriate (Table B), and data on the size of the male and female population of the country in 1990 (Table C).

Table A

Age group	Fertility rates
15–19	0.0390
20–24	0.1251
25–29	0.1178
30–34	0.0692
35–39	0.0347
40–44	0.0118
45–49	0.0017

BOX 10.1. continued

Table B: 'West, Level 23' Model Life Table

Age (x)	l_x	$_nm_x$	$_nq_x$	$_nL_x$	$_5L_{x+5}/_5L_x$	e_x
			Females			
0	100,000	0.0154	0.0152	98,629	0.9840[a]	75.00
1	98,484	0.0006	0.0024	393,346	0.9979[b]	75.15
5	98,248	0.0003	0.0013	490,926	0.9988	71.33
10	98,123	0.0002	0.0011	490,355	0.9986	66.42
15	98,019	0.0004	0.0018	489,662	0.9979	61.49
20	97,846	0.0005	0.0025	488,610	0.9971	56.59
25	97,598	0.0006	0.0032	487,207	0.9963	51.73
30	97,285	0.0008	0.0041	485,417	0.9950	46.89
35	96,882	0.0012	0.0058	483,004	0.9927	42.07
40	96,319	0.0018	0.0089	479,464	0.9883	37.30
45	95,466	0.0029	0.0146	473,851	0.9813	32.61
50	94,074	0.0046	0.0228	465,006	0.9707	28.06
55	91,928	0.0073	0.0360	451,369	0.9531	23.66
60	88,619	0.0120	0.0582	430,193	0.9211	19.44
65	83,458	0.0212	0.1008	396,265	0.8652	15.49
70	75,048	0.0378	0.1727	342,839	0.7759	11.95
75	62,087	0.0668	0.2862	266,015	0.5197	8.92
80	44,318	0.1540	—	287,843	—	6.50
			Males			
0	100,000	0.0219	0.0214	98,080	0.9774[a]	71.19
1	97,856	0.0009	0.0034	390,618	0.9967[b]	71.75
5	97,521	0.0005	0.0022	487,062	0.9979	67.99
10	97,303	0.0004	0.0019	486,055	0.9972	63.13
15	97,119	0.0007	0.0037	484,692	0.9956	58.25
20	96,758	0.0010	0.0051	482,547	0.9949	53.46
25	96,261	0.0010	0.0051	480,084	0.9946	48.72
30	95,773	0.0011	0.0057	477,500	0.9934	43.95
35	95,227	0.0015	0.0075	474,348	0.9905	39.19
40	94,512	0.0023	0.0116	469,820	0.9843	34.47
45	93,416	0.0040	0.0199	462,430	0.9734	29.85
50	91,556	0.0068	0.0334	450,149	0.9553	25.40
55	88,503	0.0116	0.0564	430,029	0.9273	21.19
60	83,508	0.0188	0.0900	398,759	0.8849	17.31
65	75,995	0.0307	0.1427	352,874	0.8200	13.77
70	65,154	0.0503	0.2235	289,364	0.7259	10.65
75	50,591	0.0817	0.3394	210,034	0.4806	7.99
80	33,422	0.1720	—	194,314	—	5.81

[a] Proportion surviving from birth to 0–4.
[b] $_5L_5/_5L_0$

Source: A. J. Coale and P. Demeny, *Regional Model Life Tables and Stable Populations* (Princeton University Press, Princeton, NJ, 1966).

BOX 10.1. continued

Table C: Population by age and sex, Singapore, 1990

Age group	Male	Female	Total
0–4	111,163	103,393	214,556
5–9	108,194	100,595	208,789
10–14	100,619	92,542	193,161
15–19	115,418	107,856	223,274
20–24	120,015	114,352	234,367
25–29	146,818	138,643	285,461
30–34	151,173	142,670	293,843
35–39	127,779	123,236	251,015
40–44	105,447	102,585	208,032
45–49	66,737	65,690	132,427
50–54	62,683	62,960	125,643
55–59	49,273	49,699	98,972
60–64	40,570	40,886	81,456
65–69	27,975	29,618	57,593
70–74	19,440	23,393	42,833
75–79	12,541	17,148	29,689
80+	7,567	12,805	20,372
Total	1,373,412	1,328,071	2,701,483

To project five years forward, simply multiply each age group by the appropriate survival ratio from the life table column headed $_nL_{x+n}/_nL_x$. For example, the 15–19 male cohort is survived as follows:

$$115,418 \times 0.9956 = 114,910.$$

We do this for all the age groups from 0–4 up to 55–9 (although the exercise could continue on to ages beyond those usually spent in the labour force), as Table D shows.

Table D

Age	Male population
0–4	—
5–9	110,796
10–14	107,967
15–19	100,337
20–24	114,910
25–29	119,403
30–34	146,025
35–39	150,175
40–44	126,565
45–49	103,791
50–54	64,962
55–59	59,881

Principles of Population and Development

BOX 10.1. continued

Special care is needed to make sure the 0–4 age group is multiplied by the correct survival ratio. The footnote at the bottom of the column of survival ratios must be correctly interpreted. In model life tables that include l_1 (after l_0 and before l_5), it is the second figure in the survival ratio column that is required, i.e., $111,163 \times 0.9967 = 110,796$.

This procedure yields the projected population by age except for the future 0–4 year age group. Projecting this age group involves estimating births over the five-year period. Precision would require annual projections of women and their births. Abridged data merit only abridged methods, however, and the estimate can be based on the female population of childbearing age by five-year age group currently and projected for five years' time (obtained in the same way as for men). First, the average population of women in each age group during the projection interval is calculated (see Table E).

Table E

Age	Current women	Projected women	Average women
15–19	107,856	92,412	100,134
20–24	114,352	107,630	110,991
25–29	138,643	114,020	126,332
30–34	142,670	138,130	140,400
35–39	123,236	141,957	132,596
40–44	102,585	122,336	112,460
45–49	65,690	101,385	83,538

Multiplying the population in each of these age groups by the appropriate age-specific fertility rate for the projection period (supplied earlier) gives the annual average number of births shown in Table F.

Table F

Mother's age	Births
15–19	3,905
20–24	13,885
25–29	14,882
30–34	9,716
35–39	4,601
40–44	1,327
45–49	142
Total	48,458

Next, multiply by 5 to obtain total births over the next five years:

$$48,458 \times 5 = 242,290.$$

Finally, to convert these to the male births for use in a male population projection, divide by (1 + female:male sex ratio at birth). If the male:female sex ratio at birth is 1.05, then the female:male ratio is about 0.95:

$$242,290 \div (1 + 0.95) = 124,251.$$

BOX 10.1. continued

This number represents the boys that will be born during the next five years. They will form the cohort aged 0–4 years in five years' time. Unfortunately, not all of them will survive to be 1, 2, 3, 4 years etc., owing to infant and child mortality. Therefore, the births must be multiplied by a survival ratio appropriate for the age group as a whole. This is tabulated either separately, for example at the bottom of the life table, or as the first figure in the survival ratio column. Again, interpret the footnote with care. The result is as follows:

$$124{,}251 \times 0.9774 = 121{,}443.$$

Thus, the projected male population is:

0–4 = 121,443, and

5–9 = 110,796, etc., as above.

To project ahead for further five-year periods, one simply repeats the entire procedure using the projected population as input rather than the baseline population. This can be done using either the same fertility and mortality rates for all projection periods or different ones for each period.

foreign exchange. The Government of Thailand has actually considered the export of labour as one of its planning objectives. Similarly, the Government of the Philippines has trained nurses for deployment overseas.

The countries of East Asia, particularly Japan and Singapore, have largely resisted the temptation to solve their emerging labour shortages by allowing major increases in immigration. Labour commutes from Malaysia to Singapore daily, a pattern that has some of the advantages for Singapore that circular migration from neighbouring countries has had for South Africa (see Chapter 9). The main response in East Asia to the need to use increasing capital without driving up wages, however, has been to invest capital overseas (in the same way as Western capitalists did earlier). Japan, in particular, has sought out locations in South-East Asia where cheap labour is abundant to establish overseas companies with plant and equipment.

It should be apparent by now that the economic responses to the emerging differences in the demographic position in Asia (illustrated in Figure 10.1) have been many and diverse. Labour is seen as a resource to be developed. Both labour and capital are becoming more mobile, quickening the pace of internationalization in the world economy.

Notes

1. This need not always be a bad thing. Fairly wealthy populations might prefer to have more children to enjoy their wealth rather than simply to accumulate more for themselves. Even poorer populations might share this view, though on the whole the human race seem to be choosing fewer children and more income per head rather than the reverse option.

2. Economists use the term capital-deepening to indicate that the level of capital per member of the labour force is actually increasing. Capital-widening means simply that more capital is being supplied to the labour force. If the latter is growing, this may not result in deepening.

3. The full picture is more complicated than we have indicated in the text. If capital is substituted for labour in the industrial sector, the rate of reinvestment of profits from industry back into industry may go up. This could be because capitalists save more than labourers (who have to consume most of their income to stay alive). Increasing reinvestment will mean faster rates of industrial growth and hence faster rates of increase in the demand for labour from agriculture. This is a well-known development paradox. Less employment today could lead to greater employment in the future. This is not always true. After all, capitalists might consume their incomes by importing luxuries rather than save.

4. Economists familiar with dual-economy models will recognize that increased population growth tends to delay the turning-point at which the marginal product of labour in agriculture begins to rise above zero. The latter condition drives up the wage level in industry that is required to continue the transfer of labour between the sectors. This requirement is therefore also delayed by population growth.

5. Such models are constructed from the experience of those populations that have both good registration data and appropriate levels of life expectancy. For example, Taiwan has had almost complete registration of births and deaths since the 1920s, a time when it still had low life expectancy. The same was true of Western Europe in the late nineteenth century. In a similar way, one can obtain model age-specific fertility rates.

Further Reading

Cassen R., ed., *Population and Development: Old Debates, New Conclusions* (Transaction Publishers, Oxford, 1994).

Findlay, A., and Findlay, A., *Population and Development in the Third World* (Routledge, London, 1991).

Jones, H. R., *A Population Geography* (Harper & Row, London, 1981).

Livi-Bacci, M., *A Concise History of World Population* (Blackwell, Oxford, 1992).

McEvedy, C., and Jones, R., *Atlas of World Population History* (Penguin, Harmondsworth, 1985).

Newell, C., *Methods and Models in Demography* (Wiley, Chichester, 1994).

Pressat, R., *Population* (Penguin, Harmondsworth, 1973).

Stockwell, E. G., Shryock, H. S., and Siegel, J. S., *The Methods and Materials of Demography* (Academic Press, New York, NY, 1976).

Thomas, I., *Population Growth* (Macmillan, Basingstoke and London, 1980).

Chapter 1

Alison, A., *The Principles of Population and their Connection with Human Happiness* (Thomas Cadell, London, 1840).

Boserup, E., 'Environment and Technology in Primitive Societies', *Population and Development Review*, 2 (1976), 21–36.

—— *Population and Technology* (Blackwell, Oxford, 1981).

Engels, F. (1844), 'Outline of a Critique of Political Economy', in *Friedrich Engels: Selected writings*, ed. W. O. Henderson (Penguin, Harmondsworth, 1967). Section on population.

George, H., *Progress and Poverty* (Doubleday, New York, NY, 1907). Section on Malthus.

Grigg, D., 'Ester Boserup's Theory of Agrarian Change: A Critical Review', *Progress in Human Geography*, 3 (1979), 64–84.

Malthus, T. R. (1798), 'An Essay on the Principle of Population', in *Malthus: An Essay on the Principle of Population*, ed. A. Flew (Penguin, Harmondsworth, 1970).

—— (1830), 'A Summary View of the Principle of Population', in *Malthus: An Essay on the Principle of Population*, ed. A. Flew (Penguin, Harmondsworth, 1970).

Marx, K. (1887), 'The General Law of Capitalist Accumulation', in *Capital* (Penguin, Harmondsworth, 1973), Volume I, Chapter 25, Sections 3 and 4 on relative surplus population.

Ricardo, D. (1821), 'On Wages', in *The Principles of Political Economy and Taxation*, with an introduction by D. Winch (Dent, London, 1973), Chapter 5.

United Nations, Department of Economic and Social Affairs, 'Population Theory', in *The Determinants and Consequences of Population Trends*, *Population Studies*, no. 50 (United Nations, New York, NY, 1973), Volume I, Chapter 3.

Woods, R., *Theoretical Population Geography* (Longman, London, 1982), Chapter 1.

Chapter 2

Berg, A., *The Nutrition Factor* (The Brookings Institution, Washington, DC, 1973), Chapters 1–5.

Boserup, E., 'Technical Change and Human Fertility in Rural Areas of Developing Countries', in *Rural Development and Human Fertility*, W. A. Schutjer and C. S. Stokes, eds. (Macmillan, New York, NY, 1984).

Chayanov, A. V. (1925), *The Theory of the Peasant Economy*, ed. D. Thorner (University of Wisconsin Press, Madison, WI, 1986), Chapter 1.

Mueller, E., 'The Impact of Agricultural Change on Demographic Development in the Third World', in *Population Growth and Economic Development in the Third World*, L. Tabah, ed. (Ordina Editions, Liège, 1975).

——'Income Aspirations and Fertility in Rural Areas of Less Developed Countries', in *Rural Development and Human Fertility*, W. A. Schutjer and C. S. Stokes, eds. (Macmillan, New York, NY, 1984).

Pryer, J., and Crook, N., *Cities of Hunger: Urban Malnutrition in Developing Countries* (Oxfam, Oxford, 1988).

Revelle, R. 'Food and Population', in *The Human Population*, Scientific American Books (W. H. Freeman, San Francisco, CA, 1974).

Chapter 3

Barclay, G. W., Coale, A. J., Stoto, M. O., and Trussell, T. J., 'A Re-assessment of the Demography of Traditional Rural China', *Population Index*, 42 (1976), 606–35.

Cassen, R., *India: Population, Economy, Society* (Macmillan, London and Basingstoke, 1978), Chapter 4.

Coale, A. J., and Watkins, S. C., *The Decline of Fertility in Europe* (Princeton University Press, Princeton, NJ, 1986).

Davis, K., *The Population of India and Pakistan* (Princeton University Press, Princeton, NJ, 1951), Chapter 6.

Dyson, T., ed., *India's Historical Demography* (Curzon, London, 1989).

Geertz, C., *Agricultural Involution: The Processes of Ecological Change in Indonesia* (University of California Press, Berkeley, CA, 1968), Chapter 6.

Hajnal, J., 'European Marriage Patterns in Perspective', in *Population in History: Essays in Historical Demography*, D. V. Glass and D. E. C. Eversley, eds. (Edward Arnold, London, 1965).

Hanley, S. B., and Yamamura, K., *Economic and Demographic Change in Pre-Industrial Japan 1600–1868* (Princeton University Press, Princeton, NJ, 1977), Chapter 9.

Hayami, A., 'Population Change', in *Japan in Transition from Tokugawa to Meiji*, M. Jansen and G. Rozman, eds. (Princeton University Press, Princeton, NJ, 1986).

Ho Ping-ti, *Studies on the Population of China 1368–1953* (Harvard University Press, Cambridge, MA, 1959).

Mosk, C., 'The Decline of Marital Fertility in Japan', *Population Studies*, 33 (1979), 19–38.

Morris, D., and Smith, T. C., 'Fertility and Mortality in an Outcaste Village in Japan', in *Family and Population in East Asian History*, S. B. Hanley and A. P. Wolf, eds. (Stanford University Press, Stanford, CA, 1985).

Ohbuchi, H., 'Demographic Transition in the Process of Japanese Industrialisation', in *Japanese Industrialisation and its Social Consequences*, H. Patrick, ed. (University of California Press, Berkeley, CA, 1976).

Owen, N. G., 'Introduction', in *Death and Disease in Southeast Asia* (Oxford University Press, Singapore, 1987).

——'Population and Society in Southeast Asia before 1900' (Mimeographed, 1989).

Perkins, D. H., *Agricultural Development in China, 1368–1968* (Edinburgh University Press, Edinburgh, 1969).

Visaria, L., and Visaria, P., 'Population', in *The Cambridge Economic History of India*, Volume 2 (Cambridge University Press, Cambridge, 1983).

Wrigley, E. A., and Schofield, R. S., *The Population History of England 1541–1871: A Reconstruction* (Edward Arnold, London 1981). Summarized in *Malthus Past and Present*, J. Dupaquier, ed. (Academic Press, London, 1983).

Chapter 4

Blaikie, P., *The Political Economy of Soil Erosion in Developing Countries* (Longman, London, 1985), Chapter 20.

Cohen, J. E., *How Many People Can the Earth Support?* (Norton, New York, NY, 1994).

Ehrlich, P. R., *The Population Bomb* (Simon and Schuster, New York, NY, 1971), Chapter 1.

——and Ehrlich, A. H. *The Population Explosion* (Pan, London, 1990).

Gleave, M. B., 'Population Pressure in West Africa: Academics' Views and Real-World Experience' (University of Salford Working Paper, 1988).

——'Population Density, Population Change, Agriculture and the Environment in the Third World', in *Environment and Population Change*, B. Zaba and J. Clarke, eds. (Ordina Editions, Liège, 1994).

Gould, B., 'Population Growth, Environmental Stability and Migration in Western Province, Kenya', in *Environment and Population Change*, B. Zaba and J. Clarke, eds. (Ordina Editions, Liège, 1994).

Jodha, N. S., 'Population Growth and the Decline of Common Property Resources in India', *Population and Development Review*, 11 (1985), 247–64.

Meadows, D. H., Meadows, D. L., Randers, J., and Behrens, W. W., *The Limits to Growth: A Report for the Club of Rome's Project on the Predicament of Mankind* (Universe, New York, 1972).

Repetto, R., and Holmes, T., 'The Role of Population in Resource Depletion in Developing Countries', *Population and Development Review*, 9 (1983), 609–32.

Ware, H., 'Desertification and Population in Sub-Saharan Africa', in *Desertification*, M. H. Glantz, ed. (Westview, Boulder, CO, 1977).

World Bank, *World Development Report 1992: Development and the Environment* (Oxford University Press, New York, NY, 1992), Chapters 3 and 7.

Chapter 5

Ashton, B., Hill, K., Piazza, A., and Zeitz, R., 'Famine in China 1958–61', *Population and Development Review*, 10 (1984), 613–45.

Further Reading

Dreze, J., and Sen, A., *Hunger and Public Action* (Clarendon Press, Oxford, 1989).

Dyson, T., 'On the Demography of South Asian Famines', Parts 1 and 2, *Population Studies*, 45 (1991), 5–25 and 279–97.

Ghose, A. K., 'Food Supply and Starvation: A Study of Famines with Reference to the Indian Subcontinent', *Oxford Economic Papers*, 34 (1982), 368–89.

Harrison, G. A., *Famine* (Oxford University Press, Oxford, 1988).

Kane, P., *Famine in China 1959–61: Demographic and Social Implications* (Macmillan, Basingstoke, 1988).

McAlpin, M. B., *Subject to Famine* (Princeton University Press, Princeton, NJ, 1983), Chapter 3.

Sen, A., *Poverty and Famines* (Clarendon Press, Oxford, 1981).

Chapter 6

Banerji, D., 'Social and Cultural Foundations of Health Services Systems', *Economic and Political Weekly*, 32–34, (1974), 1333–46.

Beaver, M. W., 'Population, Infant Mortality and Milk', *Population Studies*, 27 (1973), 243–54.

Curtin, P. D., *Death by Migration* (Cambridge University Press, Cambridge, 1989).

Doyal, L., *The Political Economy of Health* (Pluto, London, 1979), Chapters 1–4 and 7.

Gray, R. H., 'The Decline of Mortality in Ceylon and the Demographic Effects of Malaria Control', *Population Studies*, 28 (1974), 205–29.

Henderson, D., 'The Eradication of Smallpox', *Scientific American*, 235 (1976), 25–33.

McKeown, T., and Record, R. G., 'Reasons for the Decline in Mortality in England and Wales during the Nineteenth Century', *Population Studies*, 16 (1962), 94–122.

Mercer, A., *Disease, Mortality and Population in Transition* (Leicester University Press, Leicester, 1990).

Pryer, J., and Crook, N., *Cities of Hunger: Urban Malnutrition in Developing Countries* (Oxfam, Oxford, 1988).

World Bank, *World Development Report 1992: Development and the Environment* (Oxford University Press, New York, NY, 1992), Chapter 5.

Chapter 7

Banks, J. A., and Banks, O., 'The Bradlaugh-Besant Trial and the English Newspapers', *Population Studies*, 8 (1954), 22–34.

Jones, H. R., *A Population Geography* (Harper & Row, London, 1981), Chapters 4, 5, and 7.

Mueller, E., 'The Impact of Agricultural Change on Demographic Development in the Third World', in *Population Growth and Economic Development in the Third World*, L. Tabah, ed. (Ordina Editions, Liège, 1975).

Seccombe, W., 'Marxism and Demography', *New Left Review*, 137 (1983), 22–47, especially Parts 2 and 3.

Todaro, M. P., *Economic Development in the Third World* (Longman, London, 1977), Chapter 7.

Chapter 8

Banister, J., *China's Changing Population* (Stanford University Press, Stanford, CA, 1987), Chapter 7.

Caldwell, J., 'In Search of a Theory of Fertility Decline for India and Sri Lanka', in *Dynamics of Population and Family Welfare 1983*, K. Srinivasan and S. Mukerji, eds. (Himalaya, Bombay, 1983).

Cassen, R., *India: Population, Economy, Society* (Macmillan, London, 1978).

Croll, E., Davin D., and Kane, P., eds., *China's One-Child Family Policy* (Macmillan, London, 1985).

Greenhalgh, S., 'Shifts in China's population policy', *Population and Development Review*, 12 (1986), 491–515.

Hartmann, B., and Standing, H., *The Poverty of Population Control: Family Planning and Health Policy in Bangladesh* (Bangladesh International Action Group, London, 1989).

Liu, Z., and Song, J., *China's Population: Problems and Prospects* (New World Press, Beijing, 1981).

Mamdani, M., *The Myth of Population Control* (Monthly Review Press, New York, NY, 1972).

Nag, M., and Kak, N., 'Demographic Transition in a Punjab Village', *Population and Development Review*, 10 (1984), 661–78.

Sathar, Z., Crook, N., Callum, C., and Kazi, S., 'Women's Status and Fertility in Pakistan', *Population and Development Review*, 14 (1988), 415–32.

Soni, V., 'The Development and Current Organization of the Family Planning Programme', in *India's Demography: Essays on the Contemporary Population*, T. Dyson and N. Crook, eds. (South Asian Publishers, New Delhi, 1984).

Chapter 9

Boserup, E., *Population and Technology* (Basil Blackwell, Oxford, 1981), Chapter 10.

Connell, J., DasGupta, B., Laishly, R., and Lipton, M., *Migration from Rural Areas* (Oxford University Press, Delhi, 1976), Chapters 1 and 2.

Crook, N. R., *India's Industrial Cities: Essays in Economy and Demography* (Oxford University Press, Delhi, 1993), Chapters 3 and 7.

Hoselitz, B. F., 'The Role of Cities in the Economic Growth of Underdeveloped Countries', *Journal of Political Economy*, 61 (1953), 195–208.

Marx, K., and Engels, F. (1844), 'Division of Labour, Towns and Country', in *The German Ideology* (Lawrence and Wishart, London, 1974), Part 1c.

Morris, M. D., 'The Recruitment of an Industrial Labour Force in India', *Comparative Studies in Society and History*, 2 (1960), 305–28.

Peek, P., and Standing, G., 'Rural-Urban Migration and Government Policies in Low-Income Countries', *International Labour Review*, 118 (1979), 747–62.

Preston, S. H., 'Urban Growth in Developing Countries: A Demographic Reappraisal', *Population and Development Review*, 5 (1979), 159–215.

Richardson, H. W., *The Economics of Urban Size* (Saxon House/Lexington Books, Farnborough and Lexington, 1973).

Further Reading

Sethuraman, S. V., *Jakarta: Urban Development and Employment* (International Labour Office, Geneva, 1976).

Sivaramakrishnan, K. C., and Green, L., *Metropolitan Management: the Asian Experience* (Oxford University Press, New York, NY, 1986).

Standing, G., 'Migration and Modes of Exploitation', *Journal of Peasant Studies*, 8 (1981), 173–211.

Timæus, I., and Graham, W., 'Labour Circulation, Marriage and Fertility in Southern Africa', in *Reproduction and Social Organization in Sub-Saharan Africa*, R. Lesthaeghe, ed. (University of California Press, Berkeley, CA, 1989).

Todaro, M. P., *Economic Development in the Third World* (Longman, London, 1981), Chapter 9.

Weber, A. F. (1899), *The Growth of Cities in the Nineteenth Century* (Greenwood, New York, NY, 1969), Chapters 3 and 5.

Wrigley, E. A., *Population and History* (Weidenfeld & Nicolson, London, 1969).

Zelinsky, W., 'The Hypothesis of the Mobility Transition', *Geographical Review*, 61 (1971), 219–49.

Chapter 10

Amjad, R., ed., *To the Gulf and Back: Studies on the Economic Impact of Asian Labour Migration* (International Labour Organization—Asian Employment Programme, New Delhi, 1989).

Bauer, J., 'Demographic Change and Asian Labour Markets in the 1990s', *Population and Development Review*, 16 (1990), 615–45.

James, W. E., Naya, S., and Meier, G. M., *Asian Development: Economic Success and Policy Lessons* (University of Wisconsin Press, London, 1989), Chapter 6.

McNicoll, G., 'Consequences of Rapid Population Growth: Overview and Assessment', *Population and Development Review*, 10 (1984), 177–240.

Oshima, H., 'The Industrial and Demographic Transition in East Asia', *Population and Development Review*, 9 (1983), 583–607.

United Nations, Economic and Social Commission for Asia and the Pacific, 'Implications of Changing Age Structure for Current and Future Development Planning', *Population Research Leads*, 25 (1987), 1–10.

Index

Index

Index